Private Passions and
Public Sins

*National Rhythms, African Roots: The Deep History of
Latin American Popular Dance*—John Charles Chasteen

*The Great Festivals of Colonial Mexico City:
Performing Power and Identity*—Linda A. Curcio-Nagy

*The Souls of Purgatory: The Spiritual Diary of a Seventeenth-Century
Afro-Peruvian Mystic, Ursula de Jesús*—Nancy E. van Deusen

*Dutra's World: Wealth and Family in
Nineteenth-Century Rio de Janeiro*—Zephyr L. Frank

*Death, Dismemberment, and Memory:
Body Politics in Latin America*—Edited by Lyman L. Johnson

Plaza of Sacrifices: Gender, Power, and Terror in 1968 Mexico—Elaine Carey

*Women in the Crucible of Conquest: The Gendered Genesis of
Spanish American Society, 1500–1600*—Karen Vieira Powers

*Beyond Black and Red: African-Native Relations in
Colonial Latin America*—Edited by Matthew Restall

Mexico OtherWise: Modern Mexico in the Eyes of Foreign Observers—
Edited and translated by Jürgen Buchenau,

Local Religion in Colonial Mexico—Edited by Martin Austin Nesvig

*Malintzin's Choices: An Indian Woman in the
Conquest of Mexico*—Camilla Townsend

From Slavery to Freedom in Brazil: Bahia, 1835–1900—Dale Torston Graden

Slaves, Subjects, and Subversives: Blacks in Colonial Latin America—
Edited by Jane G. Landers and Barry M. Robinson

*Making the Americas: The United States and Latin America
from the Age of Revolutions to the Era of Globalization*—Thomas F. O'Brien

**Series advisory editor: Lyman L. Johnson,
University of North Carolina at Charlotte**

Private Passions and Public Sins

Men and Women in

Seventeenth-Century Lima

María Emma Mannarelli

Translated by Sidney Evans
and Meredith D. Dodge

University of New Mexico Press ❧ Albuquerque

PRINTED IN THE UNITED STATES OF AMERICA

LIBRARY OF CONGRESS CATALOGING-IN-PUBLICATION DATA
Mannarelli, María Emma, 1954–
[Pecados públicos. English]
Private passions and public sins :
men and women in seventeenth-century Lima / María Emma Mannarelli ;
translated by Sidney Evans and Meredith D. Dodge.
p. cm.
Includes bibliographical references and index.
ISBN 978-0-8263-2279-1 (PBK. : ALK. PAPER)
1. Adultery—Peru—Lima—History—17th century.
2. Illegitimacy—Peru—Lima—History—17th century.
3. Sexism—Peru—Lima—History—17th century. I. Title.

HQ806.M3613 2007
306.73'609852509033—dc22

2007002219

⚹

Book and cover design and typography by Kathleen Sparkes
This book is typeset using Minion Pro Open Type 10.5/13.5, 26P
Display type is Latino Elongated and Trajan Pro

Contents

∂

INTRODUCTION • ix

CHAPTER ONE
The Spanish Invasion and New Patterns of
Relations Between Men and Women • 1

CHAPTER TWO
The Scene
Separation and Convergence in Seventeenth-Century Lima • 19

CHAPTER THREE
Unwed Couples
Eating, Drinking, and Sleeping under the Same Roof • 39

CHAPTER FOUR
Adultery
Sinning against Charity and Justice • 57

CHAPTER FIVE
Illegitimate Children
Bonds of Love and Discharge of Conscience • 73

CHAPTER SIX
Female Dishonor and Social Hierarchies • 97

CHAPTER SEVEN
Abandonment, Affection, and Institutional Response • 127

GLOSSARY • 151

NOTES • 153

BIBLIOGRAPHY • 189

INDEX • 199

Introduction

It is commonplace that in Lima's colonial society marriage was apparently an institution of somewhat limited scope. How widespread a phenomenon this was and what it meant, however, have not been studied with the necessary care.[1] Extramarital relationships were endemic throughout the capital, particularly in the seventeenth century, and as a result, out of wedlock births were an important feature of the everyday life of the city. This situation was rooted in the colonial condition itself, in the submission and differentiation among social groups that emerged around the sixteenth century, and in the nature of relationships between men and women. This study explores the frequency and significance of two historical phenomena: illegitimacy and extramarital relationships in Lima's urban society during the seventeenth century.

There have always been children born outside of marriage.[2] Illegitimacy can also, however, reflect the social conditions of a precise historical moment or draw attention to a structural phenomenon that is an essential part of the society under study. Illegitimate offspring can result from either stable relationships or ephemeral contacts between men and women.[3] The picture becomes more complex if the marital status of these partners, as well as ethnic differences and gender inequalities, are brought into consideration.

Marriage occupies a central place in society and in the lives of individuals. It perpetuates social structures, allows the emergence of classes and alliances, and regulates how property is passed on. It also serves to control the libido and passions. Furthermore, it is undoubtedly linked to the passing down of culture, values, and attitudes from one generation to the next.[4] The nature and frequency of marriage in a given society express specific social processes. In the same fashion, marriage patterns can contribute to understanding the substantive, internal workings of society.

Marriage, family formation, and the establishment of family ties have inevitably implied specific behaviors and attitudes among men and women. Thus, each society and social group possesses some kind of affective, sexual culture that incorporates masculine and feminine ways of being. Here it becomes relevant to ask how a society, where marriage is not an institution of mutual consensus, is organized. In other words, how is the "disorganized" side of society put in order?

Despite the long tradition of studies on marriage and family in preindustrial European societies, the approach of French and British historians to the study of extramarital relationships and illegitimacy has been indirect. Such is the case with the classic works of Lawrence Stone, Jean Louis Flandrin, and Georges Duby, among others.[5] They suggest how frequently these phenomena occurred, but there are few studies that deal with their significance. This evidently has to do with the relative lack of importance of these problems for those societies, especially in comparison to Latin America. Proof of this is the interest these topics have sparked there, particularly where plantations and slavery played a dominant role. Colonial Brazil and the Caribbean, where matrifocal families have considerable importance, are a case in point.[6]

The historiography of colonial Peru has contributed indirectly to the topic. Although highly suggestive, Pablo Macera's work on indifference toward marriage among Lima's elite during the eighteenth century or Claude Mazet's effort to systematize the information found in baptismal records are just the tip of the iceberg. Other research, such as that of Bernard Lavallé or Alberto Flores Galindo and Magdalena Chocano on the problem of divorce in colonial Peru, are valuable references.[7] Studies on urban slavery, particularly those of Frederick Bowser and Christine Hunefeldt, also provide a conceptual and historical framework that has contributed to this work.[8]

When speaking about intimacy between men and women sexuality must be referred to.[9] In colonial Latin America and especially in Peru, sexuality was often acted upon outside of marriage. Premarital sexual activity, consensual relations, bigamy, polygamy, out of wedlock births, and clandestine affairs between clergy and laity were quite common components of daily life in colonial society. Studies of sexuality in Mexican colonial society also provide insights useful for understanding this.[10]

Lima was chosen for this study for reasons of a different sort. As the administrative, commercial, and religious center of the Viceroyalty of Peru, the city had complex, varied social characteristics. Many ethnic and social groups converged there, and studying their interactions, as well as how their identities were formed, proved irresistibly inviting. Attempting to know a city like Lima inevitably brings the historian into contact with a fascinating spectrum of social behavior patterns.

Research was initially limited to the seventeenth century. By century's end, the city's future configuration, defined by its streets, parishes, and power centers, was clear. Residential segregation aside, Lima was already a multiethnic city.

Furthermore, the seventeenth century is paradigmatic for understanding how the colony worked. It was at this time, after the civil wars among the Spaniards and the defeat of armed indigenous opposition, that the typical patterns of colonial exploitation were introduced and a stable colonial society emerged.[11] It was only during the last third of the sixteenth century that the firm establishment of such a society became possible. As the labor reforms of the viceroy, don Francisco de Toledo (1568–80), took hold, they became the norm for how Peru's economic and social system would function in the following century.

For the Spanish empire, colonization meant, above all, the organization of productive extractive activities. It also brought regulation of an increasingly complex constellation of social groups. For this, peninsular authorities imposed policies in Spain's new territories that were intended to domesticate the bodies and souls of both stubborn natives and Europeans under the spell of New World myths.

As a result, the norms for city life were established between the late sixteenth and early seventeenth centuries. Although they exhibited traits characteristic of Western civilization, the maelstrom of the colonial world marked them with a special stamp. Patterns of family life and sexual relationships had, by 1600 and particularly in Lima, already gone beyond their European origins.

The eighteenth century, according to most studies of colonial Peruvian society, displayed distinctive characteristics on several levels. When Bourbon rule replaced the Habsburg monarchy in Spain, the resulting administrative change had considerable social consequences for the colonial world. During the latter half of the century, the advent of independence was foretold by successive waves of indigenous and peasant rebellions. This period also saw different ways of controlling both sexual behavior and the tensions between the sexes. Changes in European society, particularly those originating with the Enlightenment, had some repercussions in the colonial world, mainly with regard to how sexuality was managed.[12]

As frequently happens with this type of undertaking, the initial object of research changed over time. At the beginning, the focus was illegitimacy. How extensive was it? How was it expressed among different groups in the city? These questions led me to baptismal records. I chose two multiethnic parishes in the city: the cathedral parish, El Sagrario, the oldest and largest, and a smaller neighboring parish, San Marcelo. Together they were home to at least 65 percent of the city's population.

Generally speaking, despite the usual tendency to underrecord illegitimate births, my initial research showed that nearly half the births of the seventeenth century were of this kind. Furthermore, the figures suggested other topics worthy of investigation: varying rates of paternal desertion, according to ethnicity and social condition; matricentrality; consensus; and child abandonment.

To find some human meaning in the figures, I examined the records of the royal audiencia's civil trials. Here, the claims of illegitimate men and women to be acknowledged by the civil authorities increasingly revealed the identity of the main characters in this story. These files and the wills contained in notarial records enriched my work, revealing a universe of personal attitudes and intimate motivations. From reams of bureaucratic paper work emerged words, dialogues, men's accusations, masters' statements, slaves' reproaches, and women's laments. It was no longer one story of a problem, but many stories. The illegitimate children were no longer the main characters, as the fathers and mothers who were part of those experiences also became key to their meaning. This then became even more complex, as servants, slaves, relatives, neighbors, and friends entered the picture.

The involvement of all these individuals and the attempt to interpret it inevitably led to a broadening of the topic. What were the connections between men and women in seventeenth-century Lima? What was the organization of a society where traditional marriage and family, whether nuclear or extended, already had only limited currency? To answer these questions in part, I reconstructed and interpreted the interaction of public authorities, such as the church and the colonial state, with private ones, such as the family and slave owners. All this occurred within the framework of a stratified system that combined values like honor and social realities like slavery.

The church defined how people should act on their sexuality, determining what feelings were permitted under what conditions and with whom. It also had the last word on separation, divorce, and marriage annulment. With regard to sexuality, the church intervened on the one hand to configure intimate spaces. On the other, it used its power in public spaces to regulate the sexual behavior of the urban population. Sexual transgression had a particular public connotation. Clear examples of this were the periodic ecclesiastical inspections that took place regularly in different city parishes to detect cases of cohabitation. Church inspectors, in compliance with the mandates of the Council of Trent (1545–63), invaded the beds and sat at the tables of couples clandestinely cohabiting. The testimony of witnesses, needed in trials against cohabitation, confirmed the public nature of the church's investigation of illicit sexuality.

The state's discourse, though less relevant than the church's, cannot be overlooked. It was especially important for inheritances and their distribution to illegitimate or natural offspring. These were matters that fell under the jurisdiction of the royal audiencia, a decidedly civil institution. While its judges had nothing else to say regarding relationships between the sexes, when they issued decisions they usually took into consideration moral aspects, such as a woman's virtuous and retired life, that were usually within the church's domain. The civil judiciary was also in charge of punishing the city's inhabitants for their sexual misbehavior, since they looked into crimes like adultery.

To a great extent, however, private codes regulated sexuality, and especially female sexuality. Men, as heads of their families, and masters, as owners of slaves, controlled much of the sexual regulatory system. Men in general did so through dowries, the power they exercised over female family members, and the code of honor. As for slave owners, property rights had precedence over slaves' very actions and diminished the influence of public authorities. Slavery itself protected masters from the sexual transgressions of their slaves. The rules emanating from the code of honor and slavery established the general coordinates that governed the lives of Lima's people.

Quantitative data from Lima's parochial baptismal records and qualitative evidence from civil and ecclesiastical trials gradually revealed patterns of relationships between the genders that could only be explained by reference to the past. Did these behavior patterns correspond to an affective culture that was essentially colonial? Were there Spanish components emerging in the colonial world? To answer these questions, chapter one deals with the Iberian family tradition, ties between men and women, and extramarital relations in fifteenth-century Spain.

The patterns of gender relations prevalent in the colonial period began to take shape at the beginning of the European invasion. This is why it is pertinent to examine the attitudes of the first conquerors toward women, the type of links they established with them, and the incidence of illegitimate offspring and how they were treated.

Unfortunately, the testimonies of indigenous women on this point are practically nonexistent. Only the chroniclers' versions of these women's feelings about their unions with the Spaniards are known. For this reason, I present some of the mechanisms regulating the relationships between men and women in Indian society, especially the exchange of women. Combining such mechanisms with certain characteristics of Spanish society of the time established the foundation for interpreting gender relationships. As chapter one will demonstrate, these models or their particular characteristics evolved and became more complex during the next century. Some of their features will be examined, but many others remain to be explored.

Chapter two reconstructs the urban scenario where the stories took place. Census and demographic information made it possible to trace by ethnic group the unequal numbers of men and women in Lima's population throughout the century. This clearly showed competition among women in the urban marriage market and in some cases linked population imbalances between the sexes with the trend toward illegitimacy. Following this is an analysis of the influence of bureaucrats, both civil, military, and religious; merchants; and slaves on how men and women interacted. The structure of ethnic and gender segregation and the configuration of public and private spaces with their own particular characteristics produced a tableau organized and differentiated by ethnic criteria. This was done using contemporary chronicles and testimonies, monographs about the city, and quantitative information from both primary and secondary sources.

Chapter three deals with how civil authorities and ordinary people of the time perceived extramarital relationships; the response of church officials is also noted. An attempt is made here to understand a problem dealt with at length elsewhere: the coexistence of several moral codes in colonial society, the result of the division of power between the private and public spheres. The chapter ends with discussion of a topic central to this work, the relationships between men of the social elite and women belonging to subordinate groups.

Chapter four explores a specific aspect of extramarital relations: adultery. Some features of colonial society, including matchmaking and the relative lack of importance accorded personal choice, the availability of subordinate women, and men's geographic mobility, weakened the marital link and led to out of wedlock relationships. Files from the Archivo Arzobispal in Lima concerning divorce actions and trials against cohabitation provided material for this discussion.

Illegitimacy and its significance in Lima's urban society are dealt with in chapter five. The meaning of illegitimacy emerged from numerical and qualitative material, especially testimonies from illegitimate men and women. These demonstrated how birth outside of marriage became a criterion for social stratification that nourished the gender and social hierarchies of colonial society. Fragments from these life stories led to an understanding of the dynamic between private and public and the conditions in which allegedly natural children could be acknowledged.

In these circumstances, consensual unions became only relatively important, since illegitimacy was more directly linked to abandonment by fathers and matrifocal families. Illegitimacy was a matter of degree, and this became clear when the attitudes of men toward their illegitimate offspring were examined. It was further shown by the barriers that could keep natural children from sharing in paternal goods: legal marriage; the presence of heirs, whether direct or collateral; the slave status of a mother; the weight of masculine wishes; and the public, though uncertain, pressures illegitimate children could bring to bear on them. The material illustrating this appears in wills taken from the records of the city's scribes and the civil files of the royal audiencia in the Archivo General de la Nación in Lima.

The relationship between illegitimacy and women is the focus of chapter six, where a panoramic view of the identity of colonial women, with its emphasis on control of sexuality, is presented. The seclusion of women, the dowry system, and the code of honor interacted with pressure from women seeking to broaden the restricted scope of action the hierarchical order assigned to them. Two fundamental issues appear here: the position of public and private authority in relation to women's sexual behavior and the variety of moral codes sustaining the different forms of discrimination that affected women. The different ways women of the aristocracy experienced motherhood outside of marriage is analyzed, as well as the formation of an affective culture where illegitimacy and the emotional values based on extramarital relations were not seen as socially stigmatic, especially among women of the urban middle sectors.

Finally, the meaning of illegitimacy among the female slave population is discussed. The analysis presented is based on quantitative sources, the civil files of the royal Audiencia of Lima, and wills from notarial archives.

The problem of child abandonment resulting from extramarital relationships is dealt with in chapter seven. The estimated number of children in this population and their characteristics are given. The study of two institutions, the Hospital de los Niños Huérfanos and the Colegio de Niñas Expósitas de Santa Cruz de Atocha, highlights the institutional response to this problem. Finally, the trajectories of life for abandoned children and the adults involved with them are traced, which provides an enhanced view of the fate of children without parents in colonial society and the feelings their stories produced.

In conclusion, it must be said that this work does not attempt to explain the origin of a problem that has persisted for centuries in Peru. Rather the intent is to offer a model for interpreting the ways in which social hierarchies are combined with inequalities between men and women.

CHAPTER ONE

The Spanish Invasion and New Patterns of Relations Between Men and Women

❧

Ychach munani, Ychach manamunani[1]
(Maybe I want to, maybe I don't).

*Yo no me caso si no vendo estos yndios por dies y seis mil pesos
que me dan por ellos en barras y en plata. Y si estuviera en esta
ciudad la hija de Tomás Vásquez, vezino del Cuzco, que me
daba más, me casara con ella.*[2]

*(I will not get married if I cannot sell these Indians for sixteen
thousand pesos in ingots and silver. And if the daughter of
Tomás Vásquez, a vecino of Cuzco, were in this city, he would
give me more, and I would marry her.)*

Following the wars of the conquest, the Spaniards' physical appropriation, abduction, and rape of women mirrored similar wartime experiences elsewhere. Fascination with power and wealth also affected in a very special way the libidos of those who took part in the war and gave rise to gender relations characterized by domination. The vicissitudes of war surely had a peculiar impact on the minds and behaviors of those who were involved in it as well. At the same time, patterns of relations between men and women began to emerge in response both to the wars and to the colonial system that was beginning to take shape. To reconstruct and interpret the dynamics of these relationships in the context of the Spanish invasion, Iberian traditions must be taken into account. A good part of this dynamic can be explained by how the major actors of this drama transferred these patterns to the Indies and how relationships crossed lines of power, ethnicity, and culture.

Spanish family structure of the times was hierarchical, and each member held a position with clearly defined functions. The family was conceived of as a natural organism bound to remain unaltered forever. Each of its members had well-defined rights and duties. Relations among its members were based on assumptions of superiority and inferiority and command and obedience.[3] Iberian patriarchal families were inclusive entities. Relations both between and within families included a substantial number of individuals and established varying degrees through which the wealthiest and noblest were related to the neediest, like slaves and orphans. This structure also included illegitimate offspring who were treated as both relatives and servants.[4]

Despite the strongly patriarchal Christian tradition, Spain's Muslim legacy, and the importance of codes of honor that subordinated women, women nevertheless had access to property and inheritance, while enjoying considerable customary and formal rights. The *Siete Partidas* and the Laws of Toro established the legal foundation of Iberian society for centuries, and men and women had, at least in principle, equal rights to family patrimonies.[5] Nonetheless, there were times, as was the case with *mayorazgos* (entails), when male privileges took precedence over those of females. Moreover, women had a limited field of action in the public arena, since masculine tutelage prevailed in configuring social interaction. Paternal wishes, for example, directed women's marriage choices.[6] Even among those of humble condition, material interests took precedence over emotional or aesthetic considerations.[7]

Spanish conquistadores inherited a tradition in which the status of women was debatable. Religious authorities had argued for the inferiority of women, an idea repeated throughout the Western tradition.[8] Such notions were compiled and condensed in the fifteenth century in a handbook for inquisitors entitled *Malleus Maleficarum* (Hammer of Witches), which emphasized women's moral and intellectual inferiority.[9] In particular, women were prone to evil and too weak to resist temptation, making them easy tools for the work of the devil. These characteristics necessarily placed them under masculine tutelage, be it of their fathers, husbands, or priests, and ascribed to them the status of minors.

During the final centuries of medieval Spain, matrimony was respected as an institution and a sacrament, and sexual relations outside marriage were considered a grave failing. The church condemned sexual misconduct as sin, but it was also subject to civil sanctions and punishment. Although legislation busied itself exerting control over the many types of existing extramarital relations, cohabitation and adultery were widespread phenomena in Spanish cities in the sixteenth and seventeenth centuries.[10] The clergy, the aristocracy, and dominant groups in general, far from being strict observers of sexual rules, engaged in rather loose sexual behavior.[11] Spanish society tolerated extramarital relations and the situations resulting from them. Such acceptance is revealed by the ease with which offspring from forbidden couplings were legitimized and sexual crimes forgiven.[12]

Indicative of the high rates of extramarital relations and illegitimacy is Spain's fifteenth century having been dubbed the century of bastards.[13] Illegitimate children were deprived of a number of rights.[14] This could be overcome, however, if they obtained their legitimacy through a letter signed by the king himself. A common way of presenting this legitimacy request personally to the monarch was by serving him, and there was no better way to do this than by conquering "infidel" Indians. The compensatory and redeeming value of the conquest to its participants, many of whom were illegitimate, cannot, therefore, be underestimated.[15]

The diffusion of extramarital relations and illegitimacy throughout the Iberian peninsula indicates that they were essential features of both Spanish identity and Hispanic emotional culture. This must have significantly influenced in general attitudes about women and conjugal relations.

The social practices of native groups also contributed to this process of defining relationships between men and women. Local marriage patterns varied from region to region throughout the Andes, so it would be misleading to make a general statement about preconquest relations between men and women. The types of domination men exerted over women and of female subordination certainly differed from group to group.[16] One widespread practice deserves special mention here, however: the exchange of women to establish marriage alliances. This phenomenon was extremely important in clearly delimiting the distribution of rights by gender and consequently the forms of subordination and dependence between spouses.[17] Appropriation of women was a source of authority and prestige, and it implied recognition of a man's power.[18] Moreover, a woman's status in those exchanges was defined, at least in part, by the rank of the man giving her away.

The Inca had at his disposal a number of women he gave to important nobles, whether to honor them or prove his power. In this case, giving women away demonstrated the Inca's supremacy, and accepting the gift meant the recipient acknowledged his position as vassal to the Quechua lord. The exchange of women sealed the political alliance that had been established.

This practice also suggested the existence of different rights for men and women. Men had rights over women that women did not exercise over men or other women. This is not to say that women could not receive women as gifts and therefore be awarded a degree of recognition. Huayna Cápac, for instance, bestowed numerous attendants, including three hundred women, on one of his noble wives, the lady of Tocas and Huaylas, who was the curaca of Contarhuacho.[19] Although the exchange of women presupposes that men and women did not enjoy equal rights, reciprocity between genders gave women rights within their new reference group.

Similarly, the exchange of women between groups implied their reciprocal alliance. Moreover, parallel succession rights among Quechua groups ensured women access to the means of subsistence and control of their own political and religious institutions.[20]

A clearly established set of sexual-control guidelines regulated the exchange of women in Inca society. Adultery was harshly punished, and the rules for relations between the sexes were quite rigid. Felipe Guamán Poma de Ayala wrote at the beginning of the seventeenth century that "no lost woman has ever been found, nor a lost woman gotten married, or an adulteress been found. Law-breaking young women or men were killed. They were left hanging alive from a rock, as were male and female adulterers; justice is severe."[21]

In contrast to what occurred with regard to adultery and illegitimacy in fifteenth-century Spain, these phenomena seem to have been isolated within native ethnic groups under Inca rule. These were agricultural societies with incipient urban centers and limited trade. Social organization was built on the internal articulation of social components through specific and well-defined kinship relations. As in most societies of this kind, marriage patterns had to conform to relatively strict rules so that access to property, whether patrilineal, matrilineal, or bilateral, common or individual, and the resulting productive processes would achieve the best results.[22]

The Spanish invasion radically changed the lives of most native women. Spanish aristocratic traditions allowed Indian noblewomen to retain their access to landed property. This access, which in many cases had been previously limited to independent feminine cults, was nevertheless restricted in the emerging colonial order. Formally, a local tradition giving women unconditional hereditary rights through feminine descent from ancestors was severed.[23] Without a doubt, aristocratic native women passed from one patriarchal system to another. Research to date shows, however, that under the Spanish system their prestige was undermined.[24]

The small number of Spanish women and the mutual sexual impulses and attraction that could occur between conquistadores of Peru and native women led to some relatively enduring consensual relations.[25] This was certainly intensified by the desire for power and the lure of the new that attracted the mostly young men who were the protagonists of the conquest.[26]

When referring strictly to the physical aspect of the Spaniards' desire for native women (if this is possible at all) their beauty and exotic appearance surely aroused Spanish men. There is some testimony to this effect. Decades before, Columbus had written in his travel log that Indian women had "very beautiful bodies."[27] Nevertheless, a different color skin was quickly associated with aesthetic qualities; a dark complexion meant less beauty. Garcilaso's revealing remarks about Cusi Huarcay, the wife of his relative, Sayri Túpac, suggest this. "She was extremely beautiful and would be even more so if her dark color did not detract from her beauty."[28]

Honor was important for understanding why Spanish males established consensual relationships with native women but refused to marry them later. The principle of honor discriminated among social strata and behaviors and served to distribute privilege.[29] The desire for honor and fame defined the Spaniards' code of conduct, a code derived from the *Siete Partidas*. A man acquired his reputation by virtue of his rank, deeds, and courage. Honor moved him to action and ascribed his place in the social hierarchy, transcending even the value of an individual's life. The poor based their honor on virtue alone. Women, according to men, protected their honor with sexual modesty.[30] The code of honor considered women as their husbands' property, thus giving rise to a double moral standard that had profound social and personal implications.[31] The physical appropriation of women and the taking of their personal services were also legitimized by a certain idea of honor.

From the standpoint of the conquest, of triumph and glory, values like honor increased in importance. According to Américo Castro, the era was characterized by an intense desire for personal dominion in a way unknown before.[32] No matter how low the social rank of the Spanish soldier, the glory and legitimacy gained through wars in the Indies placed him in the enviable position of satisfying these personal aspirations. Marriage to an Indian woman, no matter how noble, could not grant a Spanish male the same prestige that could be attained through marriage to a Spanish woman, since honor was associated with being an Old Christian, and this in turn presupposed "purity of blood."[33] Indians had been worshippers of idols and only recently been converted. Such a trait cast a shadow on any family aspiring to recognition in Hispanic society.

In the decades before Isabel and Ferdinand unified the Spanish kingdoms, various cultural and ethnic groups had lived together in relative peace and harmony on the Iberian peninsula. A consolidated state and centralized monarchy had led, among other things, to xenophobia. Persecution of Jews and Moors redefined the rules that had permitted cohabitation among these groups, exacerbated feelings of discrimination, and contributed to the emergence of racial prejudices that also played a role in colonial Spanish America.[34] It is important to place this fact in the context of the Spanish male code of honor, however, since that code was intimately linked to female sexual behavior and to women's virginity in particular. Whatever women's virginity may have meant in native societies, Spaniards apparently thought Indians did not much value it. Spaniards feared Indian promiscuity threatened their own honor, and this discouraged them from considering marriage with indigenous women.[35]

Garcilaso asserted that the Spanish conquistadores reined in their sexual conduct with Spanish women. This was apparently also a matter of honor, as Spaniards could not sexually use the daughters, wives, and mothers of their own group. The attitude of Spanish men toward women was based not on what women meant in and of themselves, but on their relationships to their fathers and husbands. Their connections to men defined their identity. Respecting a woman was a way of honoring her male relations. "They were likewise abstinent and temperate in eating and drinking as well as in restraining their sensuality, especially toward the women of Castile, because it seemed to them they could not act otherwise without prejudice to their neighbors' daughters or wives."[36]

Such feelings were the basis of gender relations among Spaniards, but the conquistadores displayed a range of behaviors. Gonzalo Pizarro was described as "giving himself too much out to women, either Indians or those from Castile."[37] Melchor Verdugo, one of the Men of Cajamarca, had an illicit affair with the married daughter of his companion, Francisco Fuentes. Both these instances reveal that the code of honor provided imperfect protection when it came to relations with women who belonged to one's own group.[38]

Other forces shaped the relations between men and women of the times as well. In principle, the alliances conquistadores formed with women of the native nobility facilitated their exercise of power over the native populace. Perhaps the most telling case was the relationship between Francisco Pizarro and Inés Huaylas Yupanqui. Quispe Sisa, as she was named at birth, was given to Francisco Pizarro by her brother, Atahualpa, and they were together in Cajamarca, Jauja, Cuzco, and Lima. Stories told by contemporaries relate that Pizarro made a formal, public commitment to Quispe Sisa. He introduced her to his friends as his wife in a sort of betrothal ceremony, saying "Here you see my woman."[39] Later, during the uprising led by Manco Inca (1536–37), Contarhuacho, a leading woman of the Huaylas principality and a relative of Quispe Sisa, possibly her mother, sent one thousand Indians from her domains to help Pizarro.[40] Certainly this contributed substantially to defeating the Indian siege of Lima. Then, sometime between 1636 and 1637, the relationship ended.

Not every Spanish alliance was merely a device for winning the war. The attitudes of the Indian population also influenced these relationships. There is evidence that sometimes Indians were satisfied to see their women marry conquistadores. In this regard, Garcilaso wrote that "in those initial years, when the Indians saw an Indian woman pregnant by a Spaniard, all her kinfolk would get together, pay their respects, and serve the Spaniard as if he were their idol, because he had become their relative. And so they helped greatly to conquer the Indies."[41]

Bartolomé de las Casas tells us that "the unfortunate maidens and their families were deceived by the Spaniards, who took them at their will. The natives thought their daughters were being taken as legitimate wives."[42] At any rate, arranging women's lives was a practice the Spaniards continued. Marrying off their children's mothers to members of their own social group or other male clients was a Spanish habit of the time. Capt. Gonzalo Pizarro, father of Francisco, had seduced his son's mother, Francisca, when she worked as a humble maid in a monastery. He later gave her in marriage to a certain Martín.[43] Two very distinct patriarchal traditions meet at this point. Atahualpa gave Quispe Sisa, his sister and daughter of Huayna Cápac, to Francisco Pizarro, probably to signal his intent to establish an alliance or demonstrate his power. Within a few years he had had two children with her. The conquistador then gave Quispe Sisa, now Inés Huaylas Yupanqui, in marriage to Francisco de Ampuero, a subordinate of his entourage.[44] Pizarro then granted Ampuero an encomienda at Chaclla.[45] By 1539, Francisco Pizarro was cohabiting again, this time with Angelina Yupanqui, a woman of the native elite. With Pizarro's death, Angelina became the wife of Juan de Betanzos in a marriage decided upon by Gonzalo Pizarro.[46]

After the end of her relationship with Garcilaso's father, Garcilaso's own mother, the Palla (princess), Isabel Chimpu Ocllo, married Juan del Pedroche in a deal arranged between the two men. Aurelio Miró Quesada assumes that Garcilaso's father provided Chimpu Ocllo's dowry.[47] Leonor Curicuillor had been married to Quilaco, who acted as a sort of ambassador to Pizarro. During the years of the conquest, she became Hernando de Soto's wife.[48] Diego de Almagro, Pizarro's partner and later bitter rival, also had a concubine from the Indian nobility in Marca Chimbo, daughter of Huayna Cápac and his sister. After a period of cohabitation, Marca Chimbo married the Spaniard Juan Balsa.[49] Tocto Chimbu, wife to Atahualpa and daughter of Huayna Cápac, is another case in point. Atahualpa's successor to the Inca throne gave her to Hernando de Soto, one of the main conquistadores.[50]

These examples lead to the impression that lovers behaved like fathers: they provided their concubines with dowries to facilitate their marriages. They also chose husbands for them and left them bequests. It was as if the role of patriarch unfolded into those of lover and protective father, a perverse relationship that seemed inherent in a transaction in which women were objects without independent options.

There were women from the elite who refused to become cogs in the machinery of power set up by the native rulers and the Spaniards or among the Spaniards themselves. The attitude of the Coya (princess) Azarpay, a sister of Atahualpa, demonstrated such resistance. According to Pedro Pizarro, one Spaniard from Navarre who was close to Francisco Pizarro asked him for Azarpay as his wife. Azarpay, however, fled to Cajamarca where she was captured and taken to Pizarro.[51]

Both before and immediately after the Inca's capture at Cajamarca, local rulers were already giving women away to the conquistadores rather freely, though this pattern later changed. Gonzalo Pizarro's demand that Coya Cura Ocllo, Manco Inca's sister, be given to him was rejected by the Villac Umu.[52] Over time, the behavior of Spaniards toward native women had an impact on the Inca nobility, as miscegenation and concubinage started to affect their interests. Quispe Tito, says John Hemming, was extremely interested in bringing his son together with a girl of direct descent from the native nobility.[53]

Men who maintained relationships that could be defined as legitimate within their original families generally tended to reproduce such values. A look at the history of members of the Pizarro family demonstrates this. The only legitimate member of the family, Hernando, returned to Spain, where he lived with a concubine and finally married his niece, Francisca Pizarro.[54] By contrast, Francisco Pizarro was an illegitimate son, and there was no evidence suggesting that his father would recognize and legitimize him.[55] He lived with Inés Huaylas Yupanqui, daughter of Tupac Yupanqui and Mama Anahuarque, from the conquest of Cuzco in 1534 until the siege of Lima. The lives of his brothers, Gonzalo and Juan Pizarro, also born out of wedlock, more closely resembled the life of Francisco Pizarro than that of Hernando Pizarro.[56]

Another prominent case illustrates the repetition of behavior patterns. Garcilaso de la Vega, another illegitimate son of a native woman and a Spaniard, himself had an illegitimate son with one of his female attendants after leaving Peru.[57] Reproducing these types of relationships between men and women in the colonial context gradually became a key component of colonial social relations generally.

Many Spaniards lived with whatever women they had at their disposal, principally those who served them. Some were Indian women brought from far away as war booty. Alonso de Toro, among others, had a stable, lasting relationship with his Indian maid.[58] Alonso de Mesa cohabited with all the Indian women who labored for him at the same time, while Francisco de Vargas had a daughter of mixed blood with his Indian maid.[59] Juan de Valdivieso had a son with a Cañari woman who belonged to his entourage of servants.[60] Juan García lived with a Peruvian Indian who was in his service.[61] Finally, Miguel Ruiz, himself born from an earlier relationship between a Spaniard and his slave, maintained an ongoing relationship with one of the Nicaraguan female servants who traveled with the conquistadores.[62]

The children born from these cohabitations between native noblewomen and Spanish conquistadores were in some cases joyfully welcomed by both. This happened with Francisca Pizarro, born in Jauja in 1534 from the union of Francisco Pizarro and Inés Huaylas Yupanqui.[63]

The offspring of this passing union were not left in their mother's care. The two mestizo children, Francisca and Gonzalo, were taken from her and given to Francisco Martín de Alcántara, the conquistador's stepbrother, and his wife, Inés Muñoz,[64] who raised them in the purest Hispanic tradition.[65]

Two more children were born from Francisco Pizarro's later relation-ship with Angelina Yupanqui. Unlike the earlier two, however, Angelina's sons Francisco and Juan were not legitimized. This probably permitted them to maintain closer ties to their mother Angelina. Francisco remained in Cuzco by his mother's side until he was about eleven years old, when he left for Spain. All four of these Pizarro children were at least for some time under the tutelage of their uncle, Gonzalo Pizarro, and all ultimately occu-pied good positions in the local Hispanic community. Gonzalo Pizarro's own two legitimized mestizo children also went to Spain.[66]

Pizarro's lieutenant Sebastián Benalcázar also legitimized three natural children, presumably all mestizos. On a later trip to Spain, he arranged a marriage for his adult son, Francisco, who had accompanied him, to María de Herrera of Burgos.[67] Francisco became lieutenant governor in Popayán and founded a family illustrious for generations. It can thus be seen how a father's recognition meant breaking away from the mother's cultural matrix, although that was compensated for by acquiring a good position in Hispanic society. Legitimization by a Spanish father thus meant depriving Indian women of their relationship with their descendants.

Efforts to keep illegitimate mestizo children away from the native cultural universe were not limited to individual conquistadores. This attitude also influ-enced the establishment of institutions such as the Santa Clara retreat for girls of mixed blood founded in Cuzco in 1551.[68] Young women like Beatriz Coya were secluded in these establishments. Even in Lima a similar, though smaller, institution was founded under the name of San Juan de la Penitencia. It turned out to be much less important than its Cuzco counterpart, however, and disap-peared after only two decades. Its rapid decline was linked to the type of women it took in, who were the unacknowledged offspring of ordinary Spaniards, and it quickly lost its social significance in Lima, the City of Kings.

The will of the conquistadores did not alone determine the fate of illegit-imate children. The interests of the Spanish crown also played a role in defin-ing the lives of illegitimate mestizos. Pedro de la Gasca, the peacemaker, wanted to bestow the Yucay encomienda and the Avisca coca leaf planta-tions, which had been granted to Francisco Pizarro, on his son Francisco. He also recommended that Francisco be legitimized like his sister, although he could remain under the care of his mother Angelina. The crown, however, only granted Francisco the revenues from those properties, stating that they should be returned to the crown after his death. Isabel, daughter of Juan Pizarro, and Inés, daughter of Gonzalo Pizarro, were each to receive six thousand ducats from their cousin Francisco's revenues and then go to Spain. The king himself decided that Francisquito, Inés's brother, should go to Spain with her and his cousin, since as the son of Gonzalo Pizarro, who had rebelled against Spanish authority, he was a potential insurgent.[69]

A Spanish father's recognition of a child was an alternative to legitimization. It did not, however, allow illegitimate offspring to inherit encomiendas or hold mayorazgos, though it did imply protection by the father. Denial of formal recognition to illegitimate children was occasionally replaced by the appointment of Spanish tutors who looked after the children's future. Francisco de Vargas, who was also present at Cajamarca when the Inca ruler was captured, placed his mestiza daughter, born from his relationship with an Indian servant, with Jerónimo de Aliaga.[70] The daughter of Leonor Curicuillor and Hernando de Soto, Leonor de Soto, later married a royal scribe, García Carrillo.[71] Soto acted differently with his mestiza daughter born to Tocto Chimbu, however. He excluded her from his will, though she had been left in the care of a tutor Soto had personally chosen.[72] Juan Pizarro refused to recognize a daughter born to one of his Indian maids, but gave her a two-thousand-ducat dowry and asked his stepbrother Hernando to arrange her marriage.[73] Fear that later inheritance claims would endanger those of legitimate heirs curtailed recognition of many children, since this would transform them from illegitimate offspring to natural descendants. There were many ways for fathers to express concern for the futures of these children born from relations with native women of lower social rank and soothe their consciences.

Male attitudes toward illegitimate children were also related to marital status. Single men, like Melchor Verdugo, had no problem with legitimizing their mestizo children, making them eligible to inherit their possessions.[74] A father's later marriage, however, generally led to excluding these children from any claims on the estate. In cases where there were no legitimate children, Spanish wives, rather than the Spanish decedent's illegitimate children, inherited encomiendas and other possessions.

The absence of legitimate heirs induced Spaniards to recognize illegitimate mestizo children. Although legally married, Diego Maldonado, one of the Spaniards who captured Atahualpa, had no legitimate heirs. He therefore decided to legitimize two children he had with an Indian noblewoman.[75] In this case, regularizing their status also meant taking care of their futures by providing for their inheritance, dowries, and marriages.

Sebastián de Torres, who had two mestizo children named Fernando and

Isabel, demonstrated another pattern of behavior current in those times.[76] All that was known of the mother's social origin was that she was an Indian. Torres later married a Spanish woman, a doña, in Peru. His mestiza daughter, Francisca, lived in her father's house, away from her Indian kinfolk, as was common with mestizos whose fathers decided to bring them into the fold of Hispanic society. Her experience shows how illegitimate children were incorporated into the Spanish world, for after her father's death, she lived with his widow, doña Francisca Jiménez, in a condition of servitude.[77] In later decades, this servile lot was the common fate of a sizable number of illegitimate descendants.

Around 1544, Alonso de Mesa, eighteen years old when he arrived in Cajamarca in 1532, refused to abide by the traditional values of contemporary courtier society.[78] Mesa not only lived with his illegitimate children under the same roof in Cuzco, but also gathered in his household their Indian mothers, who numbered six at one time. He had had a child with each of them.[79] Such an example sends us back to the Andean pattern of polygamy that had been the privilege of curacas, or local chieftains, and members of the Inca nobility. In 1552, Mesa was still single. He later married Catalina Huaco Ocllo, an Indian noblewoman, with whom he had at least one legitimate son, don Florencio Hernández de Mesa. Mesa alone of the men of Cajamarca legally married an Indian woman.[80]

Mesa also owned a black slave with whom he had a son named Francisquito, whom he refused to recognize. Such actions began in those early times and became the pattern later, as the mother's social status strongly influenced whether illegitimate children would be recognized. More often than not, men refused to recognize their children born of slave mothers.

It was inconceivable that Spaniards, free men, would recognize slaves as descendants. Slaves, who were property of another, had no inheritance rights, so any heir would have been the slave's own owner. This discouraged recognition of children born to slaves unless manumitting those children was feasible. In accord with a particular situation, Spaniards tried to obtain the freedom of their slave children. This without a doubt encouraged women who were slaves to have sexual relations with free men.

The turmoil that prevailed during the initial years of the conquest could work to the advantage of Spanish men if they lived temporarily with Indian noblewomen. In many cases, Spanish men sought to marry Indian women of the elite and thus gain access to positions of high social standing from which they were excluded by their own low birth.[81]

Being married improved one's position, at least theoretically, when nego-
tiating favors from the crown. This became even more important after the
passage of the New Laws (1542), which regulated inheritance of encomiendas. Those who wished to be encomenderos and acquire the right to collect
Indian tribute were required to marry and establish a household within a
period of three years. Civil and church authorities saw that these regulations were complied with. The crown preferred married men over single
men when granting encomiendas.[82] Marriage to an Indian woman was not
as useful as marriage to a Spanish woman, but it helped if the indigenous
wife was not a plebeian. Garcilaso remarked that Spaniards would abandon their Indian women to marry Spanish ones. They "left to these children
only what their parents earned and what their mothers and relatives helped
earn."[83] Regulations from Madrid became increasingly effective, however. By
1550, two-thirds of the encomenderos in Cuzco were married; by 1563, only
thirty-two of the five hundred encomenderos in Peru were unmarried.[84]

Marriages occurred between both Spaniards and Indians and Spanish
men and women. Alliances with native women were uncommon, but some
did facilitate access to goods that could be obtained from subjugated local
power groups.[85] For some Spanish men, marriage was aimed at gaining or
preserving a bureaucratic position. Many Spaniards married Spanish women
to collect Indian tribute through encomiendas and repartimientos.[86]

Good marriages also allowed many Spaniards of a clearly inferior social
status to rapidly climb the hierarchical ladder. Through his participation
in the events of Cajamarca, a man like Pedro de Alconchel, an artisan of
obscure origins, came to associate himself with the highest aristocracy.[87]
Among the plebeians who took part in these events was García Martín, who
married well in the Indies with doña Leonor de Valenzuela. His legitimate
son eventually inherited his encomienda.[88]

Single Spanish women arriving in Peru were interested in marrying the
newly rich.

[A]ll the conquistadores [were] sitting in one great hall watching
a party; the ladies would look at the party through a door along
the side of the hall. They were behind a screen placed in front
of the door, for modesty and to remain unseen. One of them
told the others, "They say we shall marry these conquistadores."
Another one said, "Are we going to marry these rotten old men?
Marry whomever you will, but I, for one, do not plan to marry

any of them. Send them to the devil; they seem to have escaped from hell. They look like a wreck. Some are one-legged, others lack an arm, ears, an eye, or half a face. The best looking of them has one, two, or more scars on the face." The first one replied, "We shall not marry them for their kindness but to inherit the Indians they own, and anyway they are old and tired, so they will die soon and then we shall marry any young man we wish instead of the old man, like substituting a new and good pot for an old and broken one."[89]

Garcilaso's detailed transcription reveals resentment toward the conquistadores' lack of loyalty to their Indian concubines. The conquistadores exchanged their native concubines for Spanish women with these feelings and attitudes, the chronicler seems to say. At any rate, it is important to recognize the sentiments prevailing among Spanish women regarding their marriages to the Spanish men who had conquered the Inca domains.

The infrequent legal unions between Spaniards and women from the native nobility had similar designs. Marriages of convenience were a widespread practice used to form alliances aimed at the consolidation of power. Beatriz Clara Coya is a case in point. Manco Inca, the Vilcabamba rebel, had three children: Sayri Túpac, Túpac Amaru, and Cusi Huarcay Coya, who received the Christian name María Manrique. Beatriz Clara Coya was the daughter of Sayri Túpac and his sister, Coya Cusi Huarcay.[90] The Spaniards believed they had the right to determine the fates of these women. When Sayri Túpac died and doña María was left a widow, the viceroy, Francisco de Toledo (1568–80), forced her to marry Juan Fernández Coronel, "a Spanish soldier with no lineage or fortune."[91] Toledo also arranged her daughter doña Beatriz's marriage to Martín García de Loyola, a descendent of a legendary old noble house of Biscay. It is tempting to imagine Beatriz as a reward given to García de Loyola for capturing her uncle, Túpac Amaru, who had succeeded Manco Inca as ruler of Vilcabamba.

Marriage alliances of this kind gave Spaniards access to the most important repartimientos of Indian labor; doña Beatriz was heiress to a rich, important estate. At the same time, though, arranging these unions allowed peninsular authorities to control the growth and strength of local elites, perceived as a potential threat to the crown's centralized authority. This was certainly the case when Lope García de Castro strongly opposed the marriage of doña Beatriz and Cristóbal Maldonado. Maldonado, a powerful aristocrat from Cuzco, sought power among the mestizos and later fought on the side of rebel Indians.[92]

The very small number of unions between Spanish women and members of the native nobility usually resulted in legal marriage. Doña Luisa de Medina married don Martín, an Indian who had fully adopted Spanish culture. He shared in Atahualpa's ransom, received an encomienda from Pizarro, learned fluent Spanish, accepted Christianity, and abandoned his Indian attire.[93] He even traveled to Spain. The marriage of María de Esquivel and Carlos Inca is another well-known case.[94] That Spanish women did not marry Indian men, even those from the dominant local elites, was indicative of their precarious status. Since a woman's value depended on the links she could establish with men, demographics certainly played a significant role. There were substantially fewer Spanish women than men, so it was that much easier for them to establish relations with their peninsular male peers. This did not, however, necessarily lead to stable monogamous relationships.

The behavior of Lucas Martínez Vegazo illustrates how the encomienda system served to structure gender relations in these early years. He arrived in Peru as a member of Pizarro's third expedition and lived in the eye of the storm all his life. He earned, lost, and recovered his encomienda while living with his maid, a Morisca slave. Martínez and another Spaniard initially jointly owned this woman, Beatriz. "The partners also owned three horses— one dapple and two fine chestnuts—a black cobbler, and a Morisca named Beatriz. They also had houses and lands in Cuzco."[95]

Martínez had a daughter with Beatriz. Although the girl's name is unknown, she lived with her mother in Arequipa around 1565. The relationship between the encomendero and his slave was apparently a long, stable one. He sent mother and daughter Spanish clothes and other gifts and eventually freed Beatriz after giving her his own name.[96] While on his deathbed, Martínez married María Dávalos. He reached an agreement with his future mother-in-law and accepted a sixteen-thousand-peso dowry in exchange for his encomienda, which was to be passed on to his young new wife who would in turn become an encomendera.[97] What actually happened is in dispute, for James Lockhart states that Lucas married his concubine, while Efraín Trelles, in his remarkable study of this man, fails to even mention the event.

Alonso de Toro's life story is also telling.[98] Toro, barely twenty years old at Cajamarca in 1532, later showed a hard, violent side in public affairs, and his private life was similarly marked. Not even a marriage to maintain the honor of his lineage made him give up his lover of many years, an

Indian noblewoman. Toro organized his family life in the purest courtier-like manner. His extended, patriarchal family included even his father-in-law, who lived under his roof with other family members and servants. Toro was unable to break his ties with his lover, however, and lived with her in the family home. Toro's wife, Francisca de Zúñiga, initially accepted the Indian woman's presence, but after six years Toro's father-in-law killed him. As is generally the case in societies founded on patriarchal families, the law of the father in this case was supreme. The wife had to accept her husband's wishes, which in this case meant living in the same house with his lover. Such a situation also demonstrates how private power took precedence over public authority, a basic characteristic of this period.

Although arranged marriage and cohabitation prevailed in the initial years of the colony, there were also marriages in which economic interests did not play a part. This was the case with Jerónimo de Aliaga, who made a brilliant career as a bureaucrat and encomendero in Peru.[99] In 1530 he married Beatriz de Medrano for love, and later founded a mayorazgo for his legitimate heirs, but his favorite child was a mestizo son to whom he left his position as secretary of the audiencia.[100]

↩

The attempt has been made here to specify some of the coordinates for the relations between men and women in the years of the Spanish conquest of Peru. Beyond certain traits that may make the event comparable to similar occurrences elsewhere, it is uniquely interesting because of the conflict and interaction between the indigenous and Spanish societies. Spaniards held a vision of the world imbued with certain suppositions about the relations between men and women. Despite formal recognition of relative equality of rights, in particular those concerning the distribution of property, women were regarded as inferior beings deserving protection and tutelage, but subject to the will of men. Sexual relations outside marriage and illegitimate children were components of the social and emotional landscape of Spanish colonial society. The subordination of women and widespread extramarital relationships for men were interpreted and regulated by the then-current honor code. Honor was a value of exceptional importance both within Spanish society and in the events of the conquest era. It had a substantial impact on the attitudes of the conquistadores toward the women close to them and toward the children born to these women.

Honor was related to values of women's sexual virtue, Old Christian traditions, and purity of blood. From the Spanish point of view, the indigenous women they interacted with sexually and emotionally lacked these highly regarded traits. Transitory cohabitation therefore sufficed to provide access to the resources the conquistadores needed to consolidate their power.

During the earlier Inca expansion of the fifteenth century, the exchange of women had become key for creating strategic cross-ethnic alliances that were an element of the imperial rules of the game. The Inca system of exchanging women ensured the Spaniards access to native noblewomen, at least during the initial moments of the conquest. Most, though, only maintained their relationships with native women until they had an alternative that would elevate their prestige. The objective was always a good marriage with a Spanish woman so as to fulfill their goals of personal accomplishment.

The conquest wars and contact with native women were new points of reference in the evolution of Spanish ideas of courtly morality. Spanish men chose cohabitation with women of various ethnic origins, especially with native servants and African slaves. In one sense, this was a continuation of the Iberian tradition of servitude. It replicated the patriarchal pattern between the masculine head of family and the network of servants, where powerful men took sexual favors from servants. It should be recalled here that the condition of servitude implied a relationship that was hierarchical and, most important, dependent. Likewise, because Andean women came from a variety of subjugated ethnic groups in the conquered territories, a new type of sexual relationship was created. In this new pattern, servants and lovers were closely identified. To this can be added the ethnic component that, in turn, also had an established hierarchy between masculinity and femininity.

Illegitimacy was but one manifestation of the inequality that in turn strengthened the hierarchical system of colonial society. The unstable environment likewise led to a lack of clear guidelines for defining the place of the resulting mestizo children in the social structure. The patrimonial character of the Spanish state, the absence of an institutional structure, and the conditions of war gave men much leeway for their actions. The range of personal options went from freely choosing to legitimize progeny before the Spanish crown to neglecting a child absolutely. A middle course was the father's formal recognition, giving illegitimate children the status of natural offspring, and using such mechanisms as financial endowments, dowries for women, appointment of tutors, and direct delegation to others of the responsibility for educating and rearing children. Individual considerations like the conquistadores' marital status, the presence of legitimate children, the social and ethnic background of concubines, the intervention of the crown, and the Spaniards' own personal interests also influenced attitudes toward mestizo progeny.

Although individual interests predominated in this dynamic, the crown also had a role in the process. Civil wars among the Spaniards, as well as Indian and mestizo uprisings, led peninsular authorities to issue specific measures regulating the future of the conquistadores' mestizo offspring, a potential threat to civil authority.

All this went hand in hand with the incorporation, in varying degrees, of illegitimate mestizo sons and daughters into Hispanic family structures and their subsequent isolation from their mothers' native cultural traditions. This anticipated the transformation of the condition of illegitimacy into a place in the social hierarchy associated with the low status of servitude.

Because colonialism strengthened social hierarchies, it also gave rise to hierarchical relationships between men and women and the consequent degradation of the female condition. From the onset, relations of dependency permeated the colonial world. People had servants or themselves served someone. These vertical social relations particularly affected the relations between men and women. The coordinates for the exercise of power over the Indian and slave populations gradually defined relations between the sexes and the female condition. Relationships between men and women were colored by prevailing social relations, thus creating a particular type of gender hierarchy.

CHAPTER TWO

The Scene

Separation and Convergence in Seventeenth-Century Lima

※

Lima's social landscape in the seventeenth century comprised a heterogeneous mix of social and ethnic groups. Spaniards, or white people; African slaves and their descendants; a varied array of *castas*, or people of mixed blood; and Indians all lived in the city. Around 1600, the year of the first city census, population reached 14,262 inhabitants.[1] Fourteen years later the population had spiraled to 25,167.[2] This latter figure, from the census ordered by the viceroy, the Marqués de Montesclaros (1606–14), reveals an average annual growth rate of 5.8 percent.[3]

In 1619, the gender distribution of the population also showed social and ethnic diversity. In the parish of El Sagrario, Lima's cathedral parish where about 60 percent of the city's population lived, 43 percent of the inhabitants were women. The distribution of the female population by ethnic group is presented in table 2.1.

TABLE 2.1: Percentages of male and female populations
by ethnic group, El Sagrario Parish, 1619

ETHNIC GROUP	MALE	FEMALE
Spaniard and mestizo	63	37
Black	54	46
Mulatto	40	60
Indian	62	38

Source: Bowser, *El esclavo*, 410. Percentages are based on Bowser's figures.

In 1619, women represented 48 percent of the population of San Marcelo Parish. The gender balance here showed its own peculiarities by ethnic distribution. Although the figures come from a fairly reliable census, people at the time had a markedly different perception of reality that is worth examining. For instance, the chronicler, fray Antonio Calancha, wrote "There are no more than six thousand Spanish residents, but there are more than twenty-three thousand women of all conditions and ages."[4] Fr. Diego de Córdova y Salinas, who used Calancha's observations, held the same opinion about the disproportionate presence of women.[5] In his *Descripción del Virreinato del Perú* (Description of the Viceroyalty of Peru) written at the beginning of the seventeenth century, Pedro de León Portocarrero had a similar view. "Women," he wrote, "are always twice as numerous because they do not travel by sea or land, nor do they go to war. Thus they preserve themselves better and live longer."[6] Beyond the specific figures, these opinions reflect the symbolic importance of the city's female population (see table 2.2).

The gender imbalance favoring women began to change as the century wore on. By 1636, the city's archbishop submitted to the viceroy, the Conde de Chinchón (1628–38), an estimate that showed women, with 52 percent of the population, to be more numerous than men: 14,154 women compared to 12,905 men. Toward the end of the seventeenth century, the 1689 census taken during the administration of the Conde de la Monclova (1688–1705) revealed the total population had risen to 37,234 residents, including the inhabitants of the Cercado de Indios (see table 2.3).

The Spanish population totaled 15,048 residents (excluding priests and those in convents and monasteries) or half the city's total population. The other half was split among blacks, castas, and indigenous people. Nevertheless,

TABLE 2.2: Percentages of male and female populations by ethnic group, San Marcelo Parish, 1619

ETHNIC GROUP	MALE	FEMALE
Spaniard and mestizo	60	40
Black	44	56
Mulatto	60	40
Indian	57	43

Source: Bowser, *El esclavo*, 410.

TABLE 2.3: Census of city residents, 1700

CENSUS GROUPS	NUMBER	%
Royal palace	95	0.2
Archiepiscopal palace	42	0.1
3 houses of the Inquisition	36	0.09
11 districts and San Lázaro	29,293	78.6
Town of Cercado	333	0.8
Hospitals*	1,209	3.2
Monasteries*	2,155	5.7
Convents*	3,865	10.3
Houses of the devout (beaterios)*	206	0.5
Total	37,234	100.00

*Includes servants

Source: *Numeración general de todas las personas de ambos sexos, edades y calidades que se han hecho en esta ciudad de Lima el año de 1700.*

among the city's white population there still remained some gender imbalance, at least toward the end of the seventeenth century. The *Numeración general* shows that the city's white males totaled 7,031 while white women reached 8,017. Among whites there were therefore 986 more women than men. This condition undoubtedly influenced how couples were formed, marriage patterns, and gender relations more generally. Once the number of women in the city's Spanish population in 1700 is taken into account, it can be assumed that competition in the matrimonial market put women in an uncomfortable situation, to say the least. Broadly speaking, some 1,000 white women were excluded from matrimony. Married men must therefore have had the opportunity for extramarital relationships with single women from Lima's white population. This imbalance suggests the difficulties Lima's women may have faced in finding a husband as well as shedding some light on the problems of illegitimacy and extramarital sexual relations.[7]

By the end of the seventeenth century, Lima's slave population had reached 7,182, or 24 percent of the total. Black slaves proper numbered 3,519 men and 3,663 women. Slaves from other ethnic groups were not as well balanced by gender. Among mulatto slaves, for example, there were 446 men and 592 women.[8] These figures, while establishing the gender imbalances in these groups, do not help explain illegitimacy and the low marriage rate within the slave population based on those imbalances alone.

The population of free blacks and mulattoes at the end of the seventeenth century was 3,172, or 10 percent of the total city population. Compared to the slave population, these groups show a striking gender imbalance. Among free mulattoes, for example, there were only 27 men for every 100 women.[9]

The population of indigenous people exhibited patterns of its own. The low population density of Indians in the area around Lima led to the development of a Hispanic city. The city's indigenous population was increased, however, by the considerable number of Indians from encomiendas near the city who came to Lima to pay their tribute to their encomenderos, most of whom lived in the city.[10] Over time, many of these short-term Indian residents entered the population. After a few years, their numbers were such that the municipal authorities viewed them as a threat and considered gathering them in a single place, isolated from other groups. In 1568, during the administration of Viceroy Toledo, the formal decision was made, and the town of Santiago del Cercado was founded on the property of the Caccahuasi encomienda near the city boundaries. The name indicates that it was an enclosed, or walled (cercado), town whose two gates were closed every night to prevent the indigenous population from being disturbed.[11]

Despite the efforts of city authorities to isolate them from other social groups, by the end of the seventeenth century there were 3,428 Indians resident in the city, 12 percent of the total (excluding the population secluded in various institutions).[12] This urban indigenous population numbered 1,506 females and 1,277 males.[13] The sexual behavior of this group, unlike that of the castas and the blacks, permitted the establishment of relatively stable family units.[14]

The architecture of the city, in contrast to its social and ethnic mosaic, was perfectly symmetrical. Built according to the medieval urban tradition that focused on military concerns, the city met the requirements included in the *Leyes de Indias* (1523).[15] At the beginning of the seventeenth century, its external aspect still caught the eye of European visitors. The city was "divided into square blocks measuring 140 paces on each side. They can all be walked around, and all four sides are of equal length. All the streets are the same width, and all lead straight to the countryside without turns or corners."[16] Other contemporary chroniclers noted the city's architectural harmony and spatial symmetry as well.[17]

The city's civic and religious core was located on the left bank of the Rimac River and formed the northern side of the Plaza Mayor, or main square.[18] Most of the civil, religious, and military bureaucracy lived and worked in the buildings of this area, principally in the four blocks of the viceregal palace. The viceroy's private dwellings, his garden, and his servants' quarters were on the northwest lot. The group of men who surrounded the viceroy and came to serve as his court established themselves in this part of the city. These courtiers included high-ranking military officers, corregidors, audiencia judges, judges of the criminal court, maestres de campo, treasurers and accountants employed by the royal treasury, stewards, majordomos, and those bearing the honorific *gentilhombre de cámara*.[19] As the number of aristocratic women arriving in the city increased, courtly life in Lima evolved accordingly. Meanwhile, the presence of women in the viceregal court was directly related to the administration's grandeur.[20]

The royal audiencia and its civil and criminal courts were located in the southwestern quarter at the corner of Calle de la Pescadería and the plaza. The civil tribunal attracted, among others, men and women of illegitimate birth requesting recognition as natural children and hoping to gain their corresponding rights. The criminal court handled claims relating to sexual morality, such as adultery, rape, and physical violence between men and women.

Lima's large number of government officials affected the configuration of relationships between men and women who lived in the city. The marriages of members of the colonial administration were carefully overseen. Viceroys, presidents, audiencia judges, and magistrates could not marry within the districts of their jurisdiction, nor could their offspring marry locally.[21] Relatives and servants of these officials were banned from arranging marriages with women who had inherited repartimientos or encomiendas. Breaking these rules meant immediate demotion from their posts and exclusion from other high positions.

These legal provisions were aimed at preventing marriage alliances with royal officials that could strengthen local power groups and potentially threaten the crown's centralized power. Furthermore, according to colonial legislation, new kinship relationships established through marriage alliances were seen as obstacles to the proper performance of governmental duties. Members of the military were subject to similar laws. Regulations of this type reveal the private, patrimonial traits of public authority in the colony, but these restrictions also encouraged single government officials living in the city to establish relationships outside the bonds of marriage.

The eastern side of the Plaza Mayor was occupied by the cathedral, the archbishop's residence, and the archiepiscopal court, which ruled on cases of marital separation, divorce, and marriage annulment. This tribunal also heard some cases related to moral behavior. Couples found living in concubinage, for instance, were always brought before it.

The building housing the cabildo, or city council, was located on the western side of the Plaza Mayor. The cabildo issued ordinances regulating the public conduct of men and women on the city's streets: the clothes they should wear and the rules of behavior during public ceremonies. Some men and women also brought before this body accusations against those transgressing the rules governing cohabitation.

Proximity to the port of Callao lent the city a special ambience. International and domestic commerce gave Lima a distinctive character because from very early on the city attracted a substantial number of merchants. Alongside these participants in large-scale commerce were the small- and medium-sized merchants who controlled small shops and street vending. These endeavors engaged many individuals, both men and women, from a wide range of social and ethnic backgrounds.

On the south side of the Plaza Mayor were Escribanos and Botoneros, arcades that opened on the commercial quarter of town. The backbone of this area was Calle de Mercaderes where "there were at least forty stores full of all imaginable worldly goods. Here is the main business of Peru."[22] Medium-sized and large commercial activity and artisan crafts were concentrated in this quarter. From the foundation of the city and throughout the colonial period, it formed part of El Sagrario, the parish of the cathedral. Also toward the south was Calle de Roperos where the city's black residents bought clothing.[23] Calle de las Mantas also ran from the Plaza Mayor toward the west, in the direction of the sea. This was a street "as full of shops as Mercaderes, . . . but there were no longer shops selling clothing but those selling candles, candy, or there were blacksmiths and cauldron makers."[24]

Over time, life in the city took on an increasingly corporatist style. People involved in the various urban trades slowly started establishing guilds, confraternities, and brotherhoods that had their own bylaws, rituals, pastimes, and charities. These guilds gave their names to Lima's arcades and streets where shops often also served as homes.[25]

The silver-rich Viceroyalty of Peru was a strong attraction for most Spanish merchants who came to the Indies, at least during the period from 1580 to 1600.[26] It should be mentioned here that merchants were among the few whom the crown did not require to travel to the Indies with their wives. They were excused from "living in marriage" with their wives and could stay overseas for two or three years without establishing households.[27] These men who came and went followed a specific pattern of behavior toward women in the colony, forming temporary relationships with city women without formally committing themselves.

There were other squares downtown in addition to the Plaza Mayor. One was the Plaza de Santa Ana, located toward the western part of town near the road to the Indian quarter. The San Andrés and Santa Ana Hospitals; the monastery of the Descalzas, San José; and the parish church were on this plaza. Also in the city center was the Plaza del Santo Oficio, and nearby were the Universidad de San Marcos; La Caridad, the hospital that served Spanish women; and the Tribunal of the Inquisition. The Plazuela de María Escobar was located toward the west, next to the Convento de Santo Domingo. Last came the Plazuela de Santiago, which was positioned straight down from the Plaza Mayor, toward the south.

These plazas saw most everyday retail commerce, and one of the busiest markets, El Gato, was on the Plaza Mayor. Its name, derived from the Quechua *catu*, indicates the likely presence of considerable numbers of indigenous people and their role as middlemen in petty urban commerce.[28] Small-time trade brought together in the plazas men and women from the middle and lower strata of the city who peddled their goods, including flowers, fruit, and groceries.[29] Because of their commercial activity, the plazas were places where people from different social levels encountered one another. They filled a religious role as well, for they gave friars and the lay devout a stage where they could preach the postulates of the Catholic faith, including those condemning living together in sin.

The Universidad de San Marcos and the Tribunal of the Inquisition served as a bridge between the city's civic and religious core and the eastern section of town, where public institutions in which gender separation was fundamental were concentrated. The Inquisition exerted a much-feared control over certain practices, including sodomy, homosexuality, bigamy, and soliciting, priests' seduction of women in the confessional. It was also charged with reviewing all expressions of opinion about adultery, virginity, and marriage that could be considered blasphemous or at worst, heretical.

Convents, monasteries, schools, and hospitals tended to be located in the eastern part of town. Most of the religious structures built to provide separate facilities for men and women were between the city center and the Cercado. Here were found the nuns of various orders, Poor Clares, Discalced Carmelites, Mercedarians, Trinitarians, and Augustinians of Nuestra Señora del Prado, as well as those belonging to the monasteries of La Concepción and Santa Catalina.[30] The preference of the religious for this area is best explained by its distance from commercial areas. The western section, by contrast, was the part of Lima through which mule caravans passed transporting merchandise arriving at the port of Callao.

Most of the city's hospitals were in this same area, toward the south: Santa Ana, for the Indians; San Andrés, for Spanish men; San Pedro, for clerics; La Caridad, for Spanish women; and San Bartolomé, for free blacks. The Hospital de Niños Huérfanos for orphan children and the Colegio de Niñas Expósitas de Santa Cruz de Atocha, the school for abandoned girls founded in the mid-seventeenth century, were also located there. These hospitals were segregated by sex and lodged 1,079 individuals at the end of the seventeenth century. The religious schools of San Ildefonso, Santo Toribio, the Jesuit novitiate, the royal school of San Felipe, and El Príncipe, shared this urban space.

Toward the south at the city's edge was the Casa de Divorciadas, where women legally separated from their husbands could stay, together with the convent and church of San Pedro Nolasco. Finally, on the southernmost edge, stood the Franciscan school, Buenaventura, right next to the Church of Guadalupe.[31] Although few significant public institutions were located outside this space, the Augustinian and Dominican convents, two of the city's four largest, were west of the civic center.

Of the men in the most rigorously observant convents, some lived in the Dominican Recolección de la Magdalena and some in the Mercedarian Recolección de Nuestra Señora de Belén. These were located much further south near the gardens that surrounded the city. They shared this space with relatively isolated institutions such as the Beaterio de las Nazarenas and the Hospital del Espíritu Santo.

In the masculine world, toward the end of the seventeenth century the convents, schools, and most rigorously observant religious houses run by the Mercedarians, Jesuits, Dominicans, and Franciscans housed as many as 2,155 men. This included the lay brothers and slaves who lived as virtual celibates in a state of seclusion.

Around 1700, some 3,865 women, including nuns, cloistered laywomen, and servants, lived in religious seclusion in the eastern part of town. One monastery, La Encarnación, had 827 women, of whom 434 were maids serving the nuns. Santa Clara, another convent, housed 632 women, including 278 servants. La Concepción was home to 1,041 women, 561 of whom were maids. In the other convents, a similar servile population was devoted to the nuns' service.[32]

The women living apart in the six beaterios, houses of the devout, that existed in 1700 can be added to the female population in the convents. There were 210 women, including beatas, or devout women, servants, and girls, lodged in Santa Rosa de Santa María, Jesús Nazareno, Viterbo, Copacabana, and one each under the Mercedarians and Capuchins.[33]

Devout women did not live exclusively in the beaterios, however. Being a beata presumed putting into practice the vows of chastity, poverty, and prayer and living alone or in the family home. It is therefore impossible to know how many women lived outside the beaterios or even what their celibate life was like. There were also devout women living in places like El Carmen, the school established in 1619 as a small retreat for women at Catalina María, a religious house in the Cercado.[34]

There were also throughout the city private households sheltering ten or more people, usually women. According to the *Numeración general,* there were about forty-five such homes in 1700.[35] This census also mentioned other separate spaces for women. These included the Casa de Refugio; a home for women recovering from illness, which held twenty-four women; one for poor women, with fifty-nine occupants; and the Casa de Recogidas for cloistered laywomen. Around the end of the seventeenth century, a remarkable 20 percent of the city's population lived apart by gender in convents, beaterios, and hospitals.

The notion of enclosure and separation of the sexes was rather strictly enforced in these places. Contact between men and women were severely restricted. La Caridad, the school for Spanish girls, had been founded in the sixteenth century.[36] It operated for several decades as part of the hospital for Spanish women bearing the same name, though the school later became a separate entity.[37] The life of women there did not much differ from life in a women's convent. They were isolated from men and from the world, given a strict religious education, and trained to perform household chores. The futures of these women were ensured by dowry drawings that allowed them to either marry or enter a convent. Another similar institution was Santa Cruz de Atocha, the school for abandoned girls that will be discussed below. Santa Cruz differed from La Caridad, however, in that this school was for young, white Spanish girls who had been left by their parents as foundlings.

Physical separation by gender, though not by race or class, was the norm at all these institutions and houses of retreat, even in the private homes mentioned earlier. Ethnic and social distinctions inevitably emerged internally, however. In some cases they were included from the beginning in the charters creating the institution, and in others, they were introduced through more subtle means.

Segregated spaces were not completely free of worldly influences, nor were they governed by austerity and modesty. Life within monasteries was marked by mystical devotion, but this coexisted with an active social life that included both merrymaking and conflict.[38] Moreover, priests' behavior in religious convents left much to be desired. French chronicler Amedeé Frézier wrote at the beginning of the eighteenth century of the incongruity of the convents' external appearance of devotion, the number of people they sheltered, and the religious attitudes of their residents. The use of church monies for private ends and the libertine behavior of priests were both publicly well known.[39]

The city was to an extent organized for ecclesiastical purposes. There were many public places for prayer and religious observances throughout the town. A plan from the 1680s, published by Fr. Pedro de Nolasco in 1688, showed Lima's forty-three churches, indicating the importance of religious discourse in the everyday life of city residents.[40] The church prescribed how sexuality should be experienced and what it did, and did not, allow. The confessional and the pulpit were not the only places norms about sexual behavior were promulgated. Ecclesiastical regulations went beyond the universe of intimacy, as will be clearly seen in the trials of people living together outside of marriage. The profusion of public religious places in the patriarchal urban landscape was another indication of this.

The division of the city into parishes was particularly important. At the beginning of the century there were six in Lima, El Sagrario, largest and oldest of all the city parishes; San Marcelo; Santa Ana; San Sebastián; San Lázaro; and El Cercado. Huérfanos, a seventh, was founded later. Parishes were vital points of reference for city residents where they recorded the most important events in their lives, baptisms, marriages, and deaths. Although parishes in general included a mix of social and ethnic groups, reflecting the city's expansion and cultural diversity, they had their own individual characteristics. Most city notables lived in El Sagrario, rather than newer parishes founded later. Other parishes served the explicit purpose of ethnic segregation. El Cercado, for example, was reserved for indigenous people. Some parishes still showed the stages of their evolution. San Lázaro was initially composed of settlements of indigenous people. After El Cercado was created, however, its indigenous population was transferred there, and most of San Lázaro's residents were Spaniards. Nevertheless, over time San Lázaro, which was relatively isolated on the right bank of the Rimac, little by little became a barrio of nonwhites.

Ordinances regulated the city's public life, and public space was extremely important to city residents. The streets always seemed to be crowded "with so many people that, no matter how wide they are, they cannot provide enough room for those walking or strolling in them."[41] They were a stage where people of all stations acted out the norms of the social order and found meaning for their lives.[42]

The sense of the city as stage was almost literal. In the seventeenth century there were 153 public holidays, including religious feast days, Sundays, holy days of obligation, and civic celebrations.[43] The hierarchical order observed during these public events followed specific regulations and never varied.[44] The social distinctions that characterized colonial society emerged in the organization of parades and processions during the festivities. Those who performed the public rituals at these grand events were strictly limited by membership in various social groups, such as religious communities, the military and civil bureaucracies, indigenous peoples, and artisan guilds.

People of all social estates participated in some city festivities, such as those honoring the Virgin.[45] Large crowds gathered to celebrate the Immaculate Conception. Josephe de Mugaburu, Lima's seventeenth-century chronicler, noted in 1662 that one such procession brought together ten thousand people "of all types." Religious ceremonies held in the wake of earthquakes and other catastrophes brought together people of all kinds and every condition.[46] Nonetheless, the general tendency was to distinguish and separate Spaniards, indigenous people, blacks, and mulattoes among the devout, as was the case with the feast for the Virgin del Rosario.[47]

Autos de fé attracted large crowds. All gathered around the platforms placed in the middle of the Plaza Mayor to hear the sentences read. In their habits, the religious of all the orders came in procession, accompanied by banners, choirs, the richly dressed members of the military orders, and the condemned in their penitential sanbenitos. In colonial society, public punishment was highly meaningful, for it had an exemplary purpose; prisoners were flogged in the streets both to dishonor them and serve as a warning to others. The civil and ecclesiastical authorities and members of the artisan guilds and confraternities who attended these public chastisements occupied a specific place corresponding to their position and prestige in society. Men did not mix with women. Only among the plebeians watching this people's theater was the distinction between the sexes largely ignored. They were the masses, undifferentiated, hard to identify, and little understood, who saw no need to separate male from female in their public gatherings. From their vantage point, they could express their hostility to, repudiation of, or in some cases, their secret solidarity with the accused. At any rate, everyone received a stern lesson, since the Inquisition pursued men and women of different classes at different times.

Festivities such as carnival offered the opportunity to break away from the social order dramatically. In these settings, people not only intermingled, but also adopted different identities by donning disguises. This allowed them to express desires that society usually kept in check. The day after carnival, it was common to see men and women, both Spanish and indigenous, lying in the streets. Men and women roamed the streets in gangs, and sometimes aristocratic ladies took part in the merrymaking in their own way. Servants of the elite gave out sweets to revelers and threw sugar-coated grains at each other in a mock battle.[48]

Although Spanish legislation explicitly forbade women from holding public office, just as it disallowed their presence at court without their husbands' permission, successfully appealing for legal authorization was always possible. Segregating women in the city's public space followed its own logic in accord with the particular urban activity. In outdoor religious festivities that brought together large groups of people, the presence of elite women was of little importance. Since their participation in these events was restricted and carefully regulated, when they were present at all, it was as observers. Facilitating this was an architectural element characteristic of the city: the enclosed balconies, of Arabic inspiration, that allowed women to watch events in the street. With latticed shades covering the windows, they were "in some streets so numerous and long" that they seemed to "resemble houses suspended in the air."[49]

For other, more everyday, activities, like going to church, women of these and other social strata had a place that was determined by commonly held standards based on the hierarchical differences within urban society. Women of the elite, for example, were required to be modest and inconspicuous. In 1600, on the occasion of an imminent auto de fé, the cabildo discussed the way in which members' wives would be allowed to be present. "It was agreed to build the platform so as to allow every councilor's wife to be present with another woman companion from within the fourth degree of kinship, but no more because they would not be admitted . . . and that a list would be prepared with the names of the women who would be permitted to come and that no more than the two would be allowed."[50] Women could take part in these public events because of their kinship with powerful men, but always in a prearranged position and subject to special scrutiny.

They could not participate in the festivities marking the arrival of important public authorities in the city. As Fr. Bernabé Cobo mentioned in his *Historia de la fundación de Lima* (1639), arrangements were made for women of the aristocracy to meet separately in private with the newly arrived viceroy. On his first night in the city, the viceroy received the women of Lima, their faces covered, in the viceregal palace.[51]

The streets were no place for women of the ruling elite, but there were always ways to break these rules. "Although women here are not as closely guarded as they are by the Spaniards in Europe, they leave their homes infrequently during the day. When night falls, however, they are free to make their visits and go to the most unexpected places. The women who are shiest by day are the most daring by night. Then, their faces covered with a veil, their identity hidden from the world, they will do what in France is reserved to men."[52]

Against male advice, women gathered in public places that were particularly harmful to their honor and social standing, such as the open-air theaters, the *corrales de comedias*. Priests warned husbands and fathers of the "very serious improprieties caused by their wives and daughters attending the theater."[53]

In a society of hierarchies strongly reinforced by ethnic identity, and particularly by the dramatic inequalities of slavery, external controls were made manifest in a blunt manner that left no room for doubt.[54] The result was a profusion of municipal ordinances that emphasized different sanctions for each group and each gender, even though all committed the same violations. For throwing garbage in the river, for example, Spaniards paid six pesos, blacks received one hundred lashes, and indigenous men or women, sixty lashes in jail.[55]

The regulation of life in the city took gender, ethnic, and status distinctions into consideration, and discrimination guided the restrictions applied to different groups. In 1560, the viceroy, the first Marqués de Cañete (1555–59), issued an edict ordering Lima's free people of color to abandon their homes and move in with their Spanish masters within eight days; only free women of color married to Spaniards were exempt from this.[56] Lima's cabildos resorted repeatedly to ordinances policing and strictly regulating cohabitation of blacks with whites or indigenous people. It forbade black people from visiting indigenous markets or buying alcoholic beverages and harshly regulated their festivities and dances.[57] Free black men were even forbidden to have sexual relationships with indigenous women.[58] Among many other restrictions, as early as 1535 slaves were required to observe a curfew, an ordinance that was reissued several times during the seventeenth century.[59]

Legislation governing the city sought to control everyday life in an effort to emphasize differences in social status among various groups. Free black women and mulattas, for example, were forbidden to wear pearl or gold earrings or dresses or shawls made of silk, "even if married to Spaniards, under penalty of confiscation."[60] In April 1631, the viceroy, the Conde de Chinchón, issued an edict stating that no mulattas, whether free or slave, could wear dresses made of silk or Spanish-made material or "slippers with silver ornaments." Style of dress thus reflected the ethnic differentiation of women who were not white. Mulattas also had to be controlled because they were perceived as highly dangerous to the social order. They were not allowed to have canopied beds in their homes and were encouraged to "sell their labor so they could earn their own wherewithal."[61] Because internal controls lacked import, however, self-regulation of public behavior was ineffective.[62]

In the seventeenth century the city's slave population was largely devoted to domestic work. Patriarchal life in colonial Lima was inconceivable without the presence of slaves, even in society's more modest households, although in those cases, ostentation took precedence over actual need.[63] This was not the only reason for bringing slaves into the family home, however. Of city households headed by white, indigenous, mulatta, and black women,

27 percent had slaves. This seems remarkable, considering that these households had fewer resources than those headed by men, but is less so upon closer examination.[64] Households at the time were defined not as units of consumption, but as places where various economic activities took place and the labor of slaves was very important.

Slaves not only lived in the family home, but were also out on the streets of the city every day, virtually everywhere in the city's public landscape. Civil and ecclesiastical authorities were always guarded by slaves when they traveled. blacks, who carried women of the Lima aristocracy in their litters, also drove their luxurious carriages.[65] Many slaves worked away from their owners' residences, sometimes outdoors, earning a wage they then gave to their masters. Moreover, Lima was surrounded by small farms where many slaves also toiled.

City residents also invested in slaves as a way to secure some income. A good proportion of women's dowry documents included slaves, who added to the women's social value. Such investments were also a way for some Spaniards to provide for their lovers and illegitimate children from their inherited wealth.[66]

Convents and hospitals were full of black servants. More often than not, particularly in institutions of women's seclusion, female slaves served as a bridge between the cloister and the secular world. All public institutions had slaves in their service.[67] In 1700, for example, the population of women's monasteries was 3,655 women, of which 1,798 were free servants and slaves.[68]

The households of the city were organized in highly diverse ways. Side by side with multifamily units headed by men were homes of different configurations and sizes led by women. This was the case in the last decade of the seventeenth century, when at least 27 percent of all households had women as their heads.[69] These varied in structure, size, and social composition. They ranged from those made up of a single slave woman to those of aristocratic women that brought together men, women, and children, Spanish, indigenous, casta, and slave.

The nonwhite population lived with the city's Spanish population in the same homes. Of households headed by women, 145 out of 408 in one of the city's barrios had slaves, while 109 included indigenous people who shared the house with people of other ethnic groups. Of those same households 71 had residents who were free people of color.[70]

The internal order of households also revealed the nature of the relationships between individuals and groups in Lima's colonial society. The

French traveler, Frézier, described the interiors of city life and the presumed intimacies of their people. Writing about typical houses, he noted that "the first [room] is a large hall . . . leading into two or three succeeding rooms."[71] The absence of hallways to separate rooms and make them independent could be interpreted as a sign of both their little-differentiated domestic functions and the character of the relationships among members of the same household, particularly between men and women.[72] There were observations other than Frézier's that suggested similar criteria for the distribution of rooms among residents in city homes. In his study of an aristocratic house in seventeenth-century Lima, Héctor Velarde showed how all rooms communicated with each other.[73]

Frézier commented further on the indiscriminate use of domestic space. "The first hall," he remarked, "is the reception room, which is where the drawing-room furniture is. There is also a bed, placed in a corner as if this were a spacious bedroom. The main convenience, though, is a back door through which company may come in or leave privately, even doing so unannounced, without anyone noticing."[74]

Descriptions like these suggest that some kinds of personal behavior were not private and there was little desire to make distinctions when using different rooms in a home. For instance, the bed and the drawing-room furniture were found in the same room, but men and women behaved differently there. "The furniture is covered with tapestries and velvet cushions for the ladies to sit on. The chairs for the men are covered with embossed leather."[75] This arrangement was rarely disregarded, but if it was, there was always the bedroom-like corner, not very far away.

The variety of activities occurring in the house meant that homes were more public than private and women were not confined by domesticity.[76] This particular way of life, more oriented, like people themselves, to life outside the house was reflected in the interiors of homes. "The height and size of the rooms would give them an air of grandeur if [the residents] only knew how to place some openings at regular intervals. [The rooms] have very few windows, however, and they always look dark and melancholy. Because glass is not used, [the windows] are closed with turned-wood shutters that keep out the daylight even more. The furniture does nothing to enhance the poor layout of the buildings."[77] The lack of pleasure or interest in domestic furnishings also indicated how limited the idea of privacy in the home was.[78]

The small number of beds found in houses caught Frézier's attention as well. He thought this could be explained by the fact that servants (whether slave or not, he did not say) slept not in beds, but on sheepskins laid on the floor.[79] In the same way that household functions did not exist separately and apart from other activities in the home, so physical distance between master and servant did not serve to establish distinctions between them. Other kinds of indicators, such as the use of beds, worked to underscore inequality. Within a shared space, only by emphasizing differences could an appearance of order be created.[80]

჻

The visible physical nature of separation of the sexes was crucial for interpreting both the regulation of relationships between men and women and what transgressions meant. As rules dealt most often with physical actions, how men and women related to one another was very closely tied to external references that reflected the guidance those rules provided.

Quantitative differences between the city's male and female populations, or between ethnic and social groups, cannot be considered the cause of the recorded rates of illegitimacy and are even less useful in explaining their significance. At any rate, this sexual imbalance, among other things, must have put the white women of Lima at a disadvantage and therefore contributed to reducing their social status. Something similar would have occurred with the city's many casta women. Moreover, it is possible to discern a link between sexual imbalance and percentages of illegitimacy. As will be seen later, the highest percentages of illegitimacy occurred among the castas, while the indigenous population, with a more balanced gender mix, showed the lowest percentages.

Some urban characteristics typical of Lima, such as its important role in colonial administration and its being the central point of the Spanish South American trade monopoly, had a special bearing on sexual habits. The identity of social groups living in the city helps explain some of their attitudes toward women and toward married life. Civil and military bureaucrats, of high and low rank alike, merchants in general, and foreigners in particular all carried out activities that limited their feeling of belonging to the city. Administrative positions, which were short-term, and merchants' constant coming and going helped foster extramarital relationships of a passing nature. These groups were also affected by specific corporate legislation concerning marital matters that restricted their freedom to marry and was, as will be seen, one element promoting instability in the relationships between Lima's men and women.

The presence of a large slave population, 23 percent of the city's residents, also played a significant role in shaping the pattern of relationships between the sexes. Private ownership of slaves consistently hampered both crown and church intervention, particularly with regard to marriage in the slave population. The very presence of slavery suggested that female slaves were sexually available, especially to their masters and other free men. Unlike elite women who protected their sexual reputations, female slaves were not thought to enjoy honor. Moreover, sexual relationships with free men could, under certain circumstances, earn freedom for them or their children. Given the structure of urban households, physical proximity between female slaves and free men clearly encouraged physically intimate relationships. This particular blend of slavery and a hierarchical social system tended to block the development and strengthening of public life. This had special repercussions on the interactions between men and women generally, beyond the condition of slavery in which a large group of urban residents were held.

Gender differences acted as a guiding principle of urban life in Lima. This is obvious from the segregated spaces where at least 20 percent of the city's people lived; the various rules for behavior, order, and hierarchy that structured Lima's public rituals; and the separate spaces for men and women that were also found in the private sphere.

Physical separation by gender within religious institutions was synonymous with the spiritual and contemplative life. Among women, however, it also functioned to regulate their bodies and sexuality and consequently, morality at large.

The hierarchical rankings of the social order were reproduced in open spaces that were not necessarily public. Although the prevailing social discourse and legal system strictly regulated their presence in those spaces, women, including those of the elite, nevertheless managed to get around established obstacles. Private space within the home, for example, was open, though not intimate, in nature.

The city's streets and squares were not, strictly speaking, public spaces in the classical sense of the word. Rank and social status defined people's everyday presence in these spaces. To the extent individuals expressed the attributes of their status, they also did so on Lima's plazas and streets. There was no communal external characteristic that differentiated these groups when they shared any of these public spaces.

Public functions were important in the city's social life, but the emphasis on displaying social ranking and on order, where restrictions on women's behavior were crucial, strengthened the belief that people were innately different. This in turn served to undermine the establishment of a true public culture. This idea is central for interpreting experiences like extramarital relationships and illegitimacy, insofar as an individual's values in public were subordinate to the established public values of the culture.

Exterior space, which was hardly public, had its counterpart in an inner world that, like the city streets, was not meant to be personal private space. A very fine line separated private from public, and the "personal," properly speaking, could not be found in either of the two environments. The mode of being in one space and that of living in the other were strongly influenced by the group one belonged to, for it was the group that created the rules. This type of regulation, typical of hierarchical societies, strongly emphasized external controls that differed for each social group. As a result, individual internalization of external norms was of little importance in shaping social relationships.

CHAPTER THREE

Unwed Couples

Eating, Drinking, and Sleeping under the Same Roof

❧

*With the same effectiveness I was able to prevent duels and
shameless public concubinage. No exceptions were made, and
I deferred to no one, banishing in the appropriate manner
those who insisted on these excesses and vices.*

—The Conde de Castelar,
viceroy of Peru, "Memoria"

In 1625, the general vicar of the Archbishopric accused Juan Sánchez,
a married craftsman and native of Lima, and María Criolla, a twenty-
four-year-old freed widow, "which whom with little fear of God and of
her consciousness, has been more than two years publicly engaged with
Juan Sánchez . . . for great scandal of everyone who knows them. They have
been involved and had a bad friendship, meeting together day and night
in María´s house."[1]

Testimonies like this indicate that the problem of concubinage was related to different spheres of social life. It was first a religious matter, a sin and an offense against God.[2] Second was the question of individual conscience. Though subjective, this was closely linked to religious belief and made individuals question themselves. Concubinage was, finally, a public matter, as it was a crime against the social order itself.

At this time, the line separating divine intervention from human action was rather ambiguous. Concubinage, or illicit friendship, was the work of the devil, and making unwed couples abandon their "bad state" was a miraculous, supernatural feat. Priests from their pulpits and the devout in the market preached and exhorted the faithful to choose the correct path. Francisco del Castillo, a Jesuit resident in the city during the seventeenth century, presented a repertoire of stories concerning this in his autobiography. On one occasion, the priest went to aid a man who was ill who told him of his experience. He asked Castillo to "rescue my soul from the claws and slavery of the devil. When I was twenty years old, I was in a state of mortal sin and did not know the grace of God or confess as I should. Because I have been involved in a bad friendship with a woman until now, I have decided to marry her so I can be in God's grace. One afternoon at the flea market, I heard your reverence speaking to that holy bronze crucifix you carry with you. God softened my hard heart so that I could no longer resist the repeated strong signs and touches from God I am feeling. Perhaps God has inflicted this illness on me now for not having carried out his divine advice and inspiration."[3]

Illicit sexual relations resulted in a problem of conscience and caused feelings of guilt, leading an individual to expect punishment and later seek repentance. The feeling of personal wrongdoing thus assumed a religious aspect. Repentance was not easily attained, and renunciation entailed its own risks, sometimes significant.

> One Sunday afternoon a woman listened to another woman pondering the great risk and danger unwed couples find themselves in and how spending a long time in concubinage was cause for condemnation. She then left the conversation, determined to get herself out of that situation. She avoided her partner in such a way and with such great courage that she preferred to suffer the stab wounds he passionately and blindly gave her, rather than consent to committing a sin with him.[4]

Perceptions of a more relaxed, defiant nature coexisted with these attitudes. Relationships between men and women were the object of much
conversation. People expressed their opinions about fornication in the streets
and other public places. They often discussed chastity and the soul's salvation.
Men and women not only dared to publicly affirm that concubinage was an
acceptable arrangement. They further asserted that it was better, more honorable, than marriage and that married couples would not necessarily be saved
from the wrath of hell. Furthermore, there were those who rejected doctrine
and believed that illicit relations with women were venial, rather than mortal,
sins. Discussion of the perfection of the various states—virginity, celibacy,
marriage—and their ranking also provoked conflicts.[5] Contrary to the teach-
ings of contemporary theologians, many of Lima's residents held the conviction that the state of marriage was better than that of the priesthood.[6]

During the fifteenth and sixteenth centuries, the actual act of fornication seemed less important than commenting on its nature. Engaging in a
relationship out of wedlock led to ordinary punishment, but proclaiming it
defensible could be considered both blasphemous and heretical. This was
why many men and women from diverse social classes were accused, tried,
and punished by the Inquisition. Because of his comment toward the end of
the sixteenth century that simple fornication was not a sin, Diego Frías de
Miranda was later summoned to appear before Lima's Inquisition.[7] At the
beginning of the seventeenth century, men like Juan Pérez Tavares, a mule-
teer from Triana; Jerónimo de Andrade, a sailor from San Lúcar; Nicolau, a
Greek; and many others who found themselves in similar situations shared
this opinion.[8] Juan, who dared to deny the virginity of Mary, mother of
Jesus, was accused of blasphemy.[9]

This kind of complacency with regard to sex outside of marriage was
also evident from the trials of unwed couples appearing in the archiepiscopal court. A considerable number of cases were presented before Lima's
ecclesiastical court after the couple had been living together for a number
of years. In twenty of the fifty-eight cases examined for the seventeenth
century, no reference was made to how long the accused couple had been
living together. Of the thirty-eight remaining cases, only seven failed to last
one year, while five lasted longer than a year. Fourteen couples were together
for between two and five years, seven for more than five years, three for
"many years," and two for "a long period of time."[10] That so many relationships between unmarried partners endured for more than a year indicates
a high level of acceptance for these unions among city residents. In most of

the cases, witnesses claimed to have known of these illicit relationships for between two and ten years, thus further demonstrating people's tolerance for this arrangement.[11]

The sexual behavior of clerics further showed how popular the practice of concubinage was at this time. Soliciting, whereby a priest seduced a penitent during confession, was widespread throughout the viceroyalty, and Lima's Tribunal of the Inquisition accused and tried numerous priests of this crime. The confessors, whether regular or secular clergy, committed this crime in three ways: by unpremeditated acts, through illicit conversations, and with indecent propositions.[12]

Throughout the sixteenth and seventeenth centuries, priests of different orders were tried for sexually harassing women in the confessional. Women from the social elite accused priests of having carnal contact with them. Indigenous and Spanish women, as well as mulattas, testified before the tribunal, describing in detail how the priests tried to seduce them.

Many priests were apparently content merely to verbalize obscenities in the confessional. Others dared to go a step further and touched the breasts of women attending confession. Some priests even arranged meetings with these women in order to meet them outside the confessional in the sacristy or somewhere other than the church. In 1595, the tribunal punished Fr. Pedro Pacheco for soliciting the sisters from a nunnery in Lima where he was the confessor. More than forty indigenous women testified against Fr. Alonso Días for soliciting during the same period.[13]

Many accused of solicitation appeared in the auto de fé of 1600. Seventeen women testified against Pedro de Arias Lobo, a Portuguese. Pedro de Villagra, fifty-four years old, was charged with abusing a mother and daughter. Rodrigo Ortiz, a nobleman and native of Asunción, turned himself in for having had sexual contact with numerous women in the confessional itself.[14] Fr. Juan Prieto, a fifty-year-old native of Berlanga, complained about the cold-heartedness of indigenous women and pursued his Spanish penitents, "achieving much success in his adventures."[15]

Abuse by priests in the confessional reached such levels that a certain Señor Ordóñez wrote to the Council of the Indies, saying that "It appeared that there was hardly a priest who had not sinned. . . . [T]he worst part is that some of the accused told the Indian women that it was no sin to commit sinful acts with them, and so they had sex in the church."[16]

The wide acceptance of sexual activity outside of marriage is revealed by the case of the inquisitor, Gutiérrez de Ulloa. Another cleric, Zapata, denounced him, claiming in a 1582 memorandum that the inquisitor was unscrupulous in his behavior toward women.[17] Gutiérrez de Ulloa tried "to pursue any and all kinds of women, those who were important and the noble, as well as those who were not, without ever caring whether they were young maidens or married or whether this set a bad example. All he was concerned about was following his chaotic appetite, as . . . is publicly well known." Gutiérrez de Ulloa managed to get himself mixed up in scandal after scandal. He disturbed family life by seducing young maidens and arranged marriages to suit himself. He carried on a love affair with a married woman, doña Catalina Morrejón, so disgraceful that "even the Indians and blacks knew of it, since doña Catalina would hit the inquisitor with a stick in a jealous fit, which was scandalous. In order to put an end to the problem, she was banished." Gutiérrez de Ulloa had children from this relationship, and apparently from many others as well, "and they were brought up publicly in the City of Kings, causing much scandal."

Gutiérrez de Ulloa's administration of the Inquisition was severely criticized, especially because trials were so often delayed. In July 1587, 216 charges against Gutiérrez de Ulloa were presented before the tribunal; it was later proved that he had fathered children with five different women. Shortly thereafter, it was discovered that both Gutiérrez de Ulloa and Ruiz del Prado had no interest in proceeding with the trial, since both were accomplices in the tribunal's administrative delays. Furthermore, Ruiz wanted to be an inquisitor, but Gutiérrez de Ulloa, despite everything, refused to give up his position. In December 1594, Gutiérrez de Ulloa, appointed by the king as inspector of the Audiencia of Charcas, left for the city of La Plata. In his position as inquisitor, Gutiérrez de Ulloa represented the moral authority of society. His own behavior, however, demonstrated inconsistency in commonly held moral standards, as well as support for not one, but many moral principles.

Events such as these were no novelty to the city's inhabitants, who reproached the authorities for their behavior. Testimony in the case of Juan Montañés, a native of Marseilles, underscores how often this occurred and how ordinary people felt about it. The shared public interpretation was that "God would have to destroy Lima because of its many evils and the fact that all the clerics were involved in concubinage. When the witness told the offender not to become involved in that, he said that even the inquisitors failed to do what they were supposed to, acting against the poor rather than the important people of the world. The Inquisition was like the Tower of Babylon because those who entered it never figured out how to leave."[18]

Clerics' licentious behavior was evident to everyone. Even occasional visitors easily recognized the attitudes of the religious authorities, and particularly the relaxed view toward the vow of celibacy.

> Most friars live such licentious lives that there are superiors
> and provincials who take substantial funds from the convents
> under their responsibility to see to the expenses for a worldly
> life, and sometimes for vices so conspicuous that they have no
> misgivings about confessing their sins or the children they have
> fathered, to whom they sometimes pass on the cassocks in
> which they are vested.[19]

The archiepiscopal authorities were in charge of punishing unwed couples.[20] The trials, despite their bureaucratic, mostly repetitive tone, nevertheless provide an idea of the nature of the events and how the colonial church viewed relationships outside of marriage.

Cases of concubinage reached the ecclesiastical court in different ways. The authorities sought them out by periodically carrying out inspections, or *visitas*. It is clear from the testimony of witnesses that private life was extremely permeable and daily life implied a marked closeness between people. This gave religious authorities easy access into the intimate world of those being investigated. According to popular opinion in Lima, a woman going alone to a man's house at an ungodly hour, or vice versa, or someone regularly visiting the residence of another, "eating and drinking under the same roof," proved the existence of illicit sexual relations. A woman cooking for a man, or washing, starching, and ironing his clothes, for which he might give her money or a gift, provided sufficient evidence to confirm the offense. This type of relationship was related to the open nature of private life at this time, as was discussed in the previous chapter.

Outsiders peeked into bedrooms where bodies united. Men and women explored the intimacy of their neighbors. Curious eyes noted clandestine meetings. Around the beginning of the seventeenth century, the owner of a small store confessed to the ecclesiastical prosecutor that Catalina González, another shopkeeper, committed a "public sin" with Melchor de Cintar, a thirty-year-old, unmarried Portuguese merchant. Witnesses said that four years earlier, although Cintar had been on his way to Tierra Firme, he had approached González and been on friendly terms with her. Another witness, also a shopkeeper, claimed that he had seen the lovers with his own eyes "together in bed many times, as well as eating together at the same table . . . and he thought it was wrong."

Cintar denied the accusations. He asserted that he and González had maintained a business relationship; he would sell her bottles of wine that she would in turn sell at her store. He said he was worried she would lose her good "reputation and the status she had, for she was thought to be a decent woman and a very good Christian." Catalina fled the city and "could not be found."[21]

In 1632, Juan de Castro, a fifty-year-old married bricklayer from Jaén, Spain, and María de Ayllón, a free black who was thirty years old and single, scandalized an entire neighborhood in Lima. Six witnesses, among them a woman, recounted the physical abuse Castro had inflicted upon his wife, doña Juana de Herrera, as well as the hard life he had put her through "for being caught up in his vices, going out with other women." This unbearable situation had driven doña Juana to leave the city and travel to Panama to stay with her brother.

After doña Juana's departure, María de Ayllón and Juan de Castro would "dine and eat together and sometimes this witness would enter that home and that black woman would hide behind the bed, so that this witness would not see her frequently entering at night to sleep with Juan de Castro." Furthermore, this witness asked one of Juan de Castro's slaves, also named María, "whether María de Ayllón had already left." Another slave commented that "she stayed in her master's bed when he left for work in the morning." Francisco González de Castro, Juan de Castro's neighbor, stressed that "that black woman rules the house as if she were his wife. This drew much attention and caused much scandal in the neighborhood because it was such a public act."

Juan de Castro contended that his wife had been "harsh and rash" and had fled. He denied the illicit relationship with María de Ayllón, claiming she "would go to his home to heal some slaves." María admitted she knew him, but also denied all accusations. They spent a few days imprisoned, he in the archiepiscopal jail and she in the Casa del Divorcio. They were released later, though warned to behave properly.[22]

These testimonies suggest that corporal acts, such as sleeping and eating and therefore bodily contact, were not part of the "back room of social conduct."[23] Private, intimate aspects were exposed to the eyes of those outside the home; intimate relationships were not entirely private. This was evident as well in the architecture of the home, as noted earlier.

Insignificant exceptions aside, in almost all cases an official of the archbishopric made the first accusation: the procurator fiscal, the ecclesiastical prosecutor, the vicar general, the bailiff for the ecclesiastical court, or in some cases, an attorney of the royal audiencia. The ecclesiastical authorities' initiation of these trials did not preclude anyone else from denouncing those involved in illicit sexual relations. These two types of accusations were indistinguishable from one another, however, since authorities of the archbishopric always made the formal charge. In some cases, though, the militant tone of the accusations denoted a close relationship between the witnesses and the defendant, thus indicating their role in identifying the accused.

On many occasions, denouncing a relationship outside of marriage was an escape valve for existing social tensions. Such was the case with Francisco Escudero. A native of Castile, he owned a store on Calle de Pescadería and was accused of living with a married woman who was not his wife. The three witnesses who appeared in court, a craftsman and two small businessmen, lived on the same street as Escudero. All accused him of being with a married woman with whom "he has a son. The woman takes care of him, and he will soon be one year old. She usually enters Escudero's home at all hours of the day and sells him some merchandise that he deals in. . . . When her husband is at home with her, she is circumspect about going into the home of Francisco Escudero."

Escudero denied the charges, claiming that the relationship had more to do with business that he and the husband of the accused were involved in. "Some people, who are in the same business, are jealous because he bought seven mill . . . and he has given things to the woman to sell, paying her one peso for every ten, which is what he usually pays. This is why they have testified against him."

The court initially ordered Francisco Escudero to be put in jail. From there, he insisted that he did not know why he had been arrested and demanded that he be set free so he could take care of his business. The authorities finally ordered him not to have any dealings with the married woman and fined him "court expenses and ten pounds of wax to illuminate the holy sacrament." The leniency of the punishment suggests the authorities took Francisco Escudero's argument into account and that the witnesses' statements were disregarded, apparently a relatively common occurrence.[24]

The alferez, don Miguel Dávila, a native of Avila, and doña Antonia de Escobar, a Panamanian about twenty-five years old, may also have been victims of false accusations. Three young Spaniards, soldiers and artillerymen, claimed that don Miguel and doña Antonia were "eating at the same table and sleeping in the same bed" and bringing up their child. Doña

Antonia replied that she lived "like a slave," dedicated to taking care of her home and children. She denied the accusations and stated that the child in question belonged to the man with whom she lived, who happened to be out of town at the time. She was waiting for him to return so they could marry.

Don Miguel had come to Lima from Callao to see to a lawsuit he had with a mulatta and "only those mulattas. A certain Conde, the husband of one of them, was the accuser and enemy of doña Antonia and wished to do him wrong. This was so he would not continue the lawsuit he had against those women in the royal criminal court, where they have been condemned to flogging and exile. They go around looking to make trouble for him, which is how they plan to avoid the criminal complaint against them."

Don Miguel noted the irregularities in the trial. There were no witnesses who could prove they had found him with a woman. It was not the soldier who should be believed, but the "noble and important person." He knew her because "she washed and starched his shirts as she did for other people and soldiers."[25]

The ecclesiastical court called witnesses to give their testimony after the formal charge had been brought. It is difficult to know during this part of the trial whether these witnesses were the same ones who had initially sought the authorities' investigation. Witnesses' statements responded narrowly to specific questions, providing answers to an interrogatory that followed a fixed pattern. Fortunately, witnesses occasionally took pains to offer extremely detailed information.

Officially there were only three witnesses, though later women and more than three people participated.[26] They usually had some connection to the accused, whether as neighbors, members of the same trade or occupation, or kin. Less frequently, clerics took part in the proceedings. What the accused could be certain of, though, was that no witnesses would give favorable testimony.

Extramarital relationships included a wide social range, from gentlemen and ladies to Indians and slaves. Those accused of concubinage, however, came predominately from colonial society's subordinate strata. Men tended to be small and middling traders, low-ranking bureaucrats, and craftsmen. Women of the lower orders, castas, mulattas, mestizas, and *zambas*, worked as seamstresses, laundresses, and shopkeepers. Some indigenous women were also charged, as were a few women identified as doñas. Female slaves were virtually absent from the proceedings, indicating both general and official indifference to their sexual conduct.

Arrest orders came on the heels of witnesses' depositions with no opportunity to rebut the charges. Women were normally sent to retreat houses, hospitals, or the homes of respectable families, while men were locked up in the archiepiscopal jail. Women were sometimes jailed, but this was generally the fate only of slaves, Indians, or castas. In 1610, the ecclesiastical court accused Melchora de los Reyes, an unmarried mulatta seamstress about thirty-four years old, of engaging in an illicit relationship with merchant Juan Romero. Both denied the accusation, but the procurator fiscal sentenced her to prison.[27] Although exceptional, this case does indicate how gender, as well as ethnicity and economic status, came into play in these trials.

From their respective places of incarceration, men and women protested the decisions of ecclesiastical authorities. Men, both as men and as members of social groups with greater resources, formally questioned their verdicts in written appeals to the church. Women had fewer resources and different limitations. This could explain why men asked the authorities to review their verdicts more frequently than did women.

Defense of the accused followed these gender lines. In almost all cases, men presented their own defense. The voices of women directly implicated were, however, less frequently heard. This silence is explained in part because women's public intervention tarnished their honor. Still, not all women opted for silence when locked away. In 1635, thirty-year-old Isabel Escalante, a widow and native of Lima, was accused of concubinage with Francisco Espinosa, a Spanish cordmaker, whose wife was in Spain at the time. Both parties denied the accusation, but she was taken to the Casa del Divorcio, while he was locked up in the archiepiscopal jail. From her place of seclusion, she sent the following letter:

> I, Isabel de los Angeles, a respectable, retiring widow, state that at
> your order, the ecclesiastical prosecutor brought me to this Casa del
> Divorcio so that I may look after my honor and defense until they
> provide me the reasons for my imprisonment. . . . I prefer that they
> sentence me to house arrest instead of this jail because in my home
> I have family, wealth, and a child, and all this is at great risk in my
> absence. I ask and entreat your grace to release me or send me to
> my home as a form of imprisonment.

The trial was inconclusive. It is probable they only received the usual reprimand.[28]

In 1627, Margarita Gutiérrez, a thirty-year-old widow and native of Lima, was accused of having an extramarital affair with twenty-six-year-old Antonio Pérez, a cleric of minor orders and native of Potosí. Four witnesses claimed to have seen them sinning publicly for two years, "eating, drinking, and sleeping under the same roof." Proof of this was that "Margarita Gutiérrez gave birth to Antonio Pérez's child." He went to the archiepiscopal jail while Margarita went to the Casa del Divorcio. From there she wrote that

> I, Margarita Gutiérrez, widow, state that Francisco de Aguilar, magistrate for the ecclesiastical court, has notified me that they initiated proceedings, saying that I live in bad conditions with a certain unmarried man. This is why your grace has ordered my imprisonment and that I be held in the home of Marcos de Molina. Because I always obey your grace's orders, I ask and entreat you to order that my confession be taken and I be provided with the reasons for my imprisonment. I ask for justice.

Antonio Pérez was later convicted and had to pay eight pesos, while Margarita Gutiérrez was imprisoned in the Casa del Divorcio. In case of recidivism, he would be expelled from the city for one year, and Margarita would be locked up for one year in a place of the authorities' choosing.[29]

Both men and women tended to deny charges, even when proof, such as the existence of children, was present. A subterfuge men sometimes used as a defense was to admit that they had indeed engaged in an illicit friendship, but were separated from their lovers at the time of the accusation. Pedro Godoy, a swordmaker from Toledo and married for forty years, was accused in 1610 of adultery with a married woman. He defended himself by claiming that "for more than six years, this defendant had carnal relations with a certain married woman with whom he had a child. She later left with her husband for another place. This defendant was then reunited with his wife and never again dealt with that married woman . . . but only with the woman God had given him and with whom he shares a married life."

Because the judges of the archiepiscopal court found many aggravating circumstances, the fact that both individuals were married and there were children, they ordered Godoy jailed. He challenged the sentence, stating that the witnesses were his "mortal enemies because he had exchanged unpleasant words with them." Godoy was finally reprimanded and warned he would suffer exile and a one-hundred-peso fine if he repeated his offense.[30]

The conjugal state of those tried for concubinage varied. Many were unmarried: of fifty-eight cases, twenty-one dealt with single men and women. Their infraction fell within the realm of simple fornication, sexual relations between unrelated men and women outside of marriage who were not bound by a vow of celibacy. Such relationships were still considered "extremely serious and very dangerous."[31]

At this time a promise of marriage, whether secret or in writing, obligated the couple to uphold the commitments of an actual formal marriage. This was an old custom, but it also indicated that the church did not yet completely control conjugal relations. According to the church, betrothal alone did not constitute married life and could be considered concubinage. Archiepiscopal authorities in Lima tried during regular inspections to find those couples who, though they had taken the first step in formalizing their marital relationship, had not completed the process leading to full conjugal cohabitation.

There were couples who became engaged and then decided to live together. The promise to marry as an integral part of the marriage process underlay this type of concubinage. Some couples began, but did not complete, the process. Such was the case of Diego Loarte, a native of New Spain and vecino of Lima, and doña Gerónima Loyola, also a vecina of Lima. These two, "contemptuous of what synodal councils and institutions establish and order, have been promised in marriage for more than one year. They do not want the church's nuptial blessings and have not received them. They live together in a house and despite having been notified by your majesty's proceedings, . . . they have done nothing to end their stubbornness." This couple were pressured to wed within fifteen days, which they promised to do, and were married in the course of the year.[32]

Oftentimes men and women who engaged in sexual relationships did not live together but still intended to get married at some point. Such was the case of Ramón González, baker, thirty-eight years old, and Marina García, thirty-two years old. The neighbors stated that Ramón González "possesses her in the house, and they have seen them shamelessly eating and sleeping together on many occasions."

When the two were imprisoned, they wrote a letter together and afterward confessed. Ramón González claimed that he had not taken Marina García as a lover, but "had dealings with her because they were going to get married." Because he had been ill, however, he was hoping to recover so he could marry her. Marina declared the same. She was not living in concubinage, but was with Ramón González "instead of her husband, because he said they were going to marry." She insisted that they had lived together under the same roof "only since the previous Christmas season." They were reprimanded and forced to pay twelve pesos each.[33]

During a 1645 ecclesiastical inspection by the archbishop of Lima, it was discovered that Francisco de Saldaña, an unmarried Spaniard, had lived for many years under the same roof with doña María de los Reyes, a single mulatta, quadroon, or mestiza (the witnesses were uncertain about her precise ethnicity). Witnesses claimed that together they had had at least four children. Francisco de Saldaña confessed that he had "dishonorable relations with doña María de los Reyes, whom I had planned to marry in the past. After thinking about it carefully, however, I have decided not to go through with it." Having made this decision, Francisco de Saldaña informed the authorities of his firm conviction to stay away from doña María.[34]

It was not always the men who refused to marry. Sometimes women chose a limited, comfortable extramarital commitment. That was the decision Isabel, native of Llampa, made. She preferred being the concubine of thirty-year-old Sebastián Moreno, a native of Extremadura and single, who rented a farm in the outskirts of Lima. Isabel's relatives reported her concubinage. Francisco Simanas, an Indian tailor, stated that Isabel, who at the time was a prisoner in the archiepiscopal jail, "would rather be with that man than marry him, because things are going very well and she does not know whether he would make her life difficult as a husband."[35]

Mariana de Bicuña, a mulatta widow living in the city, was in a similar situation. She was accused in 1611 of engaging in a relationship outside of marriage with Sgto. Sebastián Susarte, "a man who sails and travels." One of the witnesses affirmed that it had been twelve years since they had initiated their illicit friendship, when the husband, who had only died seven months before, was still alive. The witness added, though, that Susarte commented to him that Mariana refused to marry him.[36]

Trial by the ecclesiastical court did not frighten the vecinos of Lima, for recidivism was common. In 1627, Juan Gómez, a married man from Trujillo, and Juana Ramírez, a black slave, were tried three times by the ecclesiastical court. According to the accusation, these two were lovers for six years. Two of the three witnesses claimed that a daughter of Juana Ramírez and Sebastián Gómez had been baptized in Santa Ana Parish. During this time, they added, Sebastián Gómez "had given her money in order to emancipate her." Because of this, "the mulatta child was recorded as free in the baptismal books of the parish."[37]

In 1668, don Francisco de Saldías and María Nicolasa, a zamba, were taken to the archiepiscopal court. One of the witnesses, a Spanish widow named doña Elena de Barrios, aged fifty, said she had seen them together many times in different places and they seemed to be lovers. One night doña Elena happened to meet doña Francisca de Espínola y Salamanca, don Francisco's mother. She saw that doña Francisca was in a jealous fit when she saw her son distracted because of his love affair. She confronted that zamba and grabbed her mantilla and scarf. Doña Elena noticed that don Francisco defended the zamba, "despite the respect he should have had for his mother."

Don Miguel de Saldías, don Francisco's brother, stated before the court that he knew of his brother's affair, which had already been going on for three years. He had seen them "eat and put tidbits in each other's mouths. They slept together in the same bed and lived together under the same roof near the convent of Nuestra Señora de las Mercedes." Don Miguel and other witnesses further claimed that they had repeatedly warned don Francisco to stay away from María Nicolasa, but in vain.

Because of this incident, doña Francisca pressured the authorities. Although it is unknown whether she brought formal charges, don Francisco was sent to the guardhouse, and María Nicolasa was confined to the archiepiscopal jail for six months. They were reprimanded when she finished her sentence, and María Nicolasa was warned not to see don Francisco again "not in public and not in secret or else she would be exiled." The lovers nevertheless resumed their relationship, left Lima, and moved to the port of Callao.

When they appeared before the court again the accusers requested harsher punishment. Don Miguel testified once again, finally remembering that he had reprimanded don Francisco because of "how terrible it looked for a young man from a good family to behave so badly with a wild, low-class zamba. He answered that it was impossible for him to be a man with any other woman." Immediately afterward, María Angu, a slave who spoke some Spanish, stated that she had accompanied the tenacious couple to Callao, helping them move. In one of her conversations with don Francisco, he confided to her that "this zamba was in his heart and he loved her very much because she helped him when he needed it. When he slept and ate, he was always thinking about her."[38]

Aside from expressing some signs of affection characteristic of the time, this love story also explains the essence of stable relationships outside of marriage. María Nicolasa and don Francisco were both single and free to marry without impediment, but the authorities did not order them to wed. They instead disallowed and even prohibited it. The differences in social standing and ethnicity between don Francisco and María Nicolasa counseled against such a union.

❧

Illicit relationships knew no social boundaries and played out at religious, public, and personal levels. Guilt was a sentiment common to both men and women. In relationships outside of marriage, it was basically linked to religious offense and the notion of sin. Concubinage became a theme in the public domain, treated either with horror or with naturalness and complacency. These sentiments existed side by side with attitudes defiant in the face of religious discourse.

Colonial authorities, mainly those of the church, were in charge of reining in illicit sexual relationships. There were nevertheless many obstacles to the efficacy of their efforts. So long as they were themselves involved in public concubinage, the religious, from inquisitors to lower-ranking clerics, could not effectively exercise their power to control illicit relationships. Public power of the religious sort was in the public eye, under the daily scrutiny of the capital's residents. The popular perception that authorities were corrupt diminished the influence and rigor of religious rhetoric about the expected sexual conduct of laypeople. This in turn played an important role in people's respect for the law.

Mild punishment of couples engaged in concubinage also points to the high level of tolerance for this endemic urban phenomenon. Men paid small fines in pesos, while women were usually jailed for a short time. There is no record that the infamous punishments stipulated in Spanish law, such as losing the right to wear specific clothing, whipping, or walking naked in the streets, were ever brought to bear.

Matrimonial rituals involved several stages, and those who took the first few formal steps sometimes failed to complete the process. They nevertheless had sexual contact and in some cases, lived together and had children. This made them, in the eyes of the authorities, guilty of concubinage.

It was couples of unequal social standing who most often engaged in concubinage, men from colonial society's middle and upper sectors and women from the middle or lower strata. There was a dual code of morality that differed for men and women. There were also, however, the ethnic and social hierarchies of the social system itself that produced a variety of codes that governed female sexual conduct. These implied variable levels of intensity in the efforts to control female sexual conduct and reflected the social standing of those accused of concubinage. Groups from the city's middle sectors, as well as women, were subject to tighter restrictions. Elite women were protected by prestige and their dowries, while female slaves were not thought to have any sexual or personal honor at all.

In court proceedings, women from society's highest levels and slaves rarely appeared as witnesses against concubinage. This suggests a division of labor between public and private authority for controlling female sexuality. Public powers, in this case the church, assumed responsibility for punishing transgressions involving women from the middle sectors of society. Women of the aristocracy lived under the private controls of family structure. In the case of slaves, their masters, even if uninterested in their slaves' virtue, mediated between their slaves' sexual conduct and the exercise of public authority.

How concubinage cases were prosecuted further revealed society's double standard. Sentencing and punishment differed for men and women, but ethnicity also influenced how women offenders were treated. In most cases, men and women denied the accusation. Those who admitted their guilt had either already taken the first formal steps toward marriage or had children. By contrast, the cases of recidivism suggested how deeply rooted a practice concubinage was among city people.

The ambivalence ecclesiastical authorities had about conjugal relationships was sometimes expressed in the sentences they passed. The only pressure they put on unmarried couples living in concubinage was that they should maintain a stable relationship. This was done in the hope that they might become a family, in accord with official canons. The Council of Trent had established freedom of matrimony, but in many cases the social differences between partners played an important role in influencing the attitudes of ecclesiastical authorities. In a society where social and ethnic stratification organized individuals' lives and activities, encouraging marriage between men and women of different strata was unacceptable. The colonial context was such that ecclesiastical authorities could not follow a consistent policy favoring matrimony or discouraging concubinage. Given that, the teaching of the twelfth-century church still held: "People should marry within their 'order,' the functional group in which God has placed them. There should be no unequal marriages."[39]

How concubinage relationships were described, especially by witnesses in court, revealed some features of contemporary social life and shed light on the meaning of relationships between men and women. Private life lacked intimacy and was easily viewed by those outside the home. This was fully consonant with the importance of prestige based on the opinions of others and the diminished importance of internal controls in governing individuals' sexual conduct.

CHAPTER FOUR

Adultery

Sinning against Charity and Justice

❧

Colonial legislation closely followed the precepts different Spanish bodies of law established to control adultery. This particular extramarital relationship deeply worried both civil and religious authorities. The *Siete Partidas* of Alfonso X, the Wise (1221–84), and the conciliar legislation in force during the end of the Middle Ages stipulated its punishment. In seventeenth-century Lima, the royal audiencia tried adultery cases insofar as they were secular offenses. In the archiepiscopal court, they were part of the trials against unwed couples. Incidents related to adultery were also examined in this court in an indirect fashion. When adultery was presented to the court as one of the reasons for divorce, reconstruction and interpretation of a significant part of the problem become possible.

Adultery, the extraconjugality of married couples, shared the social and religious sanctions applied to other kinds of illicit sexuality. It also had its own moral features and penalties, though, since it was the most threatening of extramarital relationships and the source of greatest discord.

It is only proper to present adultery from the point of view of the double standard. Theologians and jurists of the time asked themselves "whether the fornication future married couples commit with other people should be considered simple fornication, or does it have the wickedness of adultery, as it does for married couples?"[1] Juan Machado de Chávez y Mendoza provided a Solomonic solution that some jurists of the time had already come to. "When the engaged man commits fornication, it is neither adultery nor a circumstance that should be confessed because his status does not change. This status does indeed change when the engaged woman commits fornication, for in such a case it is believed (and with reason) that this wrongs the engaged man. For this reason, the condition changes to one of sin and that is why the engaged woman must declare it during confession."[2]

Men and women suffered different sanctions for the same offense. Male offenders incurred economic penalties while adulterous women, beyond having to pay fines, were subject to penalties intended to disgrace them, like the loss of clothing or having to walk half-naked through the streets. Sometimes the husband chose the punishment; he also had the right to kill the adulterers. There were laws restricting this, but society did not harshly judge men who acted on it.

Male adultery was scarcely considered in Spanish society at this time, appearing in formulaic language as "licentious living by married men." Although female concubines played the more sinful role and received more severe punishment, men could not exercise their prerogatives in an unlimited fashion. In 1681, the Twelfth Council of Toledo established that husbands could not abandon their wives. Those who did so and sought out the company of other women were refused communion until they returned to their wives.[3]

Adultery took two forms. Whoever violated the fidelity that a married couple should maintain committed the sin of lust. Wives, however, were further guilty of doing wrong to their husbands by their effrontery, while adulterous husbands could not live together with their spouses.[4] Adultery, a "serious mortal sin against charity and justice," remained a sin even if the injured party knowingly allowed it to occur, since harm had already been done to the holy state of matrimony.[5] In principle, because of the "mutual fidelity that both partners should maintain during marriage, both the man and the woman" sinned upon committing adultery. Nevertheless, it was the wife who was "guilty of a greater sin than the husband" because of the "shame, scandal, and harm" surrounding the uncertain identity of her children's father.[6] A husband's adultery did not dishonor his wife. A woman, though, could be accused whether she was engaged or already married.

Adultery was grounds for requesting divorce, but under civil and royal law, only the husband could bring a criminal accusation of adultery against his wife. Wives did not have this right because it was "undeniable that the same offense committed by the wife is more heinous than when it is committed by the husband. Thus it follows that a law of the kingdom expressly states that the wife cannot refuse to respond to the accusation of the husband or engaged partner by saying she wishes to prove that her husband or engaged partner also committed adultery."[7]

According to Machado de Chávez, it was a universal principle of civil and royal law that an aggrieved husband should formally accuse his adulterous wife. He could do so before either an ecclesiastical or secular judge. The ecclesiastical judge handled requests for divorce and decided whether an adulterous wife was subject to punishment, whether instead of or in addition to the divorce. The secular judge took the case if, for example, the husband sought the death penalty for his wife, on which the judge was fully empowered to act.

In 1631 Alfonso de Castro, a solicitor for the royal audiencia, had found his wife in the back room of a bookdealer "where she was waiting for a man with whom she had an illicit friendship, and he stabbed her in the temples." She died shortly thereafter in the Hospital de la Caridad. The solicitor and the adulterous bookdealer were imprisoned, though released a few days later.[8] Although the solicitor's attack fell well within the code of honor, his brother-in-law, a priest, avenged his sister's death and publicly stabbed him in the back.[9]

When the intimate lives of the powerful and subordinate produced illicit sexual conduct, adultery became part of the public domain. Juan Antonio Suardo profusely recorded detailed news about adultery cases in his *Diario de Lima*. On 18 January 1633, Juan de Reina, a notary for the ecclesiastical court of Lima, was found in flagrante with a married woman by her husband. The men dueled, and both were nearly mortally wounded.[10] A soldier was visiting his mulatta lover when her husband arrived unexpectedly. This time, the soldier stabbed the husband, and he "later died without confession."[11] In October 1630 Pablito "the Comedian," an actor in the city, fought heatedly with Julián de Lorca, a city councilman. The comedian claimed that his wife, an actress, was engaged in an illicit relationship with Lorca. The inevitable violence resulted in the near-death of the wife, shot by her husband. The authorities intervened in the matter, banishing Pablito from the city for two years and sending Lorca to the city of Trujillo for two years.[12] Obviously not every man bent on avenging his honor escaped without punishment.

Adulterous behavior worried the religious authorities. To control it they periodically inspected all the barrios and parishes of the city. This procedure became more stringent following the sixteenth-century reforms of the Council of Trent. As noted in the previous chapter, occurrences of concubinage, a designation that included adultery, were found out, and both adulterers and cohabitors were tried in a similar fashion.

In the seventeenth century unmarried individuals and single men living with married women were those most often guilty of concubinage (twelve cases). Adulterous relationships, far fewer in number, followed and included married men with married women, clergymen with married women, married men with single women, and married men and widowed women. The difference in the number of married men and women involved in these trials is also revealing: only nine men compared to seventeen women. This does not necessarily indicate the frequency with which married men and women established extramarital relations. These figures instead reveal the differing degrees of tolerance toward men and women who maintained extramarital sexual relationships: men's adulterous acts were more acceptable than women's.

In principle, married women accused of adultery could not be named in public. Diego Gil, a native of Santiago, Chile, was accused before the archiepiscopal court, of living in concubinage "with a woman who, because she is married, will not have her name stated. He is currently involved with her in a carnal way and supports her, although she causes him much grief out of jealousy."[13]

This way of protecting a woman's honor, which also served to protect her husband and family, on occasion did not work for women from subordinate groups. This was the case with Juana, an indigenous married woman whose surname was unmentioned, accused in November 1611 of living illicitly with Diego de Castro, a single merchant from the Canary Islands.[14]

Extramarital relationships between married men and single women seem to have prevailed in the city. Sebastián Gómez served as the constable in the town of Chancay in the agricultural valley north of Lima. Born in Lima, the thirty-eight-year-old family man was accused of living in concubinage with Florentina Catalán, a single woman and "daughter of Juan Catalán, the carpenter." Three male witnesses stated that Florentina and Sebastián were living "in public sin." She was very young and according to witnesses, had been involved in this "illicit friendship" since the age of fifteen. During this time, they had had two children, whom Sebastián regularly and generously supported.

Sebastián told his side of the story, though Florentina's version went unrecorded. He had known Florentina since her birth; he had also known her carnally and was the father of her children. Though he had not had sexual contact with her for the last six months, because of his past obligation "he has favored and continues to favor her, giving her bread to sustain her and her children. He aids her because she has no one to help her." Despite everything, Sebastián said, he had not failed to carry out his family responsibilities.

The ecclesiastical authorities searched for Florentina, and her parents gladly turned her over to them "of their own free will, without being forced to do so." She was immediately confined in Lima in the custody of a lawyer, Diego de Avila, so that he could put her in an appropriate place: the Hospital de la Caridad. Florentina pretended to be in labor and managed to regain her freedom. The authorities suspected that Sebastián Gómez had secured Florentina's release from the hospital, and in an attempt to clear up the matter, summoned several women from the hospital to testify, nurses as well as the abbess.

Florentina had spent enough time in the Hospital de la Caridad for the women who lived and worked there to become accomplices in her love life. They showed understanding for and solidarity with the lovers, who wrote back and forth to one another. The women knew of "the many compliments and words of love" that abounded in their communications. One of the witnesses, who took it upon herself to put the lovers in contact, said that Sebastián had written "she should be more careful and should not marry. He would promise to serve her as long as she lived. She should take care because she was the mother of their children. In the letter this witness wrote and sent to him, Florentina told him to be patient. When she left to give birth, she would petition the archbishop and tell him she wanted to stay in the city."

None of the women confessed that Sebastián had taken Florentina out of the Hospital de la Caridad. The five-year-old son of Florentina and Sebastián, however, said that "the other day, his father carried her on his back." From that moment on, an implacable persecution was launched. One of the women who lived in the Hospital de la Caridad, Juana Calderón, was locked up in the Casa del Divorcio as punishment for her complicity.

Bands of men were organized to find Sebastián Gómez, but not before a bay horse and one hundred fanegas of wheat belonging to him were seized.

They finally found Sebastián and Florentina hiding in a nearby banana grove. Sebastián emerged from a ditch, "completely soaked, without cloak or hat." He was locked up in the archiepiscopal jail while Florentina was sent to the Casa del Divorcio. While incarcerated, Sebastián wrote to the authorities and denied having taken Florentina from La Caridad. Claiming that "his wife, children, and family were in great need," he begged for liberty. The judge finally ruled that Sebastián should have no dealings with Florentina, whether secretly or in public, and that he should return "to live in the company of his wife and children."[15]

Arranged marriages were quite common at this time. While the Council of Trent had established that personal freedom in the choice of spouse was an indispensable part of the sacrament of marriage, council provisions rarely changed the practices custom had set. More than one hundred years after the Tridentine decrees, the freedom to marry in colonial Lima was relative in the face of more immediate family pressures, and erotic impulses did not always find their sincerest expression in the matrimonial bed.

In the mid-seventeenth century, doña Juana de Pedraza requested a divorce before the archiepiscopal court after a year and a half of marriage to Damián de Montesinos. Her brother had forced her to marry, threatening her with a dagger, and this beginning had led to marital tension. Her husband finally found a lover, an unmarried mestiza, "whose name doña Juana does not know. Witnesses will confirm that he keeps her on his farm where he is with her and has illicit carnal relations with her as if she were his wife."[16]

Things certainly sometimes started off badly, but a rough beginning was also related to what marriage meant and how couples were paired. At this time, physical beauty and love as libidinal expression had little importance in the choice of spouse.[17] When real or imagined convenience determined matrimonial options, the seed of adultery was sown, and this held true for all social groups in the city. The experience of Francisca de Salcedo and Francisco Corbeto in the mid-seventeenth century reveals some of the characteristics of marriage that could lead to adultery. Fifteen days into their unconsummated marriage, Francisco left the house taking all his things with him, including the bed. He returned two years later, Francisca said, this time with a mulatta, Marta Sarmiento, with whom he spent every night and "with whom he still maintains an illicit relationship in my presence."[18]

Another source of men's adultery was the widespread practice of premarital sex, a long-standing tradition. Men had sexual relations with women they had no intention of marrying because of their disparate social standings. Presented with an interesting prospect, men eventually married but continued their previous relationships. Doña Maior de Espino's accusation against her husband, Francisco Guisado, illustrates this. In 1640, the two had already been married for twelve years, but Francisco had not ended his earlier relationship with an unmarried mulatta. She was the same one "he had been involved with before marrying me," said doña Maior, lamenting her bad luck.[19]

In 1634, Francisca de la Mota requested a divorce from her Portuguese husband, Pablo Domínguez. They had only been married for ten months, but during that time, her husband had kept up a relationship with María de Salinas, an Indian. According to Francisca de la Mota, her husband had promised to marry María before he married Francisca, and they had even had children together. At the age of twelve, Francisca, "naïve in the ways of the world," had been forced to marry Pablo Domínguez "to please an aunt who had raised me." Pablo Domínguez insisted this was a lie and if anything, she should be accused of abandoning their home.[20]

Adultery and illicit relationships were very closely related to the geographic mobility that characterized the economic activities of many men. A large number owned properties, both large and small, outside the city limits and beyond, in the provinces. Men devoted to business also traveled. Some often came and went from the city, while others spent a great deal of time outside the city, away from their wives and children. During extended stays away from Lima, men often established extramarital relationships.

The case of María Magdalena de Rojas y Sandoval was rather extreme, but not all that uncommon. Around 1642, her husband, Juan Bautista de Porras, left Lima to go to Huaylas, but by 1653 he had still not returned. During that time, he "had been and is now involved in an illicit relationship with a woman named Ana de Rivera. He lived with her then, as if she were his legitimate wife, causing public scandal and uproar in the entire province." By 1653, Juan Bautista had already had children with Ana de Rivera. Furthermore, according to María Magdalena, only a short time after their marriage years earlier, he had been living with a mulatta named Dionisia.[21]

Situations such as these affected the marital relations of all the city's inhabitants, whatever their ethnicity or social standing. Josefa Bernarda, an Indian, sold fruit in the streets of Lima. Her husband often traveled to the Huaura Valley north of the city. She complained of her husband's abuse and how he had taken all the money she had made selling fruit so he could give it to the woman he was living with in the northern valley.[22] María Inés accused her husband, Juan Agustín, of the same thing in her divorce action. In 1672, after a year and a half of marriage, she denounced her husband's abuse, for he had nearly killed her with a knife. Furthermore, Juan Agustín was living in concubinage with an Indian in Chancay "on whom he spends a great deal of money and with whom he lives, as if she were his legitimate wife, without giving me enough money for my sustenance."[23]

Not all wives calmly awaited their husbands' return. Men's absence also gave women the opportunity for adultery. Clemente de Torres asked his wife, Angela de Gutiérrez, for a divorce. Although he had "given her everything," she was with other men when he traveled and took care of business. She had been "brazen and shameless, dedicated to wooing men." His wife would allow visitors at all hours, especially at night, using a back door for this particular purpose. Clemente referred to one lover in particular, though did not give his name "because of his social status and respectability"; the witnesses would have to identify him. Doña Angela managed to make her escape, however, and no one knew her whereabouts.[24]

Accusations of female adultery were very rare. Only three of the seventy cases examined dealt with husbands accusing adulterous wives. Don Juan Bravo de Laguna sought a divorce from his wife, Juana de Franco, on these grounds. The offended husband told how he found his wife in bed with one Juan Durán. At the time unarmed, he left to search for a weapon that would allow him to avenge this insult. The lovers took advantage of his absence and fled. The dishonored man related how Diego Andrés de la Rocha, a judge of the criminal court, had intervened over a long period of time to ensure that the marriage continued. Thanks to that, the couple had resumed their married life after four or five years of separation. Juana had "continued her chaotic life," however, and for the year and a half she had been away from home, "she was the concubine of a married man, living with him under the same roof, and I have seen them together acting like lovers on many occasions."[25]

Women's accusations of adultery typically evoked husbands' persistent denials, but sometimes they responded differently. María de Aspitia, a former slave, accused her husband, Francisco Portierra, of adultery. He in turn accused María of being an adulteress. Thanks to his wealth, she had been emancipated, but on three occasions he had found her with another man. He could have killed her, but did not, instead forgiving her immediately. Seizing the opportunity, however, he asked that María go live in "eternal slavery" in the convent of Santa Catalina.[26] Whatever their social rank, men like don Juan Bravo de Laguna and Francisco Portierra believed they had the right, if not the duty, to kill their unfaithful wives in defense of their own honor. The masculine honor code knew no social distinctions.

Testimonies offered in court suggest that extramarital relationships were something more than just adventures or chance occurrences. In seventeenth-century Lima, adultery was strongly related to promiscuity. Promiscuity was in turn associated with violence and in some cases, perverse situations.

In 1655, doña Francisca de Campos insisted on divorcing Juan Salvador. She had previously gone to criminal court in the hope warnings from the authorities would change her husband's ways, but in vain. They had been married for seven years, and Juan Salvador had engaged in a series of extramarital affairs the entire time. When doña Francisca sued for divorce, Juan Salvador was simultaneously involved in two adulterous relationships. One was with a mulatta named Lorenza, a slave belonging to Bernardo Meléndez, "whom he has impregnated and with whom he has had a long-standing relationship." The other was with "another young woman who is a maiden and whose name will therefore go unmentioned. The witnesses will say who she is."[27]

Doña Sebastiana de Tello wanted to divorce her husband, José de Paredes. The abuse she had received from him was the result of her husband's long-standing public involvement in an illicit relationship with doña Catalina García. They had had one child together, José. According to doña Sebastiana's representative, the accused had even dared to bring his concubine to doña Sebastiana's home under the pretext that doña Catalina was José's godmother and forced her to work like a slave. As if this were not enough, José was living shamelessly with yet another woman, doña Isabel.[28]

Doña María de Marmolejo asked the archiepiscopal court in 1600 for a divorce from her husband, Capt. Rafael Escoto. She had suffered terrible abuse during their marriage. He had "put his foot on her throat and almost choked her" and later threatened to kill her with a dagger. He had spent all the money she had brought in dowry, and she wanted it returned to her. Finally, doña María added, her husband was involved in illicit relationships with two different women, a doña Luisa Maldonado and another woman. Through his representative, Captain Escoto denied he had abused his wife. In any case, even if he had, the mistreatment was of little importance and "had to be extremely cruel for a divorce to be granted."[29]

Similar situations occurred within the middle and lower social strata of the city. In 1651, Leonor Pascuala, an Indian from Huaylas, requested a divorce from Alonso Esteban, a hatter. Ever since their marriage three years before, "he has had and continues to have illicit relationships with different Indian women and in particular, one Francisca Manto."[30] Reports of men involved in relatively stable, but serial, extramarital relationships with women of different social rank are legion in the divorce records of the seventeenth century.

Women sometimes related how their husbands took the liberty of bringing their paramours right into their own homes. This was the case with doña Blasa de Guzmán. She complained that her husband, Francisco de la Mota, unburdened by conscience and with no fear of God, had taken as lovers "different women with whom he has committed adultery. He has even dared to bring them into my home, where he has carried on with them as if each one were his legitimate wife. Because I opposed this, I was beaten."[31]

Perverted behavior that went beyond the socially acceptable conduct that merely encouraged extramarital affairs also occurred. This was certainly the case with María de las Nieves, a mestiza born in Hatunjauja, and her mestizo husband, Hernando de Cuevas. María claimed that her husband treated her like a slave, beating her so severely she miscarried three times. Hernando had taken a married woman as his lover and what was worse, had raped María's sister.[32]

Doña Juana de Avendaño was in a similar, though more extreme, situation. Requesting divorce, she explained how her husband, Antonio Rico, had "given himself over to the vice of sensuality . . . and was living illicitly and publicly with a woman. Not content with this offense and his adulterous acts, he brought his concubine into my home, where I was supposed to entertain her and give her gifts. If I did not lavish affection on her, he would slap me in the face, grab me, and threaten to kill me right in front of her."

Adultery differed from other expressions of marital discord primarily because it was closely associated with violence. In every case where adultery was cited as one of the reasons for a divorce, physical and verbal abuse also occurred. It can therefore be assumed that two conditions heightened marital violence: the inequality between men and women and the access men had to extramarital relationships with women of inferior social standing.

Male adultery was a powerful reason for requesting divorce, but many women tolerated it for years before making an accusation and asking the court for a separation or a divorce. Doña María Rodríguez de Giraldo, married to Pedro Gerónimo de Mello for twenty years, had brought a significant dowry of twenty thousand pesos to the marriage. She was now subject to the physical and verbal abuse of a husband who was involved in a relationship with a married woman. "When she had tried to take away some of her own jewelry from him, which he intended to give to that woman, . . . he hit her with a club and broke her right arm." Furthermore, because he had pursued his amusements so freely, sixteen years had passed since they had last lived together. Doña María and her son lived a miserably poor life, while he spent money "on wild women and is currently illicitly involved with a widow, causing notorious scandal. He provides for her even better than if she were his wife." Doña María demanded the return of her dowry; Pedro denied everything.[33]

As often as adultery and abuse could lead to divorce, so could mistreatment of another kind: a husband's failure to support his wife materially. Doña Ana Sabala wanted to divorce her husband in 1700 because he treated her cruelly and refused to provide for her. The cause, she found, was "his illicit relationship with a mulatta. When I found them together, he proceeded to hit me many times."[34] In 1640, Francisca de Ampuero sued Ambrosio de Torres, a mulatto, for divorce because he physically abused her and forced her to support him. He had caused her to "loathe him because of his illicit involvement with a zamba named Tomasina, which is publicly well known. All this is sufficient cause for the divorce."[35] Doña Ursula de Avilés filed suit against Manuel de Rivera in 1656 after three years of marriage because of his relationship with "a quadroon named Mariana. He lives with her as if she were his wife and has a child with her."[36] At the time of her marriage to Pedro de Valencia Bohórquez, doña Luisa de los Ríos possessed both slaves and real property. By 1633, when her representative sought her divorce in archiepiscopal court, it was clear that Pedro had availed himself of doña Luisa's wealth to finance his love life. He had carried on with different women for eight months, spending "many pesos, both his own and hers, on dresses he gave them and in particular, on a shawl embroidered with gold, some gold earrings, household linens, and gifts of food. This is enough for me to hate him and wish him dead."[37]

Abuse and lack of support aside, a husband's adultery in and of itself was sufficient grounds for seeking a divorce. Doña Catalina de Uceda cited the extramarital activities of her husband, Martín Francisco Alemán, as "the first and principal" reason she was requesting a divorce. Martín's behavior certainly left much to be desired. He had permanently taken up with his lover in a "shamelessly notorious fashion." The result was at least one bastard daughter, whom he forced doña Catalina to raise. Doña Catalina gave the girl a dowry, which allowed her to marry well, "because this was the decent thing to do." Martín failed to mend his ways, however, and because of his continued amorous pursuits was tried on several occasions for concubinage.[38]

Women of lower social standing than doña Catalina also, though infrequently, said adultery alone motivated their divorce actions. In 1653, María Gertrudis, a free mulatta, charged that her husband Jusepe had violated his marital fidelity and taken Francisca Pastrana, a free black, as his lover. She had become aware they had begun this affair some time before and therefore demanded a divorce because he "often commits adultery with this woman."[39]

Accusations of concubinage usually noted the ethnicity of the husbands' lovers, which was a way of identifying the lower social rank of these women. Social and ethnic hierarchies produced women of low social status whose availability made adulterous relationships possible. This in turn debased the female condition by dishonoring and devaluing legitimate wives and established great inequality between partners in relationships outside of marriage.

Wives' requests for divorce because of abuse, the failure to fulfill marital responsibilities, and infidelity were unaffected by social standing. In 1633, María de Andrade, an Indian, sought a divorce from her mestizo husband, Francisco de Ortega. Although María denounced her husband's abuse, what spurred her to act was her husband's involvement with an Indian woman from Calle del Cercado "with whom he has committed many adulterous acts."[40]

In the mid-seventeenth century, doña María Cuyniga, an Indian born in Huarochirí, was living with her husband, Pedro de Angulo, in Lima's San Marcelo Parish. The frequent abuse Pedro inflicted on his wife had increased to the point that María was forced to abandon her home despite her pregnancy. "He threw me out of the house. He did not take care of me when I was in labor and does not now, when I am bringing up his son and his two daughters." All this happened because Pedro had been living with Francisca de Medrano, a mulatta slave, for more than a year.[41]

In 1634, Lorenza Criolla, a free black from Lima, accused her husband, Antonio Bermúdez, a black slave, of committing adultery. According to Lorenza, Antonio had taken up with different women from the day they had married "and in particular with Felipa, a black slave from the Congo, whom he has impregnated. He spends a great deal of money on her, his own as well as others', buying her clothes and food. Because of this he hates me and has stopped living with me or providing for my needs. For this reason and because he is a terrible, incorrigible man, he has beaten me again and again because I have tried to report his concubinage."[42]

Lorenza's testimony closely resembles that of women whose status in Lima's colonial society was much higher. Such similarity indicates that with regard to gender identity, women were much closer to one another than the hierarchical social stratification formally allowed.

According to the prevailing morality, female honor arose from a woman's retiring nature, virtue, and sexual modesty, and on her virginity, if she was single, or her fidelity, if she was married. It was based, in other words, on how she behaved with respect to men. There were nevertheless some women who thought their honor depended on how their husbands carried out their conjugal duties.

In 1639, Ana Delgado requested a divorce from Francisco Rodríguez before the archiepiscopal court. Her husband, fearing neither God nor justice, was publicly engaged in concubinage, behavior demonstrating his contempt for his wife.[43] Ana María de la Zerba, seeking a divorce in 1654, argued that her husband, Martín de Espinosa, verbally abused her and treated her disrespectfully. They had been married for seven months when Martín took her dowry money and gave it to "a woman named Polonia with whom he previously had and now has an illicit relationship. *By doing so, he showed his lack of respect for me.*"[44] Another plaintiff, doña Josefa de Monterrey, in 1658 wanted to divorce Juan de Rivadeneyra after five years of marriage. He had failed to fulfill either his material or sexual responsibilities and what is more, had attempted to kill her. He had relationships with other women, in particular "a young parda named Graciela, whom he would *disrespectfully* bring to my home, showing contempt for me and, through his words and gestures, letting me know that he appreciated her more than he appreciated me."[45]

Errant husbands could devalue the respect, intimately associated with honor, that many wives wanted, but married women also suffered dishonor from the women illicitly involved with their spouses. María de Tineo argued before the archiepiscopal court in 1655 that her husband, Roque de Dueñas, verbally and physically abused her, did not support for her, and dedicated his time to gambling. Furthermore, he was publicly consorting with one doña Gregoria, vecina of Callao, "who, encouraged by my husband, *has lost all respect for me*, entering my house and insulting me with my husband's support."[46]

A non-Spanish couple, Ana Ruiz and her Portuguese husband Marcos Fernández, had traveled everywhere together until parting company in San Lúcar de Barrameda, when Marcos left for the Indies. They reunited in New Spain twelve years later, but he left again, this time for Lima, where she found him yet again. Because he had failed to carry out his obligations, he established a shop for her. From then on, Ana affirmed, "he has made me support him. I clothe him, buy him shoes, and give him what he wants, but he does not give me a kind word in return. Instead he calls me ugly names, like swindler, whore, hick, and uses other disgraceful words *against my honor and reputation*. Not happy with that, he also beats me, kicks me, slaps me, and treats me badly."[47]

Witnesses added that the women Marcos carried on with were blacks and mulattas. Marcos denied any dealings with the black woman, but admitted his sexual relations with the mulatta, for "he had spent a day in his house with that mulatta while his wife was not at home." Ana asked to be admitted into the convent of La Caridad or Santa Clara.

According to the law, a woman's adultery was simply adultery. What these cases show, however, is that wives considered their husbands' adulterous conduct a serious act with many repercussions. It dishonored the woman, showed contempt and a lack of respect, and devalued women in general. This leads to a significant conclusion: that women's notions about honor differed from what the dominant rhetoric said about relations between men and women. In contrast to the masculine point of view, which saw female honor as based solely on a woman's sexual modesty, wives could indeed be dishonored by their husbands' immoral behavior.

❧

A set of circumstances, some pertaining exclusively to the colonial world, added a unique shading to adultery. Arranged marriages and the unimportance of personal choice, both reinforced by the dowry system, could make the marital bonds extremely vulnerable. The availability of women from lower social strata exacerbated this. The geographic mobility of some men in Lima also contributed to the pervasiveness of adultery.

The authorities, backed by public morality, refused to tolerate female adultery, thus reproducing the same double standard observed in Spain. In Lima's colonial society, however, infamous punishments were unknown. Even in cases of recidivism, presumed adulteresses suffered only warnings and threats. A dishonored man's right to kill the offending partners, however, remained in force.

Adultery was often the most important reason for seeking a divorce, though it was also cited in conjunction with other offenses women considered serious: physical and verbal abuse and the lack of material support. The close association of masculine honor and widespread sexual relationships outside of marriage made Lima a city prone to violence.

Of particular note is that wives who accused their husbands of adultery shared similar points of view. Social differences aside, women equated adultery with their own devaluation by men, which diminished women's honor as a result. This was a distinct counterpoint to masculine morality, which defined women's honor by their sexual modesty. Although accusations of adultery were made more frequently against men than women, husbands were always dishonored by adulterous wives, no matter what their social standing.

Women who enjoyed a dowry were probably more prone to denounce male adultery than those who did not. Nevertheless, by the seventeenth century the female feeling of being dishonored by male behavior was also part of women from the subaltern groups of the urban colonial society. A sense of female dignity, different from the one defined by men, was expressed by both women from upper and lower groups of the city.

CHAPTER FIVE

Illegitimate Children

Bonds of Love and
Discharge of Conscience

The meaning of illegitimacy is not fixed over time. It is related to the stability of the social system in which it appears; the relations among various social groups; the ties between men and women; and the shared sentiments, values, and attitudes of the culture. Perceptions of illegitimacy are further influenced when the incidence of out of wedlock births is high, as was the case in colonial Lima.

Lima's seventeenth-century society had its own complexities. What is in question is whether marriage was valued in general as the inevitable choice for all social groups.[1] Differences between them impeded the transmission of cultural values, in this case, those of marriage. With the exception of the church, elites had little interest in controlling the sexual morality of the lower orders. Social pressure on them to marry was largely insignificant, particularly with respect to the slave population and to a lesser extent, the castas.[2]

Some studies have found a positive correlation between economic stability and the frequency of legal marriages.[3] Similarly, in societies with set forms of social organization, economic depression tends to delay marriage age, causing illegitimacy rates to rise.[4] In the seventeenth century, Peru suffered through a structural economic crisis.[5] Although the evidence is as yet incomplete, there are some indications that urban elites of the time also collapsed. Lima's merchants, with their regional and overseas ties, seem to have taken a severe pounding.[6]

This difficult economic situation would have discouraged the formation of new families. It is likely that the means necessary for this, whether from inheritance or dowry, were less available. While research irrefutably affirming this is lacking, it can at least be said that in circumstances such as these marital rates would have remained unchanged.

Disapproval of illegitimacy is related to the social disorganization it creates.[7] The rights of illegitimate children in colonial Peru were established in accordance with existing Spanish legislation. According to the *Siete Partidas*, a natural child was one born of single parents living together with no impediment to marriage, so long as the woman was the man's sole partner. The Laws of Toro defined natural children more broadly as those whose parents could marry without dispensation at the time of their conception or birth. If the father lived apart from the mother, but recognized the children as his own, it did not matter whether the parents lived together or the woman was the man's only partner.[8]

All other illegitimate children fell into distinct categories. Adulterine children were those born of an adulterous relationship, itself subject to punishment since according to the Laws of Toro, the adulteress mother incurred the death penalty. Concubines were the mothers of bastard children. Nefarious children came from the union of a progenitor with a descendant. Blood relatives within a prohibited degree produced incestuous children. Sacrilegious children were the offspring of ordained priests, monks, or nuns. Last were the *manceros*, children of prostitutes.[9]

Spurious children, those whose fathers were unknown, could not inherit mayorazgos or estates nor could one be established for them. By contrast, natural children of a noble father, who both enjoyed paternal recognition and benefited from his social standing, could inherit a father's estate.[10]

Despite these considerations, children born out of wedlock could not succeed to a mayorazgo without a father's express stipulation nor could they use his surname or coat of arms. They could claim neither kinship with nor lineage from the mayorazgo's founder. According to Juan de Solórzano y Pereyra, scholars such as Baldo, Molina, and Gregorio López were in agreement on this point.[11] Furthermore, natural children, although less discriminated against than other children born outside of marriage, could only serve as trustees of or receive mayorazgos in Spain when their fathers explicitly stated this in their wills. If they did not, the children could neither carry nor pass on the name and honorific titles or preserve the noble status of the family.[12]

Beginning in 1536, legislation reiterated the lower standing of children born outside of marriage. Adulterine and other illegitimate children could not inherit encomiendas because, lacking honor, they were "excluded from property and dignities."[13] The nobility paid no taxes and could not be imprisoned for their debts. Furthermore, their belongings, homes, horses, mules, and weapons could not be seized for debt payment.[14] Their illegitimate children did not benefit from these privileges, however, unless their fathers acknowledged them as natural children.

The restrictions on illegitimate children in the sixteenth-century Viceroyalty of Peru were far from onerous. These children, mostly mestizos, entered convents. As a result, a royal cédula issued in Madrid in January 1594 ordered the Archbishopric of Lima to prevent religious orders from accepting illegitimate, or "defective," children, in accord with the decrees of the Council of Trent. The church declared at that time that natural, illegitimate, and spurious children could not to enter religious orders because of their defect of birth.[15]

These dispositions were not strictly enforced, and in 1636 another royal cédula appeared, again prohibiting the ordination of illegitimate mestizos as clergymen. This was reconfirmed by yet another cédula of May 1676.[16] Despite these measures, illegitimate mestizos were not entirely excluded from the benefits provided legitimate children. They could obtain encomiendas by asking for a new royal grant. When such requests were sufficiently supported by services rendered, a specific dispensation was unnecessary, and the title made no mention of the recipient's "defect." Citing Antonio de León Pinelo, Solórzano added that these illegitimate children could "take advantage of the merits and services their parents and ancestors rendered, not because their own would not suffice, but instead to facilitate the process and move the spirit of the bestower."[17]

Children were legally entitled to four-fifths of their parents' estate, while parents could freely allocate only the remaining fifth.[18] Goods both material and immaterial, such as rights and obligations, could be bequeathed.[19]

TABLE 5.1: **Legitimacy and Illegitimacy among the Different Ethnic Groups at the El Sagrario Parish, Lima, Seventeenth Century**

	NATURAL	LEGIT.*	ABAND.	NO INFO.	TOTAL
Spanish	247	3027	289	658	4221
Percent	69.7	78.2	98.2	21.1	55.3
	5.8	71.7	6.8	15.6	100.0
Indian	3	105		10	118
Percent	-8.0	2.7		0.3	1.5
	2.5	89.0		8.5	100.0
Black	17	293		695	1005
Percent	4.8	7.6		22.3	13.2
	1.7	29.2		69.2	100.0
Castas	87	443	5	1749	2284
Percent	24.6	11.5	1.7	56.2	29.9
	3.8	19.4	0.2	76.6	100.0
TOTAL	354	3868	294	3112	7628
Percent	100.0	100.0	100.0	100.0	100.0
	4.6	50.7	3.9	40.8	100.0

*Legit. = Legitimate, Aband. = Abandonded, No Info. = No Information
Source: AAL, Libros de Bautizos, El Sagrario Parish, Lima.

No distinction was made on the basis of gender or age among descendants. Children legitimized after a subsequent marriage were comparable to children born legitimately. Children legitimized by the crown did not have the same rights as legitimate children had with respect to inheritances from their fathers and mothers, but they did regarding inheritances from other relatives. The Laws of Toro and the *Novísima Recopilación* amended the *Siete Partidas*, which treated natural and legitimate children equally when inheriting a mother's goods. "According to these two bodies of law, when there are no legitimate or legitimized children, natural children, and in their absence spurious children, alone would receive their mother's goods. Preference was given to those of direct descent."[20]

TABLE 5.2: **Legitimacy and Illegitimacy among the Different Ethnic Groups in the San Marcelo Parish, Lima, Seventeenth Century**

	NATURAL	LEGIT.*	ABAND.	NO INFO.	TOTAL
Spaniards	136	580	36	315	1067
Percent	47.2	58.8	94.7	26.2	42.4
	12.7	54.4	3.4	29.5	100.0
Indian	5	100		35	140
Percent	1.75	10.1		2.9	5.6
	3.6	71.4		25	100.0
Black	10	89		105	204
Percent	3.5	9		8.7	8.1
	4.9	43.6		51.5	100.0
Castas	137	217	2	747	1103
Percent	47.6	22	5.3	62.1	43.9
	12.4	19.7	0.2	67.7	100.0
TOTAL	288	986	38	1202	2514
Percent	100.0	100.0	100.0	100.0	100.0
	11.5	39.2	1.5	47.8	100.0

*Legit. = Legitimate, Aband. = Abandonded, No Info. = No Information
Source: AAL, Libros de Bautizos, San Marcelo Parish, Lima

Contemporary testimonies reveal that colonial authorities were more dismayed by sexual relations outside of marriage than by illegitimate births per se. Illegitimacy worried both the church and the social elite because of the material deprivation these children suffered. The colonial government was mindful that natural children constantly petitioned the royal audiencia for parental recognition. There is no evidence, however, that this way of dealing with the potential disorder such demands might cause was ineffective.

Illegitimacy affected all Lima's social and ethnic groups, but it meant different things to different people (see tables 5.1 and 5.2). Meaning depended on context. Gender, social standing, and ethnicity combined to influence illegitimate identity. Hierarchical social ranking and how groups related to

TABLE 5.3: Paternity Patterns among Illegitimate Children from Different Social Groups in El Sagrario Parish, Lima, Seventeenth Century

	WHITE	FREE BLACKS	SLAVES	TOTAL
Known parents	209	102	903	1214
Percent	18	22	43	32
Known Father	96	19	3	118
Percent	8	4	0	3
Known Mother	266	285	994	1545
Percent	22	60	47	41
Unknown Parents	552	27	3	582
Percent	47	6	0	16
No Information	59	40	196	295
Percent	5	8	9	8
TOTAL	1182	473	2099	3754
Percent	100	100	100	100

Source: AAL, Libros de Bautizos, El Sagrario Parish, Lima

each other also affected how illegitimacy and extramarital relationships were experienced, as did chance and the vicissitudes of life.

The kind of relationship that produced illegitimate children helped define what illegitimacy meant. It is therefore important to know whether illegitimacy resulted from a relatively stable consensual relationship or a casual sexual encounter. It is difficult to establish from the parochial records what percentage of illegitimate births corresponded to sexual relations involving cohabitation or mutual acceptance and recognition. The patterns of paternal acknowledgment of children born out of wedlock can help resolve this (see tables 5.3 and 5.4).[21]

The legitimizations appearing on baptismal certificates are one indicator that the extramarital relationship was consensual. The later marriage of the parents was one of four ways to make a child legitimate.[22] In the parish of San Marcelo during the seventeenth century, only 18 of 1,493 illegitimate children were later acknowledged. Of the 18, 11 were legitimized, while

TABLE 5.4: Paternity Patterns among Illegitimate Children from Different Social Groups in San Marcelo Parish, Lima, Seventeenth Century

	WHITE	FREE BLACKS	SLAVES	TOTAL
Known Parents	99	73	127	299
Percent	20	25	17	20
Known Father	42	10	5	57
Percent	9	3	.6	4
Known Mother	64	134	533	731
Percent	13	46	71	48
Unknown Parents	263	61	12	336
Percent	54	21	2	22
No Information	19	13	73	105
Percent	4	4	19	7
Total	487	291	750	1528
Percent	100	100	100	100

Source: AAL, Libros de Bautizos, San Marcelo Parish, Lima

7 were recognized as natural children.[23] In 1676, for example, Julián, baptized at San Marcelo six years earlier, was legitimized by his parents' marriage. Of those later legitimized, 1 had been registered only by the mother when the child was baptized, 6 appeared without parents, 2 were acknowledged by both parents, and another 2 only by the father. In the same parish, only 7 were later recognized as natural children. This paternal acknowledgment is another example of the importance of patrilineal aspects of urban society at the time. Of those later acknowledged as natural children, 5 were originally identified on their baptismal certificates as having no parents, while another 2 were acknowledged only by the father.

In El Sagrario Parish, only 40 of 3,760 illegitimate children were later acknowledged, 23 as legitimized children and 17 as natural children. Among the natural children, there is no information concerning the parents of 9 children at the time of their baptism; 4 were acknowledged only by the father and 1 by both parents. Among the 23 children legitimized at the time of their baptism, 4 were acknowledged only by the father, 9 by both parents, and the parents of the remaining 3 were unknown.

These figures show that for these two parishes, acknowledgment by both parents cannot be used to indicate consensual relationships. Other qualitative sources, especially civil documents, reveal that acknowledgment by both parents was not supported by their cohabitation or unofficial liaisons. It would appear, therefore, that consensual relationships between unmarried people were not a widespread alternative to conjugal unions in Lima during the seventeenth century.

Although legitimizations and acknowledgments were few, it is clear that children recognized by both parents, or by the father alone, were more likely to be legitimized later. The high percentage of children acknowledged only by the mother recorded in the baptismal books of the seventeenth century make it difficult to correlate illegitimacy with prenuptial sexual relationships (see tables 5.3 and 5.4).

The registration of natural and illegitimate children in the baptismal books suffered from irregularities. Nonetheless, everyday people stated that priests in charge of pouring the water on newly born children and recording their baptisms resisted registering a child as natural if the father was not present to acknowledge his paternity, a necessary condition. "Doña Blanca de Sosa, doña María Francisca's godmother, told this witness that doña Beatriz Fernández wanted the priests to write in the baptismal book that doña María Francisca was the natural daughter of Pedro Luque. The priests were hesitant to make the entry in this way because fathers were vexed when their names were spoken in their absence."[24]

In Lima's colonial society, the word of a man from the upper reaches of society was enough to persuade a third party about the legitimacy of his children. This was precisely what Antonio Pérez de Losada, a native of Salamanca, managed to do. He was a married man working as an accountant and merchant in the City of Kings. He was thought to have three legitimate children, but when he executed his will, he stated that one, Fr. Simón de Losada, twenty years old and a member of the Dominican Order, was his natural son. "When he entered the order and was given his habit, so there would be no difficulties in his receiving it, I declared that he was a legitimate son from my first marriage. Because this may eventually harm my other legitimate children, I must discharge my conscience and hereby state that he is my natural, not my legitimate, son."[25]

Nevertheless, children could be declared as natural by the mother alone, as some parish certificates show. These cases constitute a partial, though Pyrrhic, victory for women since such acknowledgment did not imply the passing on of paternal qualities. Maternal recognition might, however, alleviate a loss of prestige, at least with respect to individuals' self-perception.

Illegitimacy also involved the importance of concepts such as honor and shame in the society at large. Honor was the value forming the basis of relations among the social groups in Iberian society. In Lima, the urban aristocracy's aspirations and presumptions of nobility shared social space with the respect and honor the castas demanded. Illegitimacy crossed all social groups and helped characterize them. It can nevertheless be said that illegitimacy was perceived as the violation of a social norm. Punishment of this transgression was worked out through the code of honor and was not the same for every case. Illegitimacy placed each individual in a lower rank of honor, and the sanctions were social, not legal. The status of an illegitimate man differed from that of an illegitimate woman; at the same time, an illegitimate Spaniard could not be compared to a slave born out of wedlock. In this way, the significance of illegitimacy was linked to the criteria separating and differentiating social groups.

Being illegitimate certainly had different meanings across the social spectrum. Legitimacy was an attribute of honor, illegitimacy an inferior status that could impede social mobility.

Paternal attitudes toward children born out of wedlock varied. Considerations of a different sort influenced the possibility these children had of gaining access to paternal estates. When single men maintained relatively stable relationships with single women, illegitimate natural children were the result.

The social ranking of an illegitimate child whose parents belonged to the same social group differed from that of a child whose mother and father came from unequal social groups.[26] When the parents were social equals, their acknowledgement of a child born out of wedlock was generally endorsed. This allowed offspring to acquire the status of natural children, which made them superior to other illegitimate children, but inferior to the legitimate children of their group.

In his will, don Francisco Arce de la Parra, an unmarried merchant and native of Madrid, acknowledged four natural children, two boys and two girls. These children were brought into his family without reservation, despite the fact that he had them with three different women. The eldest son, Antonio, was appointed executor of his will, as was his son-in-law Juan de la Parra, who at the same time was named guardian of his goods. He had two of his children, Catalina de la Parra and Juan López de Sanabria, with the same woman, María del Castillo, a "single woman." With Isabel Madera, also a single woman, he later had Juana de la Parra; she married Juan de la Parra, don Francisco Arce's cousin. Finally, he declared that Mateo Arce de la Parra was his natural son. Mateo was fourteen years old at the time and lived with his father. His mother was a third unmarried woman, Mariana Montero de Espinosa.

Mateo, the youngest son, was left the same amount of money from his father's estate as Antonio de la Parra, the eldest, was. His father also left him "a canopy bed where I sleep and all my clothes, four shirts and white pairs of pants." These items, though without great material value, revealed don Francisco's affection for his youngest son. He also provided dowries for his natural daughters. He gave three thousand pesos to Catalina and fifteen hundred to Juana, even though, in his own words, he had initially offered her four thousand. In this case, the dowries functioned as advances on their inheritances. It may be that illegitimacy, despite paternal acknowledgment, exposed these children to discrimination. Children born out of wedlock, even natural children, most likely found their wish for fair treatment unfulfilled.

Don Francisco Arce de la Parra's reputation as procreator became widespread. He noted in his will that Felipa de Montoya, a mulatta, claimed that "a son she gave birth to named José is my child. This is not so, and I do not acknowledge him as such. I state this so that it may be known." Further, he added, "I also state that Antonia de Acosta, godmother of one of my children, lives in the city of Huánuco and is married to Juan de Plaza. She raised a mestizo boy named Eugenio in her home. When he was six or seven years old, she asked me to accept him into my household as a servant and refer to him as my son. I did this and kept him in my home for some time, calling him my son. At present he wanders the city because I threw him out of my house a long time ago, after telling him he was not my son and I did not know who his mother was."

Don Francisco was probably not lying. At any rate, the innuendoes about the ethnicity of the children said to be his, but whom he rejected, are worth mentioning. These kinds of references are, by contrast, absent when don Francisco mentions the relationships from which the children he acknowledged were born. Ethnic differences between partners could have served to discourage paternal acknowledgment of children.

Don Francisco Arce de la Parra's close involvement with his natural children was not necessarily a rarity. In 1682, José de Quesada, a farmer in Lima, behaved in a similar fashion. In his will he acknowledged five natural children, both boys and girls, among whom he divided his estate more or less equally. This time there was no mention of who the mothers might have been.[27]

These estate distributions indicate that fathers did not experience even the slightest inhibition in their relationships with their illegitimate progeny. These men acted as fathers typically would toward their legitimate descendants. Extramarital relationships, especially among equals, were not necessarily an obstacle to establishing traditional family patterns.

When the social standing of partners differed, however, a child born of the union was relegated to an inferior social status with fewer privileges. The most extreme, yet perhaps most common, case was the paternal refusal to recognize children whose mothers were slaves, since this relegated the illegitimate offspring to the basest social category.[28] The lower social status of women with whom they had extramarital relationships was one reason men resisted acknowledging paternity. The case of don Domingo Hernández illustrates this. Don Domingo, a Spaniard from Galicia, was a modest businessman who lived in Lima around 1630. He affirmed in his will that he had no legitimate descendants, which was why he named his soul as the heir to his goods. Nevertheless, he set aside four hundred pesos to buy the freedom of two slave girls, bequeathing "two hundred pesos to each of the two young mulatta slaves who belong to Pedro Jiménez Menacho, both named María de las Santas and daughters of Mariana Criolla, who is Pedro Jiménez Menacho's slave. This is so they will be set free. Whatever money remains will be given to them so they will be clothed. I do this because I love them and am well disposed toward them."

Hernández thought Pedro Jiménez might not manumit the two girls, so he ordered his executor to give them the clothing they needed. Deciding later that the provisions of the will were inadequate, don Domingo added a codicil wherein he clarified that Jiménez, master of the two slave girls, owed him 1,360 pesos. Hernández agreed to discount 500 pesos from Jiménez's total debt if Jiménez freed the two girls. He later modified his will yet again with a second codicil, affirming that "the aforementioned Mariana and María, mulattas, are my natural daughters. I had them with Mariana Criolla, a slave Pedro Jiménez owns, and did not state this when I made my will because they were slaves. I state this now so that it may be of record."

In the same codicil, don Domingo added a marginal note. His remaining goods should be given to Jiménez so that he could divide them equally between the two girls when they married or when they entered the convent.[29]

The slave status of women free men maintained intimate ties with in large part shaped their attitudes toward their illegitimate children. Because slaves could not inherit, any goods of significant value ended up in the hands of the woman's owner. This was why the need to free the mother or the descendant was so often mentioned. Juan de Mendoza was an unmarried sailor from Venice visiting Lima. He stated in his will that aside from his belongings, two hundred pesos, some clothes, and a slave, he also had a natural son, Alonso, whose mother, Natalia, was from Cape Verde. Her status as a slave did not cause him to refuse to acknowledge his son or Natalia herself. Moreover, he ordered his executors to purchase her liberty for two hundred pesos, adding that if they did not wish to manumit her for that amount, they could use it with whatever remained from his other belongings to do so. The affection the Venetian sailor felt for Natalia was also expressed in his bequest to her, "a small box belonging to me and the mattress and bed I sleep on, which show how well disposed I am toward her."[30]

Single men felt freer to acknowledge their natural children than married men.[31] The absence of legitimate offspring who could inherit their fathers' estates clearly played a decisive role. Personal sentiment also provided a margin for action. There was a difference between those limited to bequeathing what the law stipulated and those who left everything to their children. Antonio de Lorsa was an unmarried Spaniard. In 1668, Andrea de la Parra, exercising the power of attorney Antonio had given her, wrote a will in his name. It stated that Lorsa had two natural children by a woman who was also single and that the will was being prepared "so they will be granted what rightfully belongs to them."[32]

Diego Morales Gallinato, a scribe from Seville and member of the chapter of the confraternity of the Santísimo Sacramento, also limited himself to what was established by law. Owner of considerable goods, he left his soul as his heir, as well as a natural daughter named Catalina, "to whom, after everything is paid for and my will executed, one-sixth of the remaining goods shall be given."[33]

There were others more generous than he. Juan Martín Guillermo, Italian and unmarried, listed in his early seventeenth-century will a slave, two thousand pesos, a piece of land, and some household goods. He acknowledged Isabel de la Candelaria, "fifteen or sixteen years old," as his natural daughter and mentioned her mother, Juana López. He named Sebastián de Meneses as his executor and as Isabel de la Candelaria's guardian and tutor so he could "protect her and administer her goods until she is of age, at which time she will be given her goods." As Isabel's father, he was concerned about her future.[34]

Juan Otasso de Normat, an unmarried merchant from Navarre, owned slaves, a large amount of worked silver and merchandise, and many tools.[35] In the will he made in the mid-seventeenth century, Juan said he had a natural daughter named Micaela; he made no mention of her mother. At the time, Micaela was a professed nun in the convent of Las Descalzas in Lima. Otasso de Normat wanted to ensure that his daughter would have a permanent place in the convent, so he bequeathed her 150 pesos a year for the rest of her life "for her habits and other needs." He had earlier provided about 8,000 pesos for Micaela, "which with the income I have bequeathed her amount to much more than what she would be entitled to as a natural daughter, which is one-sixth of my goods." Otasso's generosity to his daughter had its limits, though, for he named his godson, José Gómez, as his residuary legatee "because I love him and have raised him since he was four years old."[36]

María de Salamanca, a native and vecina of Lima, was an illegitimate daughter. She had two natural children while single, Pedro and Agustina de Salamanca, and brought a dowry to her marriage. In her will, however, María de Salamanca named Pedro Rodríguez, her son from her first marriage, as her executor. She also stipulated that the same Pedro Rodríguez; Antonio de Esparsa, a natural child; and Lorenzo de la Rúa, her grandson and son of Agustina de Salamanca, should be her heirs. She enhanced the status of her natural son by giving him, from the one-third and one-fifth of her goods she could freely dispose of, "the third part and what remains of the fifth part, . . . because this is my will and does not in any way harm my other natural children."[37] Here are the criteria of a highly stratified society: men before women and legitimate children before natural ones.

Cases such as these raise the question of whether gender-based discrimination existed among the illegitimate children. Although the documents present little evidence confirming this, there were cases of natural sons acknowledged by their fathers as residuary legatees who received everything in the estate after other bequests and charges had been taken care of. No natural daughters were so acknowledged, however, even though they were granted dowries. Legitimate daughters, by contrast, were so named.

A gender difference in terms of acknowledgment by both parents was evident from baptismal certificates throughout the century. Among the free population of San Marcelo and El Sagrario, 261 sons were acknowledged by both parents, but only 226 daughters. Although the difference was not significant, the possibility must be considered that some gender discrimination did come into play when illegitimate children were acknowledged.

Men's refusal to recognize their illegitimate offspring was widespread throughout Lima's urban sector in the seventeenth century. The figures from the baptismal records of the city's parishes support this conclusion. In 43 percent of the cases, only the mothers acknowledged their illegitimate children. In the parish of San Marcelo, 48 percent of illegitimate children were acknowledged by the mother alone, while in El Sagrario only 41 percent were.

By law, children born out of wedlock could inherit one-fifth of their fathers' estates, if they chose to bequeath them. This must have created a serious conflict in the distribution of family goods and was one very important reason why people, especially married men with children, resisted acknowledging their illegitimate offspring. In 1649, don Rodrigo Paz de Orihuela, "a person of quality, a gentleman, and a nobleman . . . engaged in an illicit friendship with doña Gabriela del Aguila, a maiden. She became pregnant as a result, and Jordana was born. These people were single and free to wed."

According to doña Gabriela's testimony, don Rodrigo had provided all the necessities for doña Jordana, who at the time was about eleven years old. Despite this, he did not expressly refer to doña Jordana as his natural daughter in his will. "Further, I bequeath two thousand pesos of eight reales to a natural child from the City of Kings named doña Jordana de Paz Orihuela, daughter of Gabriela del Aguila, nine or ten years old. These will be given to her so that she may wed and for no other purpose. I also state I have supported and taken care of her since her birth. I bequeath this to her because I have loved her and been well disposed toward her since she was born."

The two thousand pesos bequeathed to doña Jordana were entrusted to one Juan Diez de Jarama; her mother had an insignificant role in these arrangements. Her father felt great affection toward doña Jordana, stipulating that "the interest from the money will be used to support her and the aforementioned Juan Diez until she marries. If she does not do so by the time she is twenty, the entire amount will be freely given to her. If she dies before this age, the money will be given to her heirs." Don Rodrigo apparently had a generous, even understanding, attitude toward her when he allowed her to inherit two thousand pesos even if she failed to marry or enter a convent. Moreover, he offered his still very young daughter the possibility of using her inheritance as she wished, despite the fact that don Rodrigo had other heirs who were legitimate. While on his death bed, however, he did not go so far as to acknowledge doña Jordana as his natural daughter. Don

Rodrigo's other heirs nonetheless advanced several arguments in court in an attempt to avoid paying the girl her due. The judges, though, were clear: doña Jordana was to be paid her two thousand pesos within eight days.[38]

Natural children usually faced many obstacles when attempting to exercise their rights. One of the main difficulties was linked to the existence of parents' legitimate unions and their legitimate children. In 1682, doña María Francisca de Cosar Bueno, arguing that she was Capt. Luque Cosar Bueno's natural daughter, claimed her inheritance from her father before the Audiencia of Lima. When she was born, she said, her parents were single and free to contract marriage. They supported and raised her, "calling me their daughter, as I called them parents." When her father married, doña María Francisca lost this support, though she now requested an advance of 300 pesos. In the face of this claim, doña Catalina de la Fontanella, Captain Cosar Bueno's wife, asked that her dowry, valued at 6,252 pesos, be returned to her. Her attorney went on to point out that don Luque had two legitimate daughters, doña Rosa and doña Clara, and that because there were creditors, doña María Francisca had rights to only 200 pesos.[39]

Capt. Lorenzo del Cerro died without mentioning in his will the two natural sons he had had with doña Antonia de Ochoa. They initiated a civil suit before the royal audiencia in 1673 so that doña Francisca de Acevedo, the captain's widow, executor, and guardian of his goods, would acknowledge their status and they could receive their inheritance from their father. Doña Francisca had her own interests to defend, since she had had two legitimate daughters with the captain. They were still young maidens and would need dowries in the future.[40]

The natural sons were between eighteen and twenty-five. As proof of their status they presented their baptismal certificates from the parish of San Sebastián. Although both parents had recognized Francisco, Antonio had been acknowledged only by his mother. The widow's attorney contended that the certificate "was not a sufficient instrument."

The witnesses presented their testimony. An unmarried mestiza stated that she had seen Lorenzo del Cerro pay the wet nurses who raised his children. Francisca de Oliva, "legitimate wife of a soldier of his excellency's mounted guard," said doña Antonia de Ochoa and her sister had moved to a house and "taken a small child with his arms still tucked in who was the captain's son." A tailor testified he was a friend of Lorenzo de Cerro "and had sewn some small clothes for Antonio and Francisco." Finally, Capt. Cristóbal de Hurtado, who supplied meat to the city, confessed that Lorenzo de Cerro had once asked him to give his sons some money. Captain Lorenzo promised to repay it, sending it from his farm "because he did not want his wife to know anything about it."

The statements of these witnesses did not provide the necessary legal proof. In the second round of witnesses, doña María Gonzales Durán assured that she had seen doña Antonia pregnant with Capt. Lorenzo del Cerro's child. Ursula de Torres, forty years old, legitimate wife of Antonio de Ulloa, testified she had been Antonia's friend since she was a young maiden, until Lorenzo del Cerro had "spoiled her." Despite this testimony, the opposing party continued to deny that the captain was the father, challenging the authenticity of the baptismal certificates. In similar circumstances, some men commonly claimed that their natural offspring were someone else's children.[41]

The defendant then presented another, more forceful argument: that the relationship between the captain and doña Antonia had developed while he was married to doña Francisca de Acevedo. This meant that the children were not natural, but spurious, and thus "entitled to only one-fifth of the inheritance." Doña Antonia's attorney alleged that the captain's position was unfounded. Doña Antonia was not an adulteress because she was unmarried.

Among the witnesses for Captain Lorenzo were those who asserted it was impossible to acknowledge children of adulterous males as natural children. The last to appear was Josefa de la Peña, a zamba, who stated she had been hired to take care of Francisco and had received money from the captain to buy bread. Francisco del Cerro, she said, "used to come at three in the morning and throw a pebble against the roof as a signal that she was to be taken to the hacienda."

Francisco and Antonio were finally acknowledged as natural children, though the amount of money they received is unknown, since some of the documents pertaining to the case are missing. It is difficult to ascertain precisely what the audiencia took into consideration when it ruled in their favor, but two points stand out. First was the presentation of the baptismal certificates that confirmed the relationship of Captain Lorenzo to his sons. Second was the statement of the wet nurse, Josefa. These two elements, the private, paternal acknowledgment at the baptismal font and the public voice of a zamba belonging to a subordinate group, helped secure the ruling that benefited the sons of Capt. Lorenzo del Cerro and doña Antonia de Ochoa.

In 1690, Bartolomé Dongo, acting for Beatriz Espinosa, asked the Audiencia of Lima both to recognize doña Baltasara de Villegas as his daughter and find that she was Juan de Villegas's natural child. Baltasara was not yet seven years old, and her mother was complaining that the guardian of Villegas's goods and executor of his will had abandoned the child.

The audiencia ruled against the petition. Juan de Villegas had been the corregidor of Ica. He was married in Spain to doña Ana de Angulo Vargas, who held a dowry valued at sixty thousand reales in vellón. Villegas owned vineyards and olive groves in Spain, as well as some large homes. He had named his wife guardian of their legitimate son, Mateo Manuel de Villegas.

Two priests confirmed that Juan de Villegas had referred to Baltasara as his daughter. One of them stated Villegas had told him he wanted to take Baltasara to Spain so that his sisters could raise her. The other, Lic. don Gregorio de Lurita, said he had paid for doña Beatriz Espinosa's stay in Lima and the cost of doña Baltasara's birth, for which Villegas had later reimbursed him. Doña Beatriz wanted to bring her daughter with her to Pisco, but don Juan took her away to live with him at his home.

Isabel, a Spanish-speaking black from the Congo who had been Juan de Villegas's slave, had witnessed the couple's illicit friendship. She had nursed Baltasara "because she was her master's daughter. He had often told her the child would accompany him to Spain." Furthermore, he stated in his will that he had another natural child, Gerónimo de Villegas, "on whom I have spent more than his share from my estate which is why I am not leaving anything to him."

Juan de Villegas did not mention Baltasara in his will. The petition on her behalf was further undermined because she was the child of an adulteress. That don Juan had a wife with a dowry with whom he had produced a legitimate son both weakened her case and reduced the importance of the witnesses' statements.[42]

Gaining a father's acknowledgement was not the only problem a natural child faced, for securing this status could also be made difficult depending on the social standing of the unmarried mother. Doña María Narváez, a member of Lima's elite, inherited a sizeable fortune from her father, Capt. Gaspar de Narváez Corral. Her daughter, Francisca Laso, was born of an extramarital affair. She later established a relationship with don Manuel Vélez de Guevara, a prosperous merchant from Madrid. Their three children, Ana, Domingo, and Nicolasa Teresa, were officially legitimized when doña María and don Manuel married. She specified in her will that her natural daughter Francisca Laso was to be given what corresponded to her from her mother's dowry "because she has been of such great assistance to us." She designated her husband as executor.

Hoping to protect his legitimate heirs, don Manuel prepared a detailed list of expenses to be charged against his wife's dowry. As a result, doña María's dowry was reduced to 1,142 pesos. Further acting against Francisca's interests, he then exercised his right to retain the movable goods from the dowry for one year. Years before, doña María, who did not know how to write, had chosen this option in writing, "waiving the rights favoring women in the Laws of Toro."

Francisca lodged her claim a year and eight months after her mother's death, but the widower refused to execute his wife's testamentary wishes favoring her natural daughter. Remarried and living in Huamanga, he contended Francisca had taken possession of some of her mother's belongings and that should suffice.[43]

The existence of a formal marriage and legitimate heirs militated against the acknowledgment of natural children and their rights as such, but not always decisively. Don Gerónimo de Oliva, native of Lima and patron of a chaplaincy, was married. His wife had been given a dowry of 5,250 pesos, and he had contributed another 1,000 pesos as his *arras* when they married. Their daughter, Francisca de Oliva, professed in the convent of La Concepción. She was don Gerónimo's residuary legatee, but he also had three natural children, Leonor, María, and Juan de Oliva. María received a dowry of unspecified amount from her father, who also gave Juan 500 pesos. Both sums were to be deducted from the portion of their father's estate, one-sixth, each would inherit.[44]

Being married did not always lead to a father's refusal to recognize the children he had with other women. Capt. Gerónimo de Montenegro, a native and vecino of Lima, had no children during his marriage. In his 1650 will, he stated that his one son, José de Montenegro, "whom I had with a single woman while I was married," had been raised in doña Clara de Ortigosa's home. He was named as heir, despite being a bastard child. Because Captain Gerónimo's legitimate wife was the executor of his will and had brought a dowry to the marriage, however, there were unresolved problems concerning José's succession.[45]

Despite the bureaucratic language of wills, the affection fathers felt for their illegitimate children is obvious. Pedro Fernández de Moreda, a native of Rioja, Navarre, was an inspector of the royal treasury. In his will, he acknowledged Pedro Fernández, his natural child from an extramarital relationship with an unmarried woman. He designated his son as the "heir to all my goods, rights, and duties, . . . so that he may enjoy them with God's blessing and my own."[46]

The bonds of affection between fathers and the children born outside of wedlock often affected how paternal estates were bequeathed. Alonso de Gameroz was a poor man from Andalusia. Despite being married, he revealed in his will that he had had an "illicit relationship" with Bernarda de Sosa, a parda, "who is pregnant. Should God our Lord shed his light upon her, and should this child be born after my death, I name the child as heir to my estate because the child is mine and should enjoy it with God's blessing and my own." He also designated one Martín Caballero as his heir and executor. This latter detail aside, it is easy to appreciate how a determined father's love could circumvent the law.[47]

Economic questions were not always central to the acknowledgment of natural children. Honor also played a part. There were fathers who had no property but still recognized their illegitimate children when they made their wills. José Carrillo de Albornoz, a native of Madrid, had been corregidor in Cajamarca and Huanta. At the end of his life, he was a merchant who had fallen on hard times. He had a daughter from his first marriage, two children from the second, and his wife was expecting a child when he wrote his will. He named all his legitimate children as heirs and his wife as executor. He further stated that his natural daughter, Catalina de Carrillo, born when he was single, was now about twenty-four. He left nothing to her, adding in a codicil that he was dying in poverty.[48]

When natural children sought recognition, they often did so with the hope of gaining access to a father's property. Acknowledgment of their status could also bring wealth of a different sort: the honors, rights, and privileges to which they might be entitled. Pedro de Mendoza asked to be acknowledged as the natural son of Juan del Monte and Luisa Flores, a mulatta. He also put forward his claim to the sixth part of his father's goods. He further stated that he should not be "forbidden from carrying a sword because it has been in my possession for more than fourteen years. I request exemption from the edict forbidding pardos and blacks from carrying swords and from everything else that may pertain to me as the son of a Spaniard and a parda." It is clear here how their illegitimacy affected castas. Acknowledgement as natural children allowed them to differentiate themselves from other castas like the pardos and blacks.[49]

The degree to which illegitimacy is stigmatized depends upon how widespread it is in a given society.[50] Disapproval of children born outside of marriage decreases during periods of social turmoil when the rate of illegitimacy is usually elevated and social control lax.[51] The diffusion of this condition throughout all social sectors weakens public control over it, and the punishments, in law and in practice, are, strictly speaking, nonexistent. The pervasiveness of illegitimacy among all social groups means it should not be seen as a kind of subculture (see tables 5.1 and 5.2).

In their everyday dealings, elite men did not always hide the existence of their illegitimate offspring. This is obvious from witnesses' testimonies and their tone. Information about these children was part of daily and familial communication. Illegitimacy, not something that could easily be kept secret, constituted a natural component of a person's identity.

In his baptismal certificate, José de Ribera was identified as the son of don Juan de Ribera and doña Rafaela de Zamudio, though his status as a natural child was unmentioned. Doña Rafaela, a rather wealthy woman, and don Juan both acknowledged José as their natural son in other documents, and the two passed away in 1659 when he was only three years old. In the document recording José's acknowledgment, the affection and concern for the future of their child are obvious. "Because I am his natural father and as such may appoint someone as the child's trustee and guardian, and knowing that no one will take better care of him and his wealth, because I love him as a father, I appoint don Francisco Cuadrado as his trustee."

Doña Rafaela arranged for her sister to care for the child until he was old enough to go to school. At that time, she decided, her executor, Fernando Cuadrado, would oversee José, acting as "his tutor and guardian. Should the child not receive good treatment in my sister's home, he should be put under Fernando Cuadrado's care."52

Perhaps influenced by guilt, a man often chose to hide the existence of his illegitimate offspring, sometimes simply leaving them a bequest. He might even mention the child in his testament, but without stating the nature of their relationship. A common practice was for a man to bequeath money in his will to his natural sons and daughters through a third party, though this was done secretly. Andrés García de Bobadilla, a native of Antequera, stated that after his death, he wanted Lic. Gerónimo de Acevedo, priest and sacristan of the cathedral, to be given "six hundred pesos of eight reales with which he is to do what I have told him. He should not be held accountable for its distribution beyond what I have made him responsible for."53

Men's conjugal state or women's social status aside, fathers' reluctance to acknowledge children born out of wedlock was also characteristic of a particular moment in the history of tensions between men and women. It is worth remembering that well into the sixteenth century in Europe, recognition of bastard children was an accepted part of social behavior; no internal or external mechanism inhibited this. Beginning in the seventeenth century, however, important changes occurred, and illegitimate paternity was often hidden.[54] According to Norbert Elias, they were related to questioning men's absolute control over women. Women began to influence public opinion, which resulted in limiting men's freedom to pursue extramarital relationships.[55] This in turn modified fathers' attitudes toward their illegitimate offspring. An increase in women's public power reduced men's proclivity for producing children out of wedlock.

❦

Illegitimacy formed a particular kind of hierarchical system. All individuals within this framework had a place, but the illegitimate child occupied an inferior position. In this system, the patterns of relations between the sexes gave rise to extramarital relationships and illegitimacy and were in turn influenced by them. Illegitimacy, however, did not have just one meaning, for there was a wide spectrum of discriminatory behavior and attitudes against those born outside of wedlock.

Illegitimacy did not always prevent men and women from ascending socially or aspiring to a place in the dominant sectors of urban colonial society. Being illegitimate nevertheless helped shape the basic identity of members of that society and established a series of guidelines governing their relationships.

Among Lima's dominant groups, illegitimate children were inferior to legitimate offspring. Natural children had a legal, though restricted, right to a percentage of their fathers' estates. Under the best of circumstances, when fathers acknowledged these children in the parochial registry and named them as heirs in their wills, executors, heirs of legitimate birth, and widows still managed to block their access to the goods fathers made available. Civil suits were then necessary to ensure recognition of the children's status and their corresponding rights.

Illegitimacy was widespread among the subordinate ethnic groups of the city and particularly among the castas. Their expectations of status were much lower, and although this made them, by definition, inferior, they still moved relatively easily within the system, provided they remained within their own social group. The colonial administration was utterly unconcerned about the people of illegitimate birth in this sector of society and had as little interest in protecting their reputations as they themselves did.

A dominant feature of the cases studied was public knowledge of children begotten out of wedlock. People close to the parents of illegitimate children, and those who were not, spoke with great familiarity about the offspring of illicit relationships. It was certainly impossible to hide pregnancy in a society where private life was subject to scrutiny. The large number of illegitimate children in Lima and the attitudes toward them meant that illegitimacy was perceived in several ways, not just as the violation of a social norm or part of a distinct subculture. It clearly was an essential part of the affective culture of the time.

Progenitors named their natural children as their full heirs only in exceptional cases. Far more common was making bequests, subject to what was established by law. When there were no heirs of legitimate birth, for example, parents designated collateral relatives as their heirs or sometimes even preferred relatives unrelated by blood, such as godchildren. In the absence of these possibilities, some men named their soul as residuary legatee, to the detriment of their illegitimate children. Legitimate half-siblings were another obstacle blocking paternal acknowledgement of natural children and their corresponding enjoyment of one-fifth of a father's estate. Illegitimate children commonly received simply a sum of money or some goods in an informal manner and not as a bequest through the will.

In colonial Lima, certain circumstances attenuated the de facto discrimination to which natural children were subjected. Mothers with money at their disposal, for instance, could grant a daughter a dowry. In a case like this, the lack of prestige inherent in illegitimacy was somewhat offset.

The public weight of institutions and men's private power worked to contain the potential social disorganization out of wedlock births might cause. In accord with their authority, men could grant to their illegitimate offspring whatever status best suited their own interests. Boys and girls formally designated as natural children, or simply recognized as such, became heirs and remained within their fathers' social group, though in a position inferior to that of legitimate offspring.

Relationships other than fatherhood, like marriage, the existence of legitimate children, or the mother's slave status inhibited the formal acknowledgment of illegitimate children in most cases. Under these circumstances, a range of individual actions was possible. Many men acted out of chivalrous morality, periodically providing money, clothes, and food; informal dowries; and secret testamentary donations.

It is important to note, however, that men strongly resisted accepting their paternity of out of wedlock children when the mothers were of low social status, and specifically, when they were slaves. Nevertheless, some negotiated with the masters of their slave lovers and made the effort necessary to manumit them by purchasing their freedom.

Natural children sought not only goods, but also status. Illegitimate children sometimes expressly requested acknowledgment as natural children so they could escape the casta system, and parents sometimes formally recognized their natural children in their wills without leaving those children an inheritance. Mothers also noted in parish registries that their children were natural, thereby hoping to improve their status.

To be acknowledged as a Spaniard's natural child meant differentiating oneself from the castas in a city where discrimination occurred on a daily basis. Illegitimacy forced individuals to be classified as castas and thus lowered their status. It was an integral component of discrimination, whose pernicious consequences were magnified when racial differences were added in.

Although illegitimate offspring pursued recognition as natural children, achieving this status depended ultimately on a father's wishes. What the father stated when recording his children in the parish register was considered to be true. A baptismal certificate could transform an illegitimate child into a natural one because of a father's acknowledgment, but he could also recant later. Only if the father asserted this in his will could a natural child claim family ties and thereby gain access to trusts and mayorazgos.

Under some circumstances, fathers could treat all their natural children as if they belonged to formally constituted families. This could occur even if the children had different mothers, provided they were unmarried and of a certain social rank. Inheritances, money, and affection flowed through relatively well-established channels, though single mothers were normally excluded from these acknowledgments and distributions of goods. In the most extreme cases, fathers could acknowledge bastard children or those begotten from adulterous relationships, thus permitting them to acquire the status of natural children. Clearly, private paternal power to determine the status of children born out of wedlock prevailed over public authority, whether civil or religious, in Lima's colonial society.

There was still, however, room for public power to counterbalance a father's commanding position. The actions of inferiors and subordinates—illegitimate children, women, and, in particular, mothers of natural children—challenged private, and therefore masculine, authority. On many occasions, the judges of the Audiencia of Lima, on the basis of witnesses' testimonies, enforced the rights of natural children. Although these children tended to receive less than what they were due, such rulings were a direct confrontation to male power. This was most likely why women and illegitimate children from throughout urban society appealed to public authority to restore their status. It is clear from this that subordinate groups were able to modify institutional attitudes, thereby increasing the importance of public power in private life.

It is worth mentioning that illegitimacy was not necessarily linked to a mutual promise to marry later, for the number of illegitimate births that preceded marriage was insignificant. Furthermore, illegitimacy was not, generally speaking, the result of stable consensual relationships. The supposition that extramarital cohabitation as an alternative for couples was widely practiced in seventeenth-century Lima is not borne out. Many social conditions militated against the spread of simple cohabitation: the tenacious control of ecclesiastical authorities over the daily life of the city's residents; the lack of intimacy in private life, which was exposed to public scrutiny; the slave status of women involved in extramarital relations; and the honor of the city's elite women and families.

The absence of a connection between illegitimacy and a subsequent marriage is further demonstrated in documents of the city's parishes. By and large, unmarried mothers alone acknowledged their natural children; when both parents were present at the baptismal font, the child was not registered as illegitimate. These practices reinforced the link between illegitimacy and lack of prestige. A father's name missing from a baptismal certificate excluded his illegitimate children from his own social group, thereby debasing them as individuals.

CHAPTER SIX

Female Dishonor and Social Hierarchies

🌿

Men acquire honor by many deeds, some by arms, others by the arts, yet others by wealth, and many of them by the nobility of their ancestors. Women only acquire it by one deed: being chaste, modest, and virtuous. According to this truth, we experience every day that a woman, no matter how humble, is honorable if she is virtuous, and princes and lords respect and venerate her.[1]

Lima lacked the rigidity of a typical stratified society, and colonial authorities failed to impose the plans for settlement that they envisioned. The segregated scheme sought by the Crown was eroded by singular types of subordination and social relations.[2]

In the social context of the times, the separation of the sexes, a complex phenomenon, was often contradictory and ambiguous. Laws regulating transfer of property did not particularly discriminate against women.[3] This relative equality was underscored in written law and acted upon in colonial reality. Daughters born of legitimate relationships shared in paternal or maternal inheritances on an equal footing with their brothers. Wives, however, rarely received anything beyond their dowry or arras, provided these were not spent during the marriage. They were also entitled to that part of their property that was outside the husbands' control, though joint property acquired during the marriage had to be distributed to both spouses.

Different treatment based on gender was sometimes clearly expressed, as when estates were created. In that case, law held that sons were to be preferred over daughters. Women were also obliged to secure their spouses' permission to initiate judicial actions, though they could also request special permission from the judge.[4] Restrictions like these intensified whenever a woman's participation in public life called into question her modesty, which the code of honor demanded of her. The lives of women were controlled, but they in turn managed to enlarge their limited public spaces in the city.

The distinct treatment of men and women was also obvious when individuals appeared before the civil and ecclesiastical courts. In the case of men, although differences existed among social groups, the characteristics defining their identity were place of birth, ancestry, where they were vecinos, and profession. Their marital status was noted only after other information had been recorded. Details about identity varied according to social standing. Those of higher social status provided ample proof of identity. In the case of mulattoes or former slaves, however, it was enough to simply say they were free; anything else was superfluous.

Women, including those from the aristocratic sectors, were generally identified in a fashion similar to men from the lower orders. Social status aside, women shared a common identity. The way they presented themselves in court demonstrates this. Immediately after stating their names, women gave their marital status, thereby clarifying their relationship to a man, a family, or a religious institution to which they belonged. The only other information of import referred to their status, such as young maiden, which also denoted their position relative to men.

The presence of an enslaved African population in colonial society, especially in urban life, considerably influenced relations between men and women. In his investigation concerning marital discord in seventeenth-century Lima, Bernard Lavallé found court testimony supporting this.

Women who denounced their husbands before the ecclesiastical court compared how their husbands treated them to the way the slave population was treated. Their husbands would whip them, but only after making them remove their clothes, in conditions that were truly degrading. In 1657, Juana de Sotomayor requested a divorce before the archiepiscopal court, claiming her husband "treated me with as much cruelty and abuse as he would have if I were his slave."[5] Many women shared this sentiment. The daily interactions of the slave and free populations injected an element of hierarchy into the interaction of men and women in general.

The vast inequalities of Hispanic society at this time were accepted in principle. Being a woman was just another status, a "feminine state" that existed along with others. Men in power and philosophers took charge of elucidating women's standing, and young maiden, married woman, widow, and nun were the resulting categories, all within the realm of domestic or religious life. Moralists of the time perceived women as inconsistent, loquacious, unstable, and emotional, all reasons they should subject themselves to men's authority, whether public or private.

Like most relations in this stratified society, those between husband and wife were explicitly spelled out. As lord and master, a husband had rights over his wife's body. Contemporary writers suggested she should be treated not as a slave, but as a companion and sister in his endeavors and life. Both civil and canon law insisted, however, that the husband was "legitimately and truly superior and could punish his wife in moderation."[6] This in no way contradicted Juan Machado de Chávez's reminder to husbands that they should also honor and respect their wives "with special signs of love and benevolence, as someone who is of their same flesh."[7]

Society maintained its own mandate concerning choice of spouse, and the stratified social system expressly defended endogamy. Violating this norm was very risky, for it brought into question the mechanisms supporting this system.[8] Marriage should take place between equals, otherwise the honor of families and their individual members would be damaged. Under the best of circumstances, families who agreed to a marriage of unequal partners, were repaid in increased prestige. Despite this, what a family never considered was allowing a woman to marry whomever she chose.[9]

Characteristic of patriarchal societies, and particularly those that are highly stratified, is the emphasis on strictly regulating women's behavior while permitting men to more or less do as they please. The rigidity of control over female sexuality varies, depending on the society. In seventeenth-century Lima, it was expressed through mechanisms such as physical separation, the dowry system, and the concept of honor.

In societies where honor is a class-based value, it is important to distinguish two interpretative models concerning control over female sexuality. Verena Martínez-Alier, who studied marriage in nineteenth-century Cuba, found that the value placed on virginity was inversely proportional to the degree of social mobility and the freedom individuals could attain in that social setting. Along these lines, the higher a woman's status in the social hierarchy, the greater the number of restrictions on her sexual conduct. The severity of punishment for a woman's deviant behavior was directly related to her family origin, which served as a source of status.[10] By contrast, Mariló Vigil's research on the daily life of Spanish women during the sixteenth and seventeenth centuries revealed that women from the middle sectors of society were under the greatest pressure to be sexually virtuous.[11]

There is, however, consensus on one point: there was little control wielded over the sexual behavior of women belonging to subordinate social groups. According to Malinowski, society would be less interested in illegitimacy occurring among the lower social orders because their position was of less importance to the larger social structure.[12] Control over women belonging to subordinate strata was insignificant in both nineteenth-century Cuba and Spain in the sixteenth and seventeenth centuries. This appears to have been the case in Lima as well, though how women who were not slaves were restricted introduces additional shades of meaning.

The institution of marriage and the social controls of the church and civil authorities were not enough to ensure that women behaved in accord with the norms of the prevailing morality. The conduct of the women who belonged to Lima's dominant sectors impressed men who visited the city and later wrote about their experiences. The Portuguese Jew, Pedro de León Portocarrero, lived there in the early seventeenth century and saw them as "the most beautiful woman in the world, with the loveliest manners. They are discreet, with an attractive enthusiasm, and are elegant and daring. They speak up openly and graciously; they are clean, curious, and able at work; and they embroider beautifully, cook anything well, and are graceful in everything. They dress in an elegant and costly fashion. They all wear silk and other rich fabrics, as well as velvet with fine gold and silver. They have thick gold chains; lots of pearls, rings, and necklaces; and flat chains made of rubies, emeralds, and amethysts. . . . They are carried to church and visits by their black porters on chairs and have very good, exquisite carriages."[13]

Restrictions were placed on women who chose to go out in public, but they resisted their husband's authority. If things became difficult for them, they simply withdrew from their husbands. Men complained about such women time and again, saying they wanted "to pursue their desires and improper pastimes. They only follow their whims, without considering what might befall them."[14] French traveler Amedeé Frézier's descriptions a century later confirmed León Portocarrero's impressions.

[These women] are generally quite pleasurable, with beautiful complexions that last a short time because of their abuse of *solimán*, a cosmetic made from mercury compounds. They have lively eyes, merry speech, and like free coquetry, which oftentimes approaches debauchery. They like to hear proposals a man would not dare make to a virtuous woman in France without meriting her indignation. Far from scandalizing them, this produces pleasure, although they are unlikely to consent to the proposals.[15]

Women resisted obeying restrictive social mandates and used their shawls to cover themselves, thus gaining a public anonymity that provided them with singular freedom. León Portocarrero, in his *Descripción del Virreinato del Perú*, related how women would cover themselves, as was only proper when appearing in public, to meet the viceroy when he first arrived in the City of Kings. It is interesting to point out here how women used hiding themselves as a way to achieve freedom, thereby changing the meaning of this act. The efforts by viceregal authorities to prevent the use of shawls are well known.[16]

Husbands attempted to control their wives by locking them away at home, but this met with strong female opposition.[17] In his 1604 report to his successor, the viceroy, Luis de Velasco (1595–1603), complained about the behavior of Lima's women. The "laziness and abundance of luxuries" were, by his account, a breeding ground for female sensuality. He requested permission to build a house of retreat where "wicked and insolent" women could be kept. This would also serve to intimidate other women and keep them from behaving in disgraceful ways.[18]

Compulsory separation of men and women was the authorities' preference. "What I had thought about, though a lack of means prevented this, was to build a place for detainment in the upper part of the court jail. These people could be gathered there, separate from men, for a limited time set by the government. They could be given sewing and other tasks to serve the hospitals. Some would be restrained by their confinement, others by example. At least their stay in prison would prevent many sins they would commit if they were free."[19]

In the course of the year 1634, city authorities failed to end the disorder attributed to the lack of control over women's behavior and continued searching for ways to "catch the dissolute, shameless women of the republic."[20] An attempt was made to prevent women from going out alone and was apparently widespread enough that it moved women to initiate divorce proceedings, or so the authorities thought. What they feared was that wives, once free of their husbands' domestic control, would become dangerous members of society. According to Francisco de Saldaña, founder of the monastery of Santa Clara, establishing a house of retreat for women separated from their husbands had helped them refrain from initiating divorce proceedings. In turn, "the few there enter there during the divorce proceedings, and many offenses against God our Lord thus cease."[21]

In 1670, the viceroy, the Conde de Lemos (1666–72), founded under royal patronage a house of retreat, the Casa de Recogidas, naming it Las Amparadas de la Purísima Concepción. Women who entered this refuge were predominantly white. "Deceived by worldly mishaps, wishing to improve their lives, they enter along the healthy road of penitence. . . . Some who are so poor and abandoned that their virtue might be jeopardized are also received."[22]

The cloister was extremely strict, and every woman dressed uniformly in gray sackcloth. They could not communicate with anyone "unless it dealt with something necessary, and then, only in the presence of an older, virtuous, and exemplary woman."[23]

Nonetheless, city authorities never ceased criticizing what they saw as inappropriately unrestrained behavior. "It is just as great a concern to remedy the public scandals and sins that some women, who lead licentious, forward lives, are accustomed to causing, especially the mulattas who are so numerous in this city."[24]

Social hierarchies were themselves one of the main obstacles to effectively controlling women's behavior. The colonial experience had produced a wide variety of groups for which no appropriate legal corpus existed. This created great confusion in resolving conflicts when they appeared. Stratified social organization, as seen in chapter two, created a special set of norms for each social group. Apart from the fact that these were sanctioned by law, they were also applied according to circumstance. In 1684, for example, the archbishop of Lima attempted to impose order in women's convents during the bull-fights that took place in the city, when the devout and lay sisters, as well as their servants, looked over the convent walls and from their bell towers to witness them. The ecclesiastical authorities prohibited this activity and ordered that

> Nuns were to be suspended from their offices for three months and religious women from their eligibility for office or voting for others. Lay women were to be ousted from those cloisters and handed over to their parents or people responsible for them. Women servants who were free were not only to be expelled, but also never to be admitted again to any convent. Those who were slaves were to be sold and sent away from this city.[25]

The authorities' views concerning female adultery were inconsistent. It was one thing for Spanish women to commit adultery and quite another when mestizas did.[26] Furthermore, for women who were not slaves, public authorities shared power with fathers and husbands. Domestic power was sufficiently strong that these city authorities had to appeal to male relatives to control their women.

The dowry system also sheds light on how women were defined in Lima's society. The first studies of the dowry and arras indicated that the dowry system in use represented the important value placed on female status in society. The payment of the arras, however, which was the price of the bride, turned women into objects, and they were literally bought.

This idea has only recently been questioned. In societies where a man's payment to secure consent to marry a woman predominated, the value of the social status of women was increasing. The dowry system therefore implied that the female condition was of little worth. Women had to receive a dowry, an added value, to be able to form a new family unit.

In principle the dowry prepared the woman to leave her original nuclear family.[27] It placed her in the best position to establish a matrimonial link and form a new family unit. The dowry was also necessary for women who wished to enter the convent through "the front door," the only honorable alternative to marriage for women of the dominant class in Peruvian colonial society. Women received their dowries from their own progenitors, usually their fathers.[28]

The dowry system favored matrimonial ties, economically protected a woman's share of property jointly held through marriage, and regulated the dynamics of hierarchical societies. It also became a way to organize female behavior and control women's choices. Among the dominant sectors of colonial society, the family dowry symbolically represented paternal endorsement of a bride's purity. Insofar as women's sexual chastity supported men's honor, the paternal dowry was a way of guaranteeing female prestige. Although no evidence has been found of daughters being deprived of their family dowries because of immodest sexual conduct, this may have occurred. Possession of a dowry assumed female chastity.

The link between the dowry system and control over female sexuality was clearly manifested by the norms pertaining to adultery. According to the Laws of Toro, one of the most important reasons women lost their dowries was because of acts of adultery. In such cases, the disgraced husband became owner of the dowry. The laws stipulated that a husband should not take the law into his own hands by killing the adulterers. In order to obtain a wife's dowry, a husband had to have them judged in a court of law.[29]

There were many white women in Lima who, because of their family background, could not rely on a dowry to secure their future. This severely restricted their competitiveness in the matrimonial market. They were particularly zealous in preserving their virtue, and control of their sexuality flowed through different channels than those for aristocratic women, very poor women, or slaves. Authorities took special measures with this group of women, and a combination of private and public power began to function.

The precariousness of colonial society, the result in part of the high mortality rate, orphaned many females. It was important to protect these infants from abandonment. Trusts, foundations, and congregations collected funds to be used to protect women without dowries. The religious confraternities, especially the Spanish ones, also provided money to be given to poor, white orphan girls for their dowries.

These bodies established requirements for allotting dowry funds to women in need. One, the seventeenth-century congregation of Nuestra Señora de la O, every year drew lots for two dowries of five hundred and one thousand pesos each to "aid women once they become nuns or marry. [They were] not intended for single women, who are excluded."[30] The women who drew lots had to meet specific criteria: they had to be poor, with no more than one thousand pesos to their name; be "Spanish," in other words, white; carry on virtuous, retiring lives; and be of legitimate birth. Women of illegitimate birth were usually excluded.

The story of Angela de Olivitos y Esquivel demonstrates how the dowry functioned as a control mechanism over female behavior and to protect the dominant groups' prestige. This young woman met the requirements of the congregation of Nuestra Señora de la O for those hoping to participate in the drawing for dowries: she was Spanish, poor, chaste, and legitimate.[31] Luck favored her, and she won the fifteen hundred pesos that would secure her future. Rather than enter a convent or marry, however, Angela took a third route, the independent road of beatitude.[32] Her work brought her a certain prestige, and this, along with sewing, provided her with money for her daily needs. After a short time, Angela, now Angelita de Cristo, was denounced to the Tribunal of the Inquisition in Lima. One of the main witnesses at her trial, an "honorable married man," insisted Angela had repeatedly seduced him. Not only that: claiming she was pregnant, she had asked him for money. Angela de Olivitos believed she was defending herself when she swore she was dominated by uncontrollable forces, but the Inquisitors attributed this to the workings of a pact with the devil.

Because of her trial, Angela lost the dowry she had won years before, and her honor was completely destroyed. Modest behavior was indispensable for women who wanted to achieve recognition in the city's social hierarchy. The behavior of these women was indeed extremely important in terms of their social status, either because they wanted to secure a permanent place or because they wanted to work their way up the social scale.

Aside from their role as biological transmitters of inheritance—their wombs sheltering the heirs of the father's goods—women were to incarnate the virtues of the prevailing morality and pass them from generation to generation. This led to the eagerness to care for those women who had less of a chance to create new nuclear families and were therefore more prone to developing behavior contrary to the values of the dominant culture.

Urban colonial society, which was highly stratified, influenced the norms governing men's and women's sexual behavior. Social status tended to be ascribed, determined by birth. Stratification was not, however, inherently static. People could lose their honor, a source of status valued within the system. In colonial Lima, individuals, despite their birth status, could perhaps rise or fall within their own social stratum. There were certainly groups within the system that were more secure and stable than others.

Honor was the basis of relations among the social groups of Iberian society. Although it changed over time in the colonial world, the code of honor still guided the behavior of men and women in a particular way. Different ideas about what honor meant also coexisted.

The social worth of individuals and families depended in good part upon the sexual virtue of their women. Vigilance over female sexuality was a central component in the social conduct of men from families who desired some social recognition. Because of this, the sanctions on shame and the loss of family honor fell much more heavily on women than men.[33] In the case of men, unlike social status, sexual virtue did not appear to affect their classification within the social system.[34] The stratified social order and the code of honor supported this double standard.

Sexual relations outside of marriage were considered a serious offense. Virginity nevertheless had a price that varied according to who the deflowered woman was. The experience of doña María Gabriela de Espinosa, a woman from Lima born from an extramarital relationship, illustrates this. Reliving part of her mother's life story, doña María Gabriela established an extramarital relationship with Tomás de Alvarado, a Spaniard, that did not end in marriage. A daughter, María, was the product of this union. The behavior of this woman, poor, though well within the mainstream of colonial society, revealed her knowledge of the rules in force. Doña María Gabriela initiated proceedings in the criminal court of the royal audiencia against Tomás, who before leaving for Spain had to pay three thousand pesos to his lover for her lost virginity.

Doña María Gabriela had managed during her life to accumulate objects of certain value: household furniture, such as a bed, chairs, and a cabinet, as well as some modest apparel. She did not marry, but "to ease her conscience and so that there is no doubt,"[35] in her will she acknowledged her daughter, María de Alvarado, five years old, as her natural child. Her illegitimacy did not prevent her mother from acknowledging her or keep her from being named as her mother's heir. Limited as it may have been, a way existed for doña María Gabriela to be compensated for her lost honor. It is unknown how many women were able to successfully pursue this course.

Some young women established extramarital relationships based on a man's promise of a future wedding. This placed their honor, a highly treasured possession, in jeopardy. The experience of doña Francisca de Morales, an aristocrat from Lima who lost her honor during the second half of the seventeenth century, illustrates this. Her story also demonstrates how men and women from different social groups perceived this situation.

One of doña Francisca's slaves told of how she "took care of her cleaning," starching the clothes of her mistress's betrothed, Capt. don Laureano Gelder. When doña Francisca saw "don Laureano would not marry her, she wept bitterly, since don Laureano had caused her to lose her honor and good reputation, and she would oftentimes cry out to God." Doña Antonia Dávila y Góngora, more than forty years old, explained that when her first cousin, doña Francisca, was single, she had "had an illicit friendship with don Laureano Gelder, who was also single. Both maintained that friendship under the promise of marriage." Doña Mariana Albina del Campo Vega y Otáñez, a thirty-year-old maiden and doña Francisca's niece, spoke of how her aunt had become involved with don Laureano, who had promised to marry her. Doña Mariana had told her aunt that she "should not believe in men's words, and doña Francisca expressed her great sorrow over this."

The promise of marriage made a couple's engagement known. It also made it possible for them to have sexual relations. Those close to don Laureano and doña Francisca were aware of their sexual relationship. Although this put doña Francisca's honor at risk, public knowledge of the situation constituted a social-control mechanism. Such control was nevertheless truly limited in this colonial society. When doña Francisca became pregnant, the engagement was still valid. Despite this, her son, Juan Jacinto Gelder, was registered in the baptismal book with the note "parents unknown." The attempt was thus still being made to protect doña Francisca's honor. She continued living apart from her future husband in the home of her brother, Dr. don Juan de Morales, a Jesuit. Don Laureano's refusal to acknowledge his son as his natural child predicted his future attitude, however.

With the same honorable desire, and "with the secrecy this matter demanded," Juan Jacinto spent the first two years of his life with María de Tapia, the midwife who had taken care of his mother and aided in his birth. Then, with "his father's consultation and consent," they took him to the home of his godfather, Luis Pérez de Tudela, where he remained until he was twenty. Don Laureano resisted aiding his son, though, and at one point doña Francisca was forced to seek the help of the Jesuits to pressure him into helping her care for their son.

Don Laureano went back on his word and decided to marry another woman, also a member of the city's aristocracy, the daughter of Capt. don Felipe de Zavala. This of course affected doña Francisca's family honor, so more pressure was applied: a duel. Don Simón del Campo y Vega Garay y Otáñez, the Marqués de Villa Rubio de Langre, gave testimony concerning this. Doña Francisca was the niece of doña Isabel Salvado Hurtado de Corcuera, the Marquesa de Villa Rubio, don Simón's wife. The marqués related how

> He had said to doña Juana de Utrera y Ocampo, Capt. Tomás Durán's widow and in his presence, "What do you think about our compadre, don Laureano Gelder, marrying Capt. Felipe de Zavala's daughter, even though he has a child by doña Francisca de Morales whom Luis Pérez de Tudela is raising?" When this witness had heard this, he had become very angry and gone to look for don Juan López de Corcuera, his brother-in-law. They went together to the home of Captain Valverde, since they were all relatives of doña Francisca, to prevent this wedding and challenge don Laureano to a duel for wishing to marry don Felipe de Zavala's daughter. They would stop the wedding and have don Laureano marry doña Francisca de Morales, whom he had promised to marry and who had a child by him.

This challenge was never carried out, for "if don Laureano had been challenged to a duel, the secret would have become known."

Shortly thereafter, don Laureano was killed in Spain by a bullet from a shotgun he himself had loaded. Doña Francisca considered his death punishment for his unfaithfulness. He had pledged to marry her and "had not kept his promise, so he found death as he did. The entire city knew he had not stood by his word, which she bitterly lamented. . . . God had permitted don Laureano Gelder to die from a gunshot. His Divine Majesty chose those weapons because that man did not keep the promise he had made. Stricken with grief, she trembled all over." Doña Francisca's honor had been destroyed, her family's dignity diminished.

The story did not end there, however. Doña Francisca had been prevented from living with her son because her brother had never forgiven her for her mistake. "So curt and aloof was Dr. don Juan de Morales toward doña Francisca . . . that when he and this witness were leaving his home, when don Juan passed doña Francisca's bedroom, he would proceed without even looking at her, even though she was standing at the door." Another witness, a priest, also mentioned the "great disdain" with which don Juan spoke to doña Francisca, arising from the "justifiable feeling he had about his sister's unfortunate deeds."

She withdrew to a "very plain room," and although she was about to marry, don Juan arranged for the wedding to be called off. As one witness noted "he did not even allow his servants to wait on doña Francisca."

Despite don Juan's hostility toward doña Francisca and her son, Juan Jacinto, the boy came into their home and ate with his mother when don Juan was not there. The link between mother and son continued throughout the years, and witnesses confirmed it on different occasions. Doña Francisca devoted herself to her son, "taking care of him, feeding and clothing him, and giving him what he needed for school and his studies. Since doña Francisca had remained close with don Juan Jacinto since his birth, she always called him son, and he always called doña Francisca mother." Because of doña Francisca's respect for her brother, though, she and her son could not live together until don Juan's death.

Doña Francisca inherited ten thousand pesos and some jewelry from her brother. When she then prepared her own will, it was obvious she was still resentful and had not freed herself from her guilt and shame. In consideration of her honor, she did not mention her son in her final will, commenting that she had done so "out of respect for her brother's soul and conscience."[36]

The control mechanism over women revealed in this story was a family matter. There was no written or public law punishing the sexual misconduct of aristocratic women. Private and domestic attitudes came into play: the brother with his heartless attitude and the family who tried to repair the damage done. These forces generated doña Francisca's feelings of guilt and shame, though they surely combined with her more private sentiments, such as the despair and anger she felt when the man she loved abandoned her.

Doña Francisca de Morales's experience differed from that of some other elite women who bore children outside of marriage. The father of don Diego Damián de León recognized him in 1664 at the Santa Ana Parish as his natural son, sixteen days after his birth, stating that the mother of the child was "unknown."[37] Though both parents were single and free to marry when the child was born, the mother remained unidentified. Even in 1690, twenty-four years after don Diego's birth, her name went unmentioned because "of the respectability of this person, who was, and still is, unmarried." Here, the honor of this unnamed woman was protected by the man's express acknowledgment of both his son and the woman's good reputation.

Such cases were not all that common, however. According to seventeenth-century parish records, among the Spanish population, only 9 percent of illegitimate children were registered in San Marcelo Parish by the father alone. In El Sagrario Parish, this was only 8 percent. These were very small percentages, and they approach insignificance when rates for the free, nonwhite population are considered: 3 percent and 4 percent respectively.

Male refusal to acknowledge children born out of wedlock damaged the status of women. Nevertheless, members of the aristocracy managed to arrange ways to live together outside of marriage, as well as to accommodate their paternity and maternity of illegitimate offspring. In the late seventeenth century, doña Jacoba de Córdova initiated a lawsuit against the heirs of Capt. Diego Ruiz de la Parra, a merchant from Seville and father of her son, Andrés, so he could be acknowledged as don Diego's natural son. The father, she claimed, "failed to fulfill his obligation in his will."

Lic. Juan Mendoza, a priest, testified he had known doña Jacoba and the captain for more than ten years. He knew of their "illicit friendship," which had lasted for a number of years when both were "single and free." Mendoza, a friend of doña Jacoba's brother, had spent time in the family home. During his visits, he had run into don Diego and seen him "speaking with and treating doña Jacoba de Córdova as if he were her husband. As a result of this relationship, she became pregnant." After the birth of Andrés de la Parra, don Diego and doña Jacoba stayed together for another eight years. The captain treated Andrés like a son, providing doña Jacoba with food and money to help raise him.

Doña Jacoba also presented as a witness the midwife who had aided in the birth of her son. Josefa Mónica de Ayala, a zamba, had known both parents for a long time. In the final months of doña Jacoba's pregnancy, don Diego had asked Josefa to be attentive, "since she was to midwife for doña Jacoba. The night she went into labor, don Diego de la Parra called this witness, and she went with him to doña Jacoba's door. After helping with Andrés de Parra's birth, she swaddled and dressed the child. She then went to don Diego de Parra's home and asked for a gift for having brought him good news. Don Diego de Parra gave her a pair of green silk stockings from Toledo and some fine cambric. He then asked her to help the mother until the child's baptism, since he was to take him to the baptismal font, which he did."

Doña Jacoba's sister, doña Luisa de Córdova, said she had also witnessed the relationship between her sister and don Diego, "who, entering the home, spent many moments alone with her." Doña Luisa's Spanish-speaking Malamba slave, Ana, told how

Diego de Parra was with Jacoba every night, when he went to see
her and have relations with her. He visited her in front of everyone
in the house. Jacoba was considered a maiden, but as a result of this
liberty and illicit friendship she became pregnant and gave birth
to a boy, Andrés de Parra. Diego de Parra knew he was his, carried
him in his arms, and gave him presents. He also gave money to
those who looked after him. He called him son in the presence
of this witness, who very often went to the shop where Diego de
Parra was with his son. This was so she could collect money for
the mother for her support and that of the child and later, when
he was older, for food and schooling.

Friends, relatives, and slaves were all aware of the relationship between
Captain Diego and doña Jacoba.

Finally, Diego de Parra's executor, who was also a merchant, presented
his testimony in favor of Andrés de Parra. He explained how don Diego de
Parra had made his will in 1685, before leaving the royal navy. Among its
clauses was one in which he asked this man to arrange for and keep three
thousand pesos to aid Andrés de Parra, his son, with its yield, and he should
receive them when he came of age. This was, don Diego stated, his responsibility and one "he was bound by as a man."

In this case, the chivalrous values of male behavior of the time were
demonstrated. Even though the captain later married another woman,
Andrés was formally acknowledged as his natural son and thus inherited
one-sixth of his father's goods.[38]

For many women, especially those who were white, or Spanish, having
children out of wedlock did not hamper their prospects for a future marriage.
Doña Juana de Lorca, for example, had given birth to Esteban, Manuela, and
Leonor Jiménez before marrying Manuel de Cuenca. All three natural children were the product of a relationship doña Juana had maintained with
Capt. Gaspar Jiménez for many years. Long-standing concubinage did not
necessarily force white women out of the matrimonial market. While only
some of the details of doña Juana's life are known, there were surely circumstances like a dowry or Captain Jiménez's public acknowledgment that saved
her from dishonor.[39]

As was seen in chapter five, civil proceedings before the royal audiencia
concerning the acknowledgment of natural children revealed the playing
out of tensions among the different actors involved. Repeated references

to the sexual behavior of engaged women were one important element in the rhetoric of these proceedings. Presumed natural daughters and their mothers had their sexual conduct exposed to public view, and witnesses from the opposing parties frequently employed judgments of it, favorable or not. Beyond whatever importance these opinions about women's sexual virtue may have had on the audiencia's final decisions, what is certain is that illegitimate status rendered women particularly vulnerable when it came to their honor.

In 1682, doña Teodora Gómez Barahona, believed to be Juan Gómez Barahona's natural daughter, presented a claim on her deceased father's estate before the Audiencia of Lima. She was still a child, between seven and twelve, and asked to be given financial support and "a dowry so I can get married when I come of age, since I am a minor and cannot appear in trials." The guardian of her father's goods claimed it was unproven that she was his natural daughter. When the baptismal certificate and witnesses were presented, the opposing party questioned the authenticity of the certificate.

A male witness gave further support to doña Teodora's position by testifying to her secluded and virtuous life. He had always seen and heard that "doña Teodora has lived and lives with great modesty, frequently receiving the sacraments. He has seen her attending the church of Nuestro Señor de los Desamparados, where this witness is a vecino, and has heard nothing contrary to what has been said."

What is clear here is the importance placed on a woman's adherence to prevailing norms, as well as her observable good behavior, such as going to church and receiving the sacraments. Another witness pointed out that the girl "was raised very modestly in her mother's company." Evidence of such behavior was a woman's residence in a respectable place such as the home of a decent family or a convent. The absence of a formal masculine presence diminished both a family's honor and a woman's reputation.

Doña Teodora had stopped living with her mother and sought refuge in the convent of Santa Clara as a laywoman; after a certain age, it was unsuitable for a daughter to continue living with her mother after failing to establish a family of her own. Manuela de Jesús, superior of the beaterio of Santa Rosa de Viterbo, said in doña Teodora's defense that she had "been brought up, and continues to live, in a modest, retiring fashion, frequently taking the sacraments, and now lives in the monastery of Santa Clara in this city." Doña Teodora won her case and was given five thousand pesos. Everything was in order, and the witnesses' statements were considered truthful.[40]

The case of the illegitimate offspring of Capt. Lorenzo del Cerro and doña Antonia de Ochoa, discussed in chapter five, further illustrates how a woman's sexual behavior could be presented in court. Doña María González Durán affirmed that Cerro had purchased a black woman to raise the children and that she was still alive. While at doña Antonia's home

> She had seen, over time, how doña Antonia was becoming heavy
> with child, so this witness asked her what was happening and
> whether maidens were supposed to do such things. Doña Antonia
> answered that Lorenzo del Cerro had brought her to ruin, but had
> offered to help her. What she had in her womb was his. Since that
> time, Lorenzo del Cerro aided doña Antonia, giving her things, and
> doña Antonia had often quarreled with her mother because of this.

Ursula de Torres, Antonio de Ulloa's wife, related how she had been doña Antonia's friend since she was a maiden, "which is why this witness often came to doña Antonia's mother's house, which was where doña Antonia lived. She saw that Lorenzo del Cerro used to visit her and did so until he got her and brought her to ruin. He continued his illicit friendship with doña Antonia for many years, and in the meantime she gave birth."

This evidence aside, the opposing party continued to deny the captain's paternity. He based his assertion principally on the many relationships doña Antonia had supposedly been involved in.[41]

Josefa de Herrera was the product of an extramarital relationship between a Spanish merchant, don Sebastián de Herrera, and a "noblewoman who was known as such," but whose name remained unmentioned so as to protect her honor. The parents were single when their daughter was born. Because of her father's death in 1679, Josefa had to leave the convent of Santa Clara where she had grown up in comfort, thanks to economic help from her father. This led her to claim her right to her paternal legitim before the audiencia. Because Josefa had not been acknowledged as a natural daughter, either at the baptismal font or in her father's will, she was forced to call witnesses to prove don Sebastián's paternity. According to their statements, immediately after doña Josefa's birth, don Sebastián de Herrera took her to doña Andrea Alvarado's home to be raised, "paying the wet nurse and providing for all her needs." When the child reached age twelve, her father brought her to the convent.

Each witness emphasized the sexual virtue of doña Josefa's mother. The witnesses, most of whom were women who had been close to Josefa throughout her life, knew her mother well and affirmed that she had "never been with any other man." This argument must have been compelling, for the judges found in doña Josefa's favor, granting her the status of natural child and fifteen hundred pesos for her support.[42]

A woman's sexual modesty and retiring life could, in such circumstances, defeat a man's will. The sum awarded was a pittance, though, given what the wealthy don Sebastián had distributed to various people and institutions of public charity, such as beaterios, houses of retreat, and shelters for convalescent Indians. The fifteen hundred pesos the court stipulated were certainly not going to make doña Josefa a rich woman. They might have allowed her to return to the convent, however, though certainly in a less comfortable position.[43]

Illegitimacy affected the lives of men and women differently. The church's rules regarding membership in religious orders, for example, were much stricter for men than women. This was a paradox of colonial society's hierarchical order, where social distinctions were the result of many combinations of classifying criteria. The case of doña Mencía Pérez Martel de San Bernardo, elected abbess of the Dominican convent of Santa Catalina in Cuzco, is a beautiful and revealing story of what illegitimacy meant for some women.

By secret vote, doña Mencía de San Bernardo became abbess of the convent rather than doña Juana de los Remedios, although a group of nuns had earlier held that sisters not born of formal marriages could not be elected. Despite doña Mencía's illegitimacy, sixteen of the thirty nuns on the electoral committee had voted for her; of those in her favor, most were themselves of illegitimate birth.

The opposing group objected to her election, basing their argument on doña Mencía's illegitimate status. Some went so far as to question her admission to the convent. They appealed to the constitutions of the Dominican Order, which, they said, stated that a difference of one vote was insufficient for election. Furthermore, all the ecclesiastical authorities that canon law required to be presented in the election had not been. In addition, only one person, rather than three, had examined the vote and authenticated the election. Finally, doña Mencía's character and honesty were questioned, for she had supposedly offered the nuns of the convent "bribes as well as gifts and foreseeing her victory, some music and dancing." Protests aside, however, a public scribe finally ratified the election results, and doña Mencía assumed her position.

Juana de los Remedios, Catalina de Jesús, Isabel de la Asunción, and María de San Josef appealed again, however, this time before Lima's metropolitan judge. Tomás Sánchez, doña Juana's attorney, claimed doña Mencía should not be allowed to be abbess because she was a bastard.

Doña Mencía de San Bernardo's attorney rose to her defense. First, he argued, according to canon law, professed nuns could not appear in court without permission from their prelates, so the claim doña Juana de los Remedios and her followers presented should not be admitted. He further maintained that illegitimate status affected male and female prelates differently. Since abbesses and prioresses had no ecclesiastical jurisdiction, they did not have to be of legitimate birth.

He supported these statements, based on papal bulls, with provisions issued at the Council of Trent. It was confirmed there that "many male religious who had professed had left their convents because of the defect [of illegitimacy]." The same did not occur with nuns of illegitimate birth, who, despite their status, remained in their convents.

Secular laws further aided doña Mencía's defense. The *Siete Partidas*, the Laws of Toro, and the *Recopilación* all concurred that natural children whose parents were noble enjoyed the same liberties and privileges as their parents and were exempt from taxation, just as if they were legitimate. Doña Mencía Pérez Martel was not just any individual of illegitimate birth. She was a natural daughter, "an illustrious noblewoman," and as such, deserved these privileges. The act of professing had been for her a "heroic act of virtue," and she did not relinquish her nobility by entering the religious life.

The principal instructor in theology of Cuzco's cathedral church approved the election, dismissing doña Mencía's accusers as malicious and recommending their punishment. The precentor of the church, the ecclesiastical judge and vicar of Cuzco, denied the unhappy nuns had any right to denounce doña Mencía and threatened to excommunicate them. When they were informed of this decision at their convent, "they stood up and turned their backs, saying they did not hear anything." Deeply convinced that a natural daughter could not be a prioress in the convent, these sisters were not ready to relent on a question of honor, despite the threat of excommunication.

Doña Juana de los Remedios was determined to pursue the case and presented an appeal in Lima, insisting on the annulment of the election. The election failed to follow the procedure set by canon law: the people who should have confirmed it were not present, and it was not verified in the proper way. The problem continued to be doña Mencía's illegitimacy.

Though female religious might have to abide by a more limited jurisdiction than their male counterparts, this did not mean that these women were excluded from positions of authority. A female prelate also exercised jurisdiction, and the "dignity of the symbolic prelature is still present."

After the second hearing the appeals court rendered its verdict. "Though mindful of the proceedings and merits of the suit, [the court finds] doña Mencía de San Bernardo has the defect of illegitimacy, which stands in the way of her election. Because the election was uncanonical, it is declared null and void, and a new election for prioress will be carried out."[44]

Other women of illegitimate origin achieved important positions in convents without having to undergo the same ordeal as doña Mencía de San Bernardo. The road was never free of impediments resulting from their status as natural children, however. Sister María Magdalena de San Juan y Santa Lucía became abbess of Lima's convent of Las Descalzas, even though she was the natural daughter of Capt. Juan de Urrutia and had not yet received the dowry granted her by her father's 1643 will. Although Captain Urrutia had not acknowledged his paternity in his testament, Sister María Magdalena's descent was registered in the parish books of San Sebastián in Lima. He had also been explicit when expressing his last wishes as to what she should receive upon his death, which occurred in 1665.

> I want . . . Magdalena de Santa Lucía, a Discalced nun in the
> convent of San José of this city, to be given two hundred patacones
> when I die. An income of four thousand patacones must then be
> given to her as long as she lives to care for her needs. When she
> dies, my heirs will inherit the principal and interest, and neither
> her convent nor any other person will have any right to this.

Captain Urrutia's fortune was substantial, sixty thousand pesos. He also had two legitimate sons. One, his father's executor, was a prebendary of Lima's cathedral church. The other was prior of the convent of San Agustín. Both were powerful and resisted giving Sister María Magdalena her bequest, claiming there was not enough money available. The royal audiencia nevertheless decided in her favor.[45]

This case shows that a woman's illegitimacy did not necessarily adversely affect her social standing and ascent to an important position. What should be noted, though, is the positive influence of her Spanish origin and elite descent. The explicit clause in her father's will also worked to benefit her.

Relationships outside of marriage, as well as illegitimacy, contributed to social classification, but at the same time they were constituent elements of people's emotional universes. Rather than forming a distinct and separate subculture among women within colonial society, they instead helped to reproduce widely held cultural values.

María de Salamanca, a vecina and native of Lima, was an illegitimate daughter who knew only her mother's name, which she mentioned in her will. While single, she had two natural children, Pedro and Agustina de Salamanca. When she wed she brought a dowry to the marriage and received the arras from her bridegroom.[46]

Little is known of Catalina Gil de Pastrana, though the codicil to her will mentioned she had three natural children, one boy and two girls. She was begotten from an informal union, but knew her parents. She later married and had two legitimate daughters.[47]

Francisca de Campoverde was a free black woman who was born in Saña but lived and died in Lima. In her 1651 will, she affirmed she was the natural daughter of a free mulatto man and a slave, both born on the island of Santo Domingo. That she knew her mother's name, but not her father's, suggests she grew up with her mother and that her father, if not a stranger, was absent from the household. Francisca belonged to eight religious confraternities, evidence of her integration in urban society. Furthermore, she had six slaves, three males and three females, as well as fine new clothes, a substantial amount of worked silver, and jewelry. She brought a dowry of 2,270 pesos to her marriage with Jacinto Sarmiento and received 2,243 in the arras. That she had both been a slave and had given birth to three children when single clearly posed no obstacle to her subsequent marriage. Although an exceptional case, this gives some idea of how flexible and accepting colonial society could be.[48]

María Pascuala de Sarmiento was an unmarried native of Lima. She was a natural daughter who remembered only the name of her father. María Pascuala had a long-standing consensual relationship with Juan Esteban de la Parra, with whom she had five children. Although they never married, it is impossible to speculate whether there was some sort of matrimonial impediment.[49]

The women involved in these extramarital situations all came from love relationships and informal family situations and may have been mimicking their mothers' behavior.[50] They were also living well within society's mainstream. They married the fathers of their children or other men, counted on a dowry and even an arras, and participated in the city's public life. All this suggests that neither matrifocal households nor illegitimacy among women from society's middle sectors generated a discrete subculture.

Illegitimacy and extramarital relationships were, however, closely linked to the existence of a slave population in general and female slaves in particular, for whom they had special meaning. In the urban centers of the Iberian colonial world, slaves were deeply involved in the life of the free society they were part of. Unlike the experience of societies where Protestantism prevailed and whites were rigidly segregated from people of color, in Spanish and Portuguese colonial societies such segregation was of a very different nature.[51]

The physical proximity of slaves and their masters was powerfully conducive to strong emotional ties between slave wet nurses and white children, the emotional declarations owners made in their wills about their slaves, and even the cruelties particular to the master-slave relationship that were fueled by daily domestic contact.[52] The sexual interaction of free men and slave women was at the center of this configuration of proximity and hierarchy.

The *Siete Partidas* established that servants could marry among themselves without their masters' permission.[53] Slaves had a right to marry, and the church intervened on their behalf in cases where married slaves belonged to different masters, such as when one owner changed residence.[54] Fernando Trazegnies points out that Spanish law favored religion over patrimony, and this guarded against a family's separation. The *Partidas* did not, however, hesitate to affirm that the slave owed obedience first to the master and only then to a spouse.[55]

Although colonial officials on many occasions attributed the public disorder and promiscuity that prevailed in the city to the slaves' behavior, they seldom disturbed the master-slave relationship, which over time determined the lives of the enslaved. These same officials yielded authority to the owners over slaves' sexual behavior. One example of this was the virtual absence of slaves implicated in court cases against those who committed concubinage, as was seen in chapter three.[56]

There was little about slaves' marriages that could benefit their masters. Such relationships were an obstacle when selling slaves or transferring them from one place to another, and masters vehemently opposed them. The master-slave bond rarely led to owners' preoccupation with sexual morality or affection toward their slaves unless this harmed them in some way.

The infrequency of marriage among the slave population and those of African descent in general reflected the strength of the relationship between master and slave. Marriage rates among blacks were low, at least until midway through the seventeenth century. Frederick Bowser's study noted that for the years 1560 to 1650, and without counting blacks who had only recently left Africa, only 6 percent of men and 10 percent of women from this group were married.[57] Slaves' marital status also depended, as did so many other aspects of their lives, upon their masters' social status. Slaves whose masters belonged to dominant social groups or whose lives were subject to public scrutiny were more likely to marry.[58]

The low marriage rate among slaves can also be explained by the constant arrival in Lima of African slaves of different ethnic origins. These recently imported Africans, unlike Hispanicized slaves, spoke a number of different languages, which made their integration into colonial culture extremely difficult. The efforts of priests, especially the Jesuits, were not always successful in establishing the communication necessary to ensure that newly arrived Africans adopted the patterns of behavior viceregal authorities expected of them.[59] This, in conjunction with slave status itself, would partially explain the high incidence of illegitimacy in the slave population.

During the seventeenth century, 19 percent of slave births in the parish of San Marcelo were legitimate, and they, in turn, represented 18 percent of all legitimate births in the parish. Another 81 percent were presumably illegitimate, for they lacked the necessary information when they were recorded; these represented 49 percent of all out of wedlock children born in the parish. During this same period, 19 percent of slaves born in the parish of El Sagrario were legitimate, while 79 percent of births lacked qualifying information at the time of inscription. Illegitimate slaves constituted 56 percent of all illegitimate births in the parish. Thus, only one out of every five slaves, 20 percent, was legitimate.[60]

Free white men acknowledged their children born of slave mothers many times. At the same time, an equally large number of wills records cases of white men liberating slave children without ever mentioning the relationship uniting them. Male intentions were reflected in baptismal records, which allow a detailed reconstruction and interpretation of illegitimacy and its significance (see tables 5.3 and 5.4).

At the parish of El Sagrario, there was no strong connection between illegitimacy and a father's absence. By contrast, in the case of San Marcelo male absence was generally associated with illegitimacy among slaves. Several conditions may explain these differences. Over the course of the seventeenth century, the parish of San Marcelo witnessed a higher percentage of slave births than did El Sagrario. El Sagrario was substantially larger than San Marcelo, and its parishioners were Lima's wealthiest and most distinguished vecinos, those who set the prevailing cultural patterns. Their slaves, who usually shared their masters' homes, were also influenced by them. It is worth noting in this regard that the percentage of legitimate births was generally higher in El Sagrario than in San Marcelo.

Another consideration was the presence of recently arrived Africans in El Sagrario. There, 12 percent of fathers of baptized children were of African origin, while in San Marcelo only 7 percent were. Although it is true that these Africans were less likely to marry, it is possible that, given the traditions of their homelands, they felt their paternal obligations strongly, and this, in turn, encouraged them to recognize their offspring at the baptismal font. In the parish of San Marcelo, illegitimate slave children acknowledged by both parents were distributed in the following manner: slave fathers recognized 41, while those who were free recognized 55. Of the illegitimate offspring acknowledged by both parents in the parish of El Sagrario, 546 were recognized by slave fathers and only 313 by fathers who were free.[61] Considering the large difference in both parishes between the number of illegitimate slave children acknowledged by both parents and those recognized only by the mother, slavery clearly specifically influenced how the group of illegitimate offspring was formed.

Because a female slave lacked honor, she could never claim to be a maiden, even if she had never had sexual relations with a man. Virginity, in society's view, did not exist as a status for female slaves. The system itself decreed this. No virtuous behavior was ever expected of them so long as their conduct did not threaten public order. This explains in part the presumed sexual availability of female slaves.

Although the institution of slavery militated against slave marriage, these women still valued marriage very highly. This would seem to suggest that even though masters resisted granting liberty, they could be persuaded to accept some minimal conditions that permitted a real married life for their slaves. Furthermore, the establishment of marital bonds created new relationships and networks that at least symbolically eroded the stigma of slavery. In the best circumstances, these links could favor real liberation. This situation worried the crown, resulting in the order that slaves were bound by their condition even if married.[62] Given all this, it is unsurprising that women in servitude, despite their lack of honor, held marriage in high regard.

When this was unattainable, which no doubt was frequently the case, female slaves found considerable advantages through sexual relationships with free men. The love that brought free men and women who were slaves together led fathers to acknowledge their children and attempt to free them. This must have been an encouraging possibility for enslaved women. Under the best of circumstances, these women could themselves be manumitted.

While the nature of the affection between free men and their slave partners is not always obvious, male sentiment about paternity sometimes emerges. In 1627 the ecclesiastical court prosecuted Juan Gómez, a married man from Trujillo, and Juana Ramírez, a black slave, for the third time. Two of the witnesses told of how a month before, the daughter of Juana Ramírez and Juan Gómez had been baptized at the parish of Santa Ana. At the time, they said, Juan Gómez had provided money to emancipate the child, and the "little mulatta girl was recorded as free" in the baptismal books of the parish.[63]

In 1632, María Arias brought suit, with the permission of her husband, don Luis de Dueñas, against her father, don Salvador Arias, for financial support. At the time, María was between fourteen and twenty-five. Her baptismal certificate said she was the "daughter of Juana, the mulatta slave of Fabiana de Vera, and an unknown father." Juana de Bonilla stated she had been a slave, as had her daughter, but that both had later purchased their freedom.

These arguments favored María Arias's claim. Her husband's status as "an honorable Spaniard" further elevated her prestige. That both parents were single when María was born, and the prosperous don Salvador had no legitimate children of his own who could inherit his wealth, also enhanced her position.

Three witnesses testified for María Arias. Diego de Leyton, an artillery-man for the royal navy; Bartola de la Torre, a married woman; and doña María de Bonilla, daughter of Fabiana de Vera, all stated they knew of the case and she was Salvador Arias's natural daughter. Don Salvador, however, denied his paternity and demanded that the manumission certificate be presented. Fabiana, the former owner, maintained that Arias had purchased freedom of each of the two women.

These facts aside, Arias's lawyer argued that Diego de Leyton could not be believed "because he had had an illicit friendship with Juana de Bonilla, mother of the opposing party." Information was then presented bearing on Juana de Bonilla's life, her numerous lovers, and her illegitimate children. The judge nevertheless granted don Luis de Dueñas three hundred pesos while the proceedings concerning Arias's paternity continued.

The statements from the masters seem to have decisively influenced the authorities' verdict in María's favor. Doña María de Bonilla claimed she had known María since her birth and they had grown up "together in her home." She added that the lovers, Juana and Salvador, had both been single when they met. She herself had advocated María's liberty before her mother when don Salvador had offered to buy his natural daughter's freedom. Furthermore, she added, his sister had taken María to her home to take care of her, saying that María was her niece, her brother's daughter.

María died during the course of the proceedings, but her children still benefited. Each one, the court ruled, should receive two hundred pesos, though "only once." This final victory showed how the daughter of a slave could become truly Spanish in the full meaning of the word.[64]

The bonds of slavery became relaxed within the stratified social order. Free men and female slaves maintained relationships and produced offspring. These children might find themselves in a superior position in the world of slaves. Under the best of circumstances, they could became Spanish and members of the free society.

﹏

The religious and secular authorities of Lima's hierarchical colonial society clearly articulated what constituted appropriate female behavior. Virginity, demureness, discretion, and subordination to father, husband, or priest were the values and conditions directing women's lives. Nevertheless, the colonial situation, with its particular social stratification, created not only a double standard of morality that differed for men and women, but also various codes of female behavior. One consequence was to differentiate women's social value, depending on their position in society, but there were others as well. A fragmented rhetoric developed regarding norms for female behavior. These hierarchical criteria, influenced by the status of illegitimacy, thus sustained different forms of discrimination.

Women did not encounter special obstacles because of their illegitimate status when entering convents. These female religious institutions lacked ecclesiastical jurisdiction and were subordinate to masculine religious power, but the defect of illegitimacy did not prevent women from choosing this life. For men, however, legitimate birth was indeed required to follow a religious vocation.

A woman's illegitimacy was not necessarily a disadvantage, for a paternal donation could ease the way to a good position in the convent. As has been seen, however, a woman's secure place in these institutions could be threatened if the delivery of money promised was interrupted or delayed or her illegitimate status was made known in circumstances where power was clearly linked to legitimacy.

Illegitimate women did not accede to ecclesiastical power through conventual life, but they did attain status by incorporation into such institutions. There was no necessary correspondence between status and power; women might gain the former, but not the latter.

The sexual conduct of women born out of wedlock came under close scrutiny because of their gender. Unlike their male counterparts, women of illegitimate birth who sought recognition as natural children in order to share in the privileges this status offered were forced to maintain their respectability and sexual honor. Sexual morality, a principle central to the ordering of the colonial social world, influenced how significant illegitimacy was under different circumstances. In the case of women, sexual conduct above suspicion was the only way to ensure civil acknowledgment of natural status and the consequent enjoyment of paternal goods. Sometimes even a woman's own participation in a public forum like the civil chamber of the royal audiencia damaged her reputation, at least according to the code of honor in place at the time. Female honor, which in this case dominant masculine rhetoric defined, played a part in the identity and destiny of natural children.

Female honor, a value specific to chaste, virtuous women in terms of sexual morality, had a particular role when illegitimacy was involved. This mechanism of female control acquires special force in societies where relationships are face-to-face and public opinion, still largely confined within the home, greatly influences people's intimate lives. This was certainly the case in Lima's colonial society, where the boundary between public and private was indistinct and intimacy did not belong exclusively to private life.

Among women, illegitimacy was a hierarchical criterion. The tendency was to expel those of illegitimate birth from the group and convert them into inferiors. White women who were illegitimate did not have easy access to family dowries, and they were excluded from certain institutions. Only by obtaining dowries from groups explicitly formed to provide them could these women enter the more prestigious convents, but even then they could encounter problems.

The social status of the father generally dictated the position of an illegitimate daughter. If a father acknowledged his paternity, granted her a dowry, and bequeathed her part of his estate, she could attain a relatively secure position of prestige in the city's hierarchy. This standing was always threatened, however, by a wife seeking to keep her marital dowry, legitimate children claiming that their father's estate was insufficient to cover a natural child's demands, or a father's later denial of paternity.

Since dowries were necessary to compete effectively in the city's matrimonial market and their availability to natural daughters was always uncertain, women of illegitimate birth faced great difficulties in attaining the married state. They were even greater for those women who failed to be recognized as natural children.

There were differences between men and women belonging to the city's dominant groups. In the case of white women, illegitimacy had specific repercussions when trying to gain a dowry, that fundamental element securing a successful future for Spanish women of the city's middle and upper sectors. The obstacles women of illegitimate birth encountered trying to access their paternal legitims must also have made establishment of new families difficult. This no doubt contributed to extramarital affairs being seen as the pattern for relationships between men and women. A vicious circle was thus created in which illegitimacy fed upon itself. Its pervasiveness tended to diminish the standing of women in the city's dominant sectors, with those of illegitimate origin suffering the most. Finally, it should also be noted that, however subtly, natural male children tended to be favored over their female siblings, even though they shared the same social status.

Evidence from women's seventeenth-century wills indicates that most women of illegitimate birth tended to have out of wedlock children themselves. This was not necessarily marginal behavior, however, for these same women could accumulate small estates, participate in religious confraternities and brotherhoods, marry, or aspire to conventual life.

Another aspect this study has explored is the emotions people in similar circumstances held in common. These sentiments, though individually experienced, expressed collectively held beliefs that had much to do with hierarchies and social differences. How one lived with discrimination or a loss of status was closely linked to the group to which one belonged. Lima's hierarchical social system and the inequalities it engendered produced a form of regulation where control over people's behavior was generally dictated by forces and restrictions external to the individual. For this reason, feelings about illegitimacy and extraconjugality, and in particular, feelings of guilt, were very closely linked to religion, to a value system based on honor, and to gender and social differences in general.

Although internal controls were weak, sexual relationships outside of marriage, particularly for women, led to feelings of shame. This was especially true when a pregnancy resulted and more so when a man deserted his partner. This was most clearly seen in the elite sectors of Lima, where the preoccupation with protecting status was greatest.

A woman's shame was part of, and closely linked to, the shame her family and social group experienced. Male acknowledgment of paternity would, however, attenuate these feelings. Baptismal certificates showed two tendencies. On the one hand, many white women, those who would be most worried about their status, found themselves with out of wedlock children whom the father refused to recognize. On the other, protecting the honor of a woman and her family rested exclusively on a father's acknowledgment of paternity. Situations such as these were of little importance in seventeenth-century Lima, however.

Illegitimacy could nevertheless diminish the prestige of women from the elite sectors of society. Although they were more concerned about their status than were members of subordinate groups, women belonging to the lower echelons of society also worried about their honor. Women of every social rank found their sexual virtue called into question in the city's courts, and this harmed them all.

Gender and illegitimacy worked differently among the city's subordinate sectors. If an illegitimate daughter, the product of a relationship between a white man and a casta woman, including a slave woman, received dowry money from her father, she could ascend socially through marriage to a white man. In this case, a woman gained status. Further investigation of marital patterns and exogamous tendencies, yet to be done, will shed more light on this.

The situation of female slaves had its own characteristics. Research indicates that slaves were not indifferent to marriage, and the institutionalization of marital bonds attenuated slavery in many ways. Furthermore, extramarital relationships between free men and indentured women led fathers to seek the freedom for their illegitimate offspring. It should be remembered, however, that even though female slaves had no claim on honor, public proceedings brought their sexual conduct to light when the offspring of these relationships sought acknowledgment as natural children.

There were many families where the mother was the sole parent, though this varied depending on her social standing. Honor kept elite women from establishing their own households to care for children. They were instead brought up in other families or in convents. Women from Lima's middle ranks had more difficulty making such arrangements, but it could be done. Still, when they sought to keep their own families intact, they suffered from the consequent damage to their status and honor. Nevertheless, they could sometimes secure their futures by claiming compensation for lost virginity, receiving an inheritance allowing them to aspire to a good marriage, or participating in the life of the city through religious confraternities. All these avenues allowed them to enter the community and prevented them from being pushed into a life at the margin of society.

Despite the frequency of paternal abandonment and children acknowledged only by mothers, it is difficult to speak of families led by women who were slaves. When an individual was the property of another, the possibility of establishing an independent family unit was severely limited. A network of relationships based on ties of blood and friendship could, and probably did, exist for slaves, but the children of slave mothers were their masters' property. Indentured women were sometimes able to gain their freedom through relationships with free men, thus allowing them to form their own households, but such opportunities were relatively rare.

Families headed by women, a social reality strongly associated with illegitimacy, implied, among other things, the absence of fathers. Because male figures represented public authority in the private world of the family, their very presence ensured certain behavioral norms. The strength of these norms diminished when the father was not part of the family unit. This could explain in part why women of illegitimate birth themselves had out of wedlock children and were willing to set up their own households.

CHAPTER SEVEN

Abandonment, Affection, and Institutional Response

๑๕

G iven that children, particularly those unacknowledged by their parents, were among the least visible members of colonial society, it is difficult to locate documentation that permits a clear understanding of their lives. Little is known about intimate reasons that led parents to rid themselves of their newly born at the baptismal font. Fortunately, there are a few sources that explore the topic and provide some insight. The baptismal registries of Lima's churches record the approximate number of children abandoned and their social origins, how this varied over time, and sometimes the circumstances resulting in paternal absence. The opinions of male authorities about this problem and the institutional response to it also help to define and explain it. Finally, testimonies, particularly from women, bearing directly or indirectly on the abandonment of newly born children can be found in diverse sources.

Several works on child abandonment in Western cities provide a context for this phenomenon. Abandonment affected many aspects of family life. It curtailed population growth, regulated inheritance, or provided a way to survive in the face of diminished material resources.[1] Some of the most obvious reasons for abandoning the newborn included physical deformity, being born from impermissible or incestuous relationships, belonging to the wrong, usually female, gender, or simply being unwanted.[2] In crowded cities, especially during periods of crisis, parents who abandoned children were increasingly likely to be unmarried: priests, single women who had been taken advantage of, prostitutes, and female domestic servants.[3] Child abandonment was also closely related to extramarital affairs and illegitimacy.[4]

Studies of family relationships, kinship relations, and childhood in particular indicate that the nature of affection among different family members varied over the centuries for a number of reasons.[5] Social transformations also led to gradual, albeit significant, changes in family relationships and how they were experienced. The seventeenth century, at least in terms of the history of the European family, marked a late stage in the development of the notion of childhood. At this time, children were about to acquire their own identity. This profoundly altered both existing family structures and the emotional content of relationships. Parents and children assumed new roles, and their mutual interaction changed. Unfortunately, nothing is known about the situation and character of children in colonial times. There are no studies on the composition of the urban family, no demographic analyses that would permit even an incomplete view of a child's place in society.

Toward the end of the seventeenth century, the population of free children in Lima totaled 6,209, 21 percent of the city's population.[6] According to the *Numeración general de Lima*, this group included 4,732 Spanish, or white, residents, 3,003 boys younger than fifteen, and 1,729 girls younger than twelve, 10 and 6 percent of the city's total population respectively. These characterizations by age and gender suggest that socially dominant groups had already developed some specific ideas about how childhood was defined.[7] This is further indicated by how city authorities compiled data on children living in Lima: boys were enumerated separately from girls only if they were white. Children of color were counted without regard to gender, and 645 Indian (2 percent of total population), 642 mulatto (2 percent), and 190 black (0.6 percent) boys and girls resided in the capital.

Children were differentiated from adults in all social groups except the slave population. In the *Numeración general*, only gender mattered. black, mulatto, and casta men of all ages were counted together, as were black women, mulattas, and casta women. The condition of enslavement was so definitive that no difference other than ethnicity was needed when identifying this social group. These kinds of classifications posit a relationship between age and membership in a particular social group. Clearly, more distinctions were made in the upper echelons of society. Elite social standing thus brought with it a more complex definition of identity.

In seventeenth-century Lima, increased urban illegitimacy produced a large number of baptized children of unknown parentage.[8] In the parish of San Marcelo, parents of 22 percent of out of wedlock children were unidentified. Another 7 percent of illegitimate children had no information at all about their parents. In other words, for one out of every three children of illegitimate birth, neither parent was present to record the baptism. Something similar was occurring in the parish of El Sagrario during the same period. For 16 percent of births, in effect illegitimate, no parents' names were recorded. In 8 percent of cases, no parents were mentioned at all. In this parish, 24 percent of children baptized were not registered by either parent.

This phenomenon seems even more widespread when the white population alone is considered. Of white children born out of wedlock in the parish of San Marcelo, the parents of 54 percent were recorded as unknown. For another 4 percent there is an absolute lack of information concerning their parents. In El Sagrario, the first group totaled 47 percent and the second, 5 percent. The failure to identify both progenitors in the parochial registry had a variety of meanings for the different social and ethnic groups in the city. This, as will be seen, makes the figures somewhat relative. Were they taken in absolute terms, they would point to mass abandonment of children.

Priests had two different ways of registering children whose parents were absent at baptism. One was to record the parents as not known or unknown. The other was to leave their names out of the entry altogether; for statistical purposes, these cases have been classified as having no information. It is difficult to determine whether there were fundamental differences between these two types of registry. An explicit reference to absent parents might indicate abandonment proper or the desire to conceal the parents' identity. The failure to record the parents' names at all might reflect indifference regarding their identity.

A close examination of baptismal records for slaves confirms this, for there the absence of parents conforms to the second pattern: there is no information. In this case, the parents' identity was often insignificant information that went unrecorded. This was not the case with the free population, however, and particularly for the Spanish population of the parish of

San Marcelo. There, children of unknown parents far outnumbered those for whom there was no information (see tables 5.3 and 5.4).

By way of contrast, San Marcelo's Indian population, which was very small, had only six births (15 percent) where the parents were unknown. Among castas and nonwhite groups generally, 25 percent of children were of unknown parentage, while in El Sagrario only 14 percent were. Among the free blacks of San Marcelo, 10 percent of illegitimate children were born of unknown parents, while in El Sagrario the figure was 17 percent.

For the slave population of San Marcelo, only 12 percent of children lacked information about their parents, while in El Sagrario 9 percent did. These low percentages are explained by the fact that a pregnant slave could scarcely conceal her condition. Because the children of slaves were in bondage by birth, owners inevitably identified the future mothers.

The existence of slaves formally lacking known progenitors was the result of owners baptizing their newly born slaves without knowing the parents' identity, in particular when the children were born out of wedlock. For this reason, it is impossible to speak about abandonment of slave children. The case of Antonio illustrates this. He was baptized in 1635 in San Marcelo, and his godparents were Juan Biafra and María Folupa. The names of the witnesses were also recorded, Juan de Medina and Francisco Pantoja. Only a marginal note reveals that Antonio was Catalina Folupa's son.[9]

These figures rise slightly if abandoned children, that is, children left by their parents at the doors of family homes or the Hospital de los Niños Huérfanos, are added. These children were identified as such in the baptismal record. They were a small percentage for each parish and were almost exclusively white. Of the 38 abandoned children recorded for San Marcelo, 36 (3 percent) were white, while in El Sagrario, 294 (4 percent) were.

According to a papal bull issued by Gregory XVI, abandoned children were considered legitimate. As such, they enjoyed the privileges accorded legitimate children and could be ordained. Based on experience, it was believed that many parents abandoned their children because they were too poor to support them, not necessarily because they were illegitimate. There was some disagreement on this, however, and according to Juan Machado de Chávez, there were those who held that illegitimate children greatly increased the number of abandoned children.[10] Pedro de León Portocarrero described how Lima's Hospital de los Niños Huérfanos operated at the beginning of the seventeenth century and explained that the children were brought there by their mothers "who had had them without their parents' permission and did not want their wrongdoing to be known."[11]

Other evidence strongly suggests that abandoned children were the fruit of illicit sexual relationships, thus confirming Machado de Chávez's comments and those in the *Descripción*. At both El Sagrario and San Marcelo there were cases of boys and girls abandoned who were later recognized by their parents, whether they had married or not. A child baptized at San Marcelo in 1645 was abandoned at the home of doña Dominga de Paula. Years later, in 1670, Francisco García, an accountant, acknowledged him as his son, stating that he had been single when the child was born.[12] In 1675, Pedro Tomás was abandoned at the home of Tomás Ortiz de Castro, a secretary, whose family was raising him when he was baptized at San Marcelo. Six years later, his father, who had married Pedro's mother, doña Isabel Rodríguez, recognized him as his legitimate son.[13]

In El Sagrario, patterns of acknowledging children resembled those of San Marcelo. A woman with the honorific doña recognized her son as natural less than a year after the child's birth.[14] Two men acknowledged their natural children although they had initially been abandoned. As in San Marcelo, one did so twenty-five years after his son's birth.[15]

These cases are too small in number to be representative, but they do reveal that illegitimate birth was one reason to abandon a baby. As a matter of honor, fathers and mothers were constrained from acknowledging their children. In the best cases, parents married and after a time formally recognized their children and assumed their parental responsibilities. In other cases, emotional reasons may have played a part.

The desire to pass down an inheritance may have led some parents to reestablish relationships with their children. Out of wedlock offspring whose descent had not been clearly recorded in the parish books could hardly gain access to paternal, and in some cases maternal, wealth. There were also those men who, at the end of their lives, no longer thought it necessary to conceal their paternity.

According to information from baptismal records, children in both parishes were usually abandoned at homes belonging to Lima's middle and upper social strata.[16] Children left there were certain to survive and might even hope to have a secure future. Leaving babies with poor families was to expose them to certain death, for they could never afford to provide the wet nurses such children required.

The simple act of abandonment deprived children of certain rights and privileges, but this could be remedied by acquiring the status of foundling. This occurred when a family, generally well off, agreed to accept and raise a child. That these children were almost always white, however, indicated how social and ethnic discrimination came into play with regard to abandoned children.

Leaving newborns at private homes, a practice only the dominant sectors of urban colonial society followed, was related to an Iberian tradition that Lima's white population adapted to the local situation.[17] The ethnic inequalities characteristic of the colonial world left their own mark on this custom, however. In Lima, the existence of abandoned white children became one more element in the hierarchical social classification. Racial segregation made it impossible for blacks, Indians, or other castas to abandon their children in the homes of whites. They were unlikely to be accepted there, but if they were, they would become servants and treated as such. At any rate, nonwhites had no reason to leave their progeny with people like themselves because their children's future would be little different from the one they would have if they had stayed in their birth homes.

It was therefore only white children who could avail themselves of foundling status, but what this condition actually meant was itself subject to interpretation. It is easy to imagine a white man arranging the future of his illegitimate mestizo offspring by placing the child with a family, thus ensuring the child's access to the privileges enjoyed by legitimate children. In this situation, the child both ceased being illegitimate and became socially white.

Many abandoned children probably never met their birth parents and always lived in the homes of families willing to shelter them. Others were not typical orphans. They might have stayed in contact with their parents, but because they had no need for formal parental acknowledgment, no traces of their lives remain. It is likely that many mothers recovered their children, but since they had nothing to pass on to them, it was pointless to carry out the necessary procedures with the parish priest. For this reason, the absence of formal acknowledgment should not lead to the conclusion that parents abandoned their children in great numbers, though the available figures might seem to suggest this.

The donations city residents made to institutions charged with caring for children without parents shed some light on how people of the time perceived and dealt with this problem. One widespread practice was to include in wills a clause giving small bequests to orphan children and institutions devoted to looking after individuals who had no close relatives to protect them. Don Andrés García de Bobadilla's 1649 testament included such a provision. "For support of and the hospital at the Casa de Nuestra Señora de Atocha in this city, fifteen pesos of eight reales, so long as the banner of the hospital is displayed at my burial."[18] His request was a common one. Orphan children regularly accompanied burial processions, "with their cloaks over their dark clothes and carrying a black banner," in exchange for a promised charitable contribution.[19]

Orphan children who had been abandoned were a physical and institutional part of the city's social landscape. Although unfortunate, the presence of these children allowed them to receive some of the income the Hospital de los Niños Huérfanos had to operate. The identity of abandoned children was also defined by the people who surrounded them every day. Bonifacia del Espíritu Santo, applying for placement at the Colegio de Santa Cruz de Atocha for abandoned girls, had been raised by doña Teresa Salazar. To prove she was an orphan, she presented a witness who stated that "everybody in the neighborhood always knew her as 'the little castaway' and they called her by that name."[20]

Not all abandoned children were lucky enough to be accepted by families or religious institutions that would look after them. Evidence of less felicitous situations were the newborn left in city streets, part of daily life in Lima.[21] Nevertheless, just as the colonial administration did not severely sanction extramarital relationships, it did not mistreat the resulting progeny.

Establishing the Hospital de los Niños Huérfanos de Atocha at the beginning of the seventeenth century was the initiative of a man known as Luis Pecador (Louis the Sinner). At the time old and blind, he lived a humble, virtuous life. Before establishing the hospital, he had traveled throughout the Andes treating people who were ill.[22] He took his inspiration from San Juan de Dios and wished to establish a public house of mercy that would accept all abandoned children. His purpose, he said, was

> To gather orphan children found at the doors of churches
> and in the streets. In some extreme cases we have rescued
> them from garbage dumps, found them almost eaten by
> dogs, and in rivers and ditches, an offense to our Lord.
> At present there are thirty babies, besides many others, we
> have placed with people who, motivated by their love of
> God, will bring them up. Still more have been placed as
> godchildren. They add up to more than one hundred twenty,
> not counting the others who have died.[23]

This situation led to the foundation in 1603 of the Casa de Niños Expósitos, also known as the Hospital de los Niños Huérfanos de Atocha.[24] The hospital sheltered white boys and girls without parents and was located in the same quarter that later became the parish of Huérfanos, or Orphans.

This institution first operated from one of the rooms of the Hospital de San Diego. Doña María de Esquivel then provisionally donated a house that was later purchased for this purpose and where the first abandoned children were taken in. Later a chapel devoted to Nuestra Señora de Atocha was built there.

Luis Pecador's efforts caught the interest of the guild of royal scribes and those working for the audiencia. They asked the viceroy, Luis de Velasco (1595–1603), to create a brotherhood devoted to looking after orphaned and abandoned children. It was formally established in November 1603 under royal patronage. Pope Paul V (1605–21) granted it official ecclesiastical authorization in 1606.[25]

The hospital was taking in fifteen hundred pesos a year by 1643. Additional donations increased the total income to six thousand pesos, which were spent throughout the year.[26] The financial situation of the hospital developed favorably in the years after its foundation, thanks to legacies and donations from members of the sponsoring brotherhood and viceregal authorities. In 1617, the viceroy, the Príncipe de Esquilache (1614–21), allotted it one-fourth of the rents from the Cuartos de la Comedia. Around 1648 the hospital employed seventy wet nurses, two teachers for the girls, and one for the older boys. This prosperity was further ensured toward the middle of 1657, when the brotherhood supporting the hospital agreed to broaden its membership by admitting "any virtuous man regardless of his profession."[27] Private and public donations kept growing as well. The viceroy, the Conde de Lemos, also granted the hospital a three-thousand-peso annual pension. This later increased to four thousand pesos a year and was used exclusively for wet nurses' wages.

The earthquake that shook Lima in 1687 marked the beginning of the hospital's financial crisis. This natural disaster destroyed the hospital building, and some children were forced to beg for money in the streets. Others sought uncertain shelter in family homes where they eventually became servants. At the same time the brotherhood responsible for supporting the institution closed its doors. A group of "illustrious persons," appointed to replace it, attempted to repair the damage to the hospital but with little success.

The hospital never recovered its early financial soundness, and by the beginning of the eighteenth century, its revenues amounted to only eight thousand pesos. This failed to meet operating expenses of twelve thousand pesos, used "to pay the nurses responsible for bringing up the children, buy clothing and everyday food, and support those who have been weaned but stay in the hospital until they become of age and leave the institution."[28] Later, during the administration of Viceroy Caraccioli, several measures were taken to improve material conditions at the hospital. Efforts were made to strengthen control over the wet nurses, and certain requisites were established to ensure their good health and behavior.[29] A royal cédula of 17 July 1710 stated that the number of abandoned children increased constantly, because of both "their parents' misery and the increase in the number of vecinos."[30]

Unfortunately, insufficient information prevents a detailed analysis of either the internal operation of the hospital or how it evolved and changed. Its bylaws had established under what conditions children would be accepted, as well as the food, clothing, and education they would receive. The orphanage had initially been established to accept only white children, but dark-skinned casta children were also abandoned. As a result, segregation was enforced within the hospital, and children were treated differently, depending on ethnicity. Girls growing up in the hospital lacked the means to secure a dowry that would allow them to marry or enter a convent. They therefore remained there and became responsible for bringing up the younger children.[31] Other Spanish children, taught to read and write, could later take up "useful, respectable professions according to each one's particular inclination."[32]

By contrast, casta children received a different education. They were obliged to serve in the hospital until they were eighteen to twenty, when they might then work as paid servants. Alternatively, they were sometimes given to city residents of good reputation who received their services in exchange for a given amount of money.[33] Nonwhite women were also offered as servants to private individuals or women's institutions, such as Lima's Casa de las Recogidas. The money paid for their work went to the hospital as repayment for the cost of their upbringing, though after twelve years they could keep their earnings.[34] In this way their condition as servants, acquired virtually by birth, was perpetuated.

Fr. Bernabé Cobo calculated in 1643 that between forty and fifty children were admitted to the hospital every year. Another eighty were in the care of wet nurses outside the hospital.[35] All told, in the mid-seventeenth century the hospital could provide for approximately 120 children of different ages and both sexes. Each wet nurse received between seven and eight pesos per month, with at least 100 children usually being breast-fed.

Wet nurses were widely used in Lima throughout the colonial period. Families with sufficient means could buy a slave whose breasts were full and have her bring up a newborn. Those who were less wealthy could rent the services of a wet nurse. It would appear from this that women who were not slaves did not nurse their children. The large number of female slaves who lived in the city, and what was probably a high infant mortality rate in the slave population, may have reinforced such a trend and left its mark on social relations generally, particularly between women and men.[36]

In Spain, moralists of the time sharply criticized women who insisted on having wet nurses breast-feed their children. The writers' objections rested not on health or emotional concerns, but on what they thought was being transmitted through the relationship between the wet nurse and her charge: moral qualities and beliefs.[37]

Abandoned children, as well as those born from legitimate marital unions, most likely found themselves in similar situations insofar as most were raised by women paid to take care of them. In the case of legitimate children, however, mothers or close relatives could have exerted some control over, and paid more attention to, how the children were reared. This might even have resulted in a lower infant mortality rate than that for children brought up exclusively by their wet nurses.[38]

Most women who sought out children at the hospital in order to breast-feed them for a given time were from subordinate social groups, slaves, black women, mulattas, and free pardas. With the money earned from this, slaves paid their masters the daily wages required of them and in the best of cases, could save enough money to manumit themselves. Free women used this income to meet their material needs.

Abandoned children went through a critical moment when they left the orphanage for a brief period to be breast-fed by their wet nurses. In many cases, children would not finish nursing with the same foster mother they started with. Paula de Atocha was left at the Hospital de los Niños Huérfanos where Gertrudis Paravicinos, Peruvian-born, picked her up to take her into her care.[39] For unknown reasons, Gertrudis returned Paula to the hospital while she was still being breast-fed. At that moment, Casimira Cabezas, a zamba living at the Portal de Botoneros on Callejón de los Clérigos, asked for a *botado*, or castaway, for her daughter Juana Meoño to nurse "until her breasts would be alleviated, since she had recently given birth." The hospital's abbess asked her to take Paula instead, only five or six months old and very weak. To please the abbess, Casimira agreed and took Paula "to her home, where her daughter started to bring her up. She became so dear to her that she never wanted to return her," and the two raised Paula, though they never sought any payment for doing so.[40]

Owners felt free to use in ways that suited them slaves who had recently given birth. María Andrea, a slave belonging to don Lorenzo de Encalada, took María Pascuala out of the Hospital de los Niños Huérfanos to keep her milk until her mistress gave birth.[41] When her mistress's child arrived, María Andrea did not want to return María Pascuala "because she loved her so much. . . . She gave María Pascuala to another black woman . . . so the child would finish nursing, but after the orphan was weaned, María Andrea did not have the courage to return her to the hospital. She has therefore supported her with her savings from the pesos her masters gave her to buy bread."[42]

Doña Josefa Pobleda told how she frequently visited Simón Zagal's shoe-shop on Calle de los Bodegones, where she met María Antonia de Atocha, whom Luganda, the shoemaker's wife, was raising. The girl was four years old when doña Josefa decided to take her away "to remove her from the streets and the abandonment in which Simón and his wife Luganda kept her." She brought up the child for the next eight years, and "although she is not very good at writing, she does know our Christian doctrine perfectly well, as well as confession and holy communion, which she frequently takes. She can also sew and make and use dusters because I have taught her to do so. She has a good disposition and is willing to do whatever she is told."[43]

Doña Josefa was like many other ordinary women who took in abandoned children, becoming self-taught educators in order to provide their charges with skills they would need in the future. Those who could not faced a dilemma. In 1787, Gabriela Argomeda, a mestiza married to Isidoro Gómez, a tailor, took María Josefa Florentina from the hospital "to nurse her for the six pesos she was paid monthly by the home's administrator. She weaned, reared, and supported the girl until she was three years old, when she handed her over to doña María Eugenia Imar and her sister, doña Eusebia. This was so María Josefa's education and instruction in Christian doctrine could continue, since Gabriela Argomeda was unable to do so."[44]

Laywomen living in convents sometimes developed relationships with children who had been abandoned. In 1743 Josefa Vivar, who resided in the monastery of Santa Clara, ordered her black slave, María Antonieta

Soberanis, to bring a Spanish girl, Vicenta de las Mercedes, from the Hospital de los Niños Huérfanos, providing the usual contribution in exchange. When Vicenta turned seven, she applied for a place in the Colegio de Santa Cruz.[45] Earlier in the century, Irena Ladrón de Guevara, a beata from Santo Domingo who served in Lima's Hospital de la Caridad, took María Juliana de Atocha from the orphanage. She brought the child up at her own expense.[46]

A Spanish girl, Alfonsa de Atocha, was left at the hospital on 24 January 1703. Fifteen days later, in exchange for the "customary alms," Luisa de Avendaño, a professed nun from La Encarnación, took her away. Doña Luisa de Avendaño and her slave Jacoba then raised Alfonsa in the convent "with all devotion and virtue" until she turned eight. At that time, she sought admission to the Colegio de Niñas Expósitas de Santa Cruz de Atocha, hoping to enjoy the dowry this institution provided to its students. After three years at the school, Alfonsa went to La Encarnación as a novice, but the prolonged illness of doña Luisa delayed her profession. When doña Luisa died, Alfonsa lost her sponsor, but worse followed. Because of an administrative mix-up she did not receive her dowry in full from the colegio, which meant she could not assume the veil at La Encarnación.

Although Alfonsa was now destitute and without protection, the nuns still managed to find a place for her in the convent. Straitened economic circumstances prevented her profession as a nun, but even her abandonment as a child did not keep her from a relatively secure and honorable life at La Encarnación.[47]

Wet nurses' intentions were sometimes marked by a combination of charity and the desire to profit. This was the case of Lorenza de Zavala, an indigenous woman. She went to the hospital "to ask for a baby she could raise, both as an act of charity and because she could get the small stipend the home usually gave to nursemaids for bringing up children." María Liberata, a young Spanish girl, lived with Lorenza for about eleven years. Lorenza brought her up, supported her, and educated her, spending "many pesos on her education and rearing just as if she were my own daughter." María then sought admission to the Colegio de Santa Cruz.[48]

Women from society's lower reaches were not the only ones appearing at the hospital door to ask for a child. Although fewer in number, elite women sometimes came, willing to nurse or even adopt a child. In 1786, don Diego Bravo de Rivero y Zavala, regimental captain in the City of Kings, appeared before the *secretario del secreto* to report about María Ascención de Atocha, an abandoned infant. His sister, the Marquesa de Vallehumbroso, had taken her from the hospital's nursery "so she could get some relief for her breasts, since she had recently given birth."[49]

Despite the late occurrence of this incident, that the marquesa would nurse this child apparently directly contradicted the notion that women of the aristocracy did not want to breast-feed their own children. At any rate, the high infant mortality in all social strata may have induced some elite women to breast-feed orphan or abandoned children, thereby simultaneously nourishing their own charitable sentiments.

Infant mortality at this time must have left a fair number of women with breasts filled with milk and no child to nurse. Many of these women picked up children from the hospital and later kept them, the fate, undoubtedly, of many illegitimate and abandoned children. This type of informal adoption drew women of all sorts—slave, free, elite, single, and beatas—into relationships with Lima's abandoned children.

The world of women's affections has been explored, insofar as the limited record permits, but what can be said about the emotions of mothers who abandoned their children? In his study on Spanish women of the sixteenth and seventeenth centuries, Vigil noted that the figure of the mother was not depicted in a distinct fashion in the literary works of the *Siglo de Oro*. The writings of moralists likewise failed to emphasize this aspect of feminine identity. This was only of concern in a few instances, as when writers wanted to underscore how important it was for mothers to breast-feed their children themselves.[50]

The concept of motherhood as it is understood today did not exist then. Further, there was no substantial difference in the affection children received from their fathers as opposed to their mothers. The absence of this notion of mother, however, does not permit drawing conclusions about maternal feelings proper: how women saw themselves in relation to their children.

To the extent the dominant affective culture of that time lacked a fundamental idea of motherhood it might be thought that giving away a newborn child would have had only an attenuated emotional and moral effect on women. For now, though, the lack of testimony regarding this most intimate act makes it almost impossible to reconstruct what feelings a woman might have had. Some fragmentary evidence does, however, indicate that abandoning a child was an event marked by great anguish.

Doña Josefa de Toro's story provides some insight on the feminine experience with regard to motherhood. Doña Josefa had named her mother as heir to all her goods, but when her mother predeceased her, she did not change her will. Doña Josefa made no mention in that testament of any other legitimate heirs, but when she died, don Diego de Villagómez sought to be acknowledged as her son. If successful he would inherit two female slaves, furniture, worked silver, and clothing, as well as some debts.

Juana de Godoy, a mulatta born in the port of Callao but then living in the parish of Nuestra Señora de Cocharcas, appeared as a witness in don Diego's suit over the estate. Because of the friendship uniting them, she said, she had assisted doña Josefa during childbirth and had therefore known don Diego from his first moment of life. She also knew that doña Josefa had given the child to doña Ana Sequera so that she could take him to the home of the man doña Josefa said was his father.

Later, though, Juana was at doña Josefa's home when doña Ana appeared and told her that she had seen her child in the hospital where orphan children were sent in exchange for alms. In the face of this news, doña Josefa begged doña María Sequera, Ana's sister, to go to the hospital and confirm what her sister had said. Doña María did so, and when she returned she stated that

> Everything was true. . . . The boy was the very same one doña Josefa
> had given birth to. Knowing this, doña Josefa was very sad, . . .
> so this witness offered to go try to get the boy out of the hospital.
> Doña Josefa insistently asked this witness to take the boy from
> the Hospital de los Niños Huérfanos. Otherwise her life would be
> at risk, since she was very sad that her son had been sent there.
> Because of the love and friendship this witness felt for doña Josefa,
> she made every effort to bring the boy back.

Upon payment of twenty pesos, the child was allowed to leave the hospital after being baptized. He then went to be raised in the home of doña María Sequera, who, fortunately for don Diego, owned a mulatta slave who could nurse him because her own infant had just died. There can be no doubt about the strength of the friendship these women shared.[51]

Abandoning children at this hospital was a wrenching experience women would have rather avoided. Some who were uncertain whether their babies would be accepted into a respectable family household had the Hospital de los Niños Huérfanos as an option, but others had not much to choose from at all. Familial sanctions could be severe, particularly for those belonging to families who wanted to protect their honor. Considering the large number of children who were abandoned, blame and remorse, or perhaps simple sadness, must have been feelings many women who gave away their infants shared.

Friendship among women was very important for those mothers without resources who suddenly found themselves with a newborn to feed. Midwives, part of a female network, filled important roles in maternity and child rearing. A midwife's job did not always end with labor and a child's birth. In some cases she assumed responsibility for raising children, even paying to hire a wet nurse to breast-feed the newborn. Female friends were always present at the moment of labor and took infants to the baptismal font. In some cases, they would personally leave the children at the homes of their presumed fathers or rescue them from the Hospital de los Niños Huérfanos.

The authorities were particularly concerned about the gradual increase in the number of abandoned white children and especially about girls growing up amidst worldly dangers. Wealthy men and women worried about the salvation of their souls constantly made donations for parentless, orphaned, and abandoned children. Brotherhoods offered dowries every year to young white women without parents, and affluent families established well-funded endowments to safeguard the honor of abandoned girls.

The seventeenth-century founding of the Colegio de Niñas Expósitas de Santa Cruz de Atocha arose from concern about the problem of illegitimacy among the city's white girls and the interest colonial authorities and the social elite had in addressing this issue. Mateo Pastor, born in La Mancha, Spain, was a vecino of Lima, where he served as a familiar of the Inquisition and had married Francisca Vélez Michel, a native of the capital. The couple had no children and decided, through a joint will, to distribute their fortune to a number of individuals and institutions. Among their charitable deeds was the 1653 establishment of the Colegio de Niñas Expósitas de Santa Cruz de Atocha, of particular interest to doña Francisca. Orphan girls' lack of "Christian instruction and education," combined with their "poverty and need," put their virtue at grave risk. Because their impoverished living conditions made marriage or acceptance into a convent an increasingly remote possibility, they could easily lose their way in the world. Don Mateo, for one, thought this situation could be remedied.

There are now and have always been girls who need to enter this place of retreat. How many will enter will depend on whatever revenues are now available, which will increase in the future.

They will always be used for girls who have been abandoned and those who were sent to the orphanage. Only these girls will be admitted, because I am establishing this colegio for these orphans, bereft of all human aid, and not for anyone else. I am providing everything else for the education and Christian instruction of these little plants, in accord with the greatest service to God our Lord. I expect them to be raised and grow in virtue and as examples, so that the lack of worldly goods does not impede them from pursuing what is spiritual.[52]

The colegio took in a number of girls who, because they were of illegitimate birth, increased the ranks of the abandoned in colonial society. Although there was no way to prove the illegitimacy of an abandoned girl, in none of the cases examined were documents like death certificates found that could confirm the death of the parents of women and girls seeking admission to the colegio. Girls who wished to enter the colegio were required to submit proof that their parents were unknown, that they had, in fact, been abandoned, and that they were Spanish, which is to say, white.

Colonial authorities paid close attention to the clothing abandoned girls wore, for this was useful in determining their ethnic origin. Highly detailed descriptions of foundlings' apparel were part of the curricula vitae submitted for girls seeking a place at Santa Cruz de Atocha. "On Wednesday, 21 October, at about quarter of nine in the evening, a newborn Spanish girl was abandoned. She was wrapped in three torn, reddish swaddling blankets from Castile; a closed Brittany cloth shirt; and around her shoulders was an old piece of cloth. There was some unbleached linen about her head, and she wore a bandage over her navel like a sash, closed with two white ribbons braided together. No papers were included."[53]

Women who requested admission to the colegio had typically spent the first part of their lives at the Casa de Huérfanos de Nuestra Señora de Atocha. The people who left the girls there concealed the parents' identity, always maintaining the children had neither mother nor father. Sometimes families who found infants abandoned on their doorstep decided to send them to the orphanage. They resisted bringing these children into their homes for several reasons. Oftentimes insufficient means made providing for the abandoned children impossible. In other cases they had no access to wet nurses who could have cared for them.

An applicant to Santa Cruz was required to present witnesses who would attest both that the girl had indeed been abandoned and that she had lived among respectable people up until that time. A Christian upbringing was considered favorably when requesting entry to the colegio, as were the ability to read and write and perform household chores.

The experience of Petronila Martínez and María del Carmen de Atocha shows how straitened economic circumstances could adversely affect an informally adopted child. In 1765, Petronila, an unmarried Indian woman, took María del Carmen from the Hospital de los Niños Huérfanos to raise her.[54] Five years later, Petronila married Pedro Chuquiñán, a barber. This and caring for their own children required so much of Petronila's time that she could not continue to bring up María del Carmen. She was further concerned because of the "laborers and apprentices who continually stay at the shop where we all live. This causes me much embarrassment and sorrow since in such small quarters a proper life may be at risk and such wickedness may increase as María grows older."

In 1772, María Manuela Menuesa, a mestiza, related how her godchild, the son of Casilda Coronel, a free black, had died. She had then suggested Casilda take in a castaway to raise, for she would eventually benefit from the payment the hospital offered. This convinced Casilda, and María Manuela fetched from the orphans' home "a boy, who was then returned when Casilda told her to bring a little girl." This was how María Dolores de Atocha, four days old, arrived at Casilda's home. From that moment until she requested admission to the Colegio de Santa Cruz de Atocha, María Dolores and Casilda were together, and Casilda supported and raised the child at her own expense. At fourteen, however, Maria Dolores's Spanish origin came into doubt. Furthermore, the authorities questioned the propriety of her life at that time. Her virtue was at risk "because she lives at a barber's shop, where she sleeps with a married couple and does not have a separate bed. . . . She may be presumed to be ruined because of the depraved habits of people who are brought up in the streets."[55]

Unlike the girls described here, boys are rarely mentioned in the documents, and their fates were most likely different. The concern the authorities demonstrated for the fortunes of white girls did not extend to white boys. There was nothing like the Colegio de Santa Cruz for them. When dealing with orphan children, the authorities' attention focused on the proper conduct of girls.

The foundation of the Colegio de Niñas Expósitas de Santa Cruz de Atocha was formalized when the inquisitor, don Cristóbal de Castilla y

Zamora, issued its charter, which made the members of the Tribunal of the Inquisition the patrons of the school. The colegio was thereafter exclusively dependent on the Holy Office, subordinate to no other secular or ecclesiastical institution. Only the inquisitors could change its charter. The rector, teachers, and students had to pledge obedience to the provisions of the school charter; violating them would constitute a mortal sin. The inquisitors also controlled appointment and removal of rectors and teachers.[56]

The rector, a woman, was in charge of the school with the assistance of a chaplain and a teacher, also a woman. Besides knowing how to read and write, the rector was to be "a zealous guardian of the well-being and upbringing of these new plants. She should also have the appropriate qualities of age, nobility, Christian behavior, authority, and respect, serving as an example." It was best if she had no close relatives or children so she could better carry out her duties. The teacher was to display the same virtues. The rector could also call on the help of an administrator and a lawyer to ensure the colegio operated properly and a physician who took care of the students' health.

The financial administration of the school was troubled. Although details are unknown, it was apparent from a 1674 inspection that all was not well. In their report, the inspectors found that many beds lacked sheets, those that had them were torn, there was a shortage of pillows, and no pillowcases at all. The wool stuffing of the mattresses was filthy. The slovenly conditions under which the women lived was obvious, even to the authorities of the time.

Immediately after Nuestra Señora de Santa Cruz de Atocha opened its doors it accepted twelve girls; another twelve were soon added. They were to receive clothing, food, education, and dowries. These students were to come exclusively from the Hospital de los Niños Huérfanos and had to be between eight and sixteen years of age.

Their education included reading, writing, instruction in Christian doctrine, sewing, music, learning to play musical instruments, and singing. In accord with their cloistered life, the girls kept to a very strict schedule. From six to seven they said the rosary, prayed, and attended mass. After breakfast, they spent the next three hours, until eleven, in the workroom, where they sewed and read spiritual literature aloud and the teacher explained Christian doctrine to them. This was the extent of their studies, most of which were devoted to religion. Out of fifteen hours of daily work, ten were devoted to religious matters. The only activities not closely related were sewing and music, although the latter was mainly of a religious sort.

They shared lunch, a main dish, stew, and dessert, in the common dining room, reading from the saints' lives during their meal. They then rested from half past noon until two, when they returned to the chapel to pray for half an hour. From half past two until half past five, they were again in the workroom for classes that consisted mainly of reading Christian doctrine aloud. They prayed the rosary and said other prayers in the chapel from six to eight and read devotional books and prayed before going to bed at half past nine. They confessed and took communion every fifteen days. Every Thursday was a free day, as were religious feasts.

Aside from the students' daily activities under the teacher's direction, which included teaching them to read, cook, wash, sweep, and do "everything else that would allow them to keep house properly when they married," they followed a routine in which "God was an important part." Examination of conscience was essential every day. At night the students were given a bit of free time before nine, as long as it was used in a virtuous manner. The administrators of the colegio also kept a watchful eye on their charges' physical contact. "They were all supposed to sleep in a chaste, composed manner, each in her own bed and never sleeping together."

Women of this social standing, in accord with the customs of the times, presumably performed no domestic labor. For these purposes they had laundresses, cooks, and servants to do their shopping. Nevertheless the girls of the colegio took turns working with the cook and the washerwoman. On Saturdays, they all cleaned the school. This domestic training suggests that most illegitimate women of unknown parentage would not acquire a social position so high that they would be relieved of household chores.

One of the students acted as a nurse in the event a schoolmate fell ill. When a physician or barber-surgeon was required, he would attend a girl who was ill only in the presence of the female rector or the teacher, and "the same would be done if the black manservant belonging to the colegio entered carrying some heavy object."

The students, forbidden to have any contact with the outside world, were isolated, for the founding charter mandated that "enclosure and confinement must be respected." Violation of the rules concerning confinement brought excommunication; a student then lost her position at the colegio and the dowry provided to her. Written correspondence was also prohibited. When contact with the outside was absolutely essential, it was made through the grate of the church or at the street door in the presence of the rector. All the doors were kept locked. Every evening the rector, the teacher, and two of the oldest students took care to ensure this and leave candles burning. The girls' dormitory was locked from within and a light left burning all night.

No male or female unconnected to the colegio could enter under any pretext. The only contact between the school and the outside world was a servant for running errands. He slept not within the school walls but in the chaplain's room nearby.

Some of the slaves of Lima found their way into the colegio. In 1674, for example, within the confines of the school were a black slave from the Congo, a Peruvian-born slave, and a mulatta, all females and all in the service of Santa Cruz. They of course slept apart from the students, in a room with "three beds where four women sleep with their own mattresses." The patrons of the school were very careful not to allow people of color into the colegio in general, however. During the annual inspection on Saint Matthew's Day, they explicitly asked the girls "whether they had allowed into the school without permission from the tribunal any black, mulatta, or mestiza to do washing or anything else."[57]

The treatment of others was to be based on respect. The informal *tú* and *vos* verb forms were always to be avoided. Love and charity should guide personal relationships, and playing favorites and taking sides were absolutely forbidden. There were to be no differences in the food consumed; the rector and the teacher ate whatever the students did and in the same amount. Everyone ate together in the refectory in the spirit of asceticism.

The students without exception wore only coarse clothing, a skirt, jacket, and scapulary, and over it, "a green cross on their chests." The servants in principle dressed just like the girls, but hierarchical differences demanded visible distinctions, so they did not wear scapularies. Silk, luxurious and sensual, was absolutely forbidden except for hosiery, "and this, only exceptionally."

Some of the funds of the colegio were given to the students so they could enter the convent or marry. Women interested in becoming nuns were favored financially. Their dowries amounted to two thousand pesos, five hundred for a trousseau and fifteen hundred for the white-veil dowry. Those who preferred marriage received one thousand pesos, enough to attract some men wishing to marry them. These potential husbands had to apply in writing to the rector of the colegio. She then evaluated the candidates and decided on their requests.

Readily obtaining a dowry depended on how long a student had resided at the colegio. Exceptions were made, however. Girls who had only recently been admitted, but wished to enter a convent, received their dowries, but without harming the precedence of those who had been there longer.

The inquisitors, who approved a girl's choice of convent or matrimony, also authorized granting a dowry and how large it would be. Girls who disobeyed the inquisitors' wishes lost their dowries. Convents were obliged to return them to the colegio if the girls died before professing their vows or abandoned the convent altogether. Husbands were likewise supposed to return them if their wives died before having children or the marriage was annulled. The dowry the school offered was an efficient way to protect the status of these women. Those who chose conventual life were accepted at the most prestigious institutions, such as La Encarnación, La Trinidad, and Santa Clara.[58]

Punishment played an important role in regulating life in the colegio. The story of Mariana de Atocha illustrates how. She began life as a little Spanish girl with no known parents or relatives, abandoned at the Casa de Niños Expósitos. Tomasa de Barahona, a married woman, took her in and breast-fed her. After weaning her, she found she could not support Mariana so she returned her to the orphanage. Doña Francisca Zumarán then removed Mariana again and brought her into her home, where she remained until she was about ten or eleven. During that time, she learned how to read and received instruction in Christian doctrine. Her good upbringing and the skills she had learned with doña Francisca allowed Mariana de Atocha y Zumarán to be accepted at the Colegio de Niñas Expósitas de Santa Cruz.

Problems arose at the colegio in 1771. Mariana, who had suddenly ceased being a little Spanish girl and become a "chola or mestiza," was accused of scratching the vice-rector's arms. She thus shamelessly lost "the respect, submission, and obedience she owed the vice-rector. This forced the school to take measures, for if such a terrible transgression were tolerated, it would be the complete ruin and perdition of the colegio."

The Inquisitional authorities then took charge, and the teacher, a servant, a student, and the vice-rector herself were called to testify. What happened, they said, was that the vice-rector had asked Manuelita del Espíritu Santo y Córdova to do the dishes. Mariana, who was responsible for Manuelita "because she was one of the youngest girls," objected, arguing that Manuelita did not have to wash the dishes because she had not used them. In the face of "such haughty, shameless behavior," the vice-rector scolded Mariana as she deserved, holding her by the hair and slapping her. Mariana then scratched the vice-rector's arms. She chose not to punish Mariana further, though, and decided against placing her in the stocks. The incident took place before all the other students.

After reviewing the testimony, the Inquisitional prosecutor made his ruling. The physical harm the vice-rector suffered resulted from Mariana's attempt to defend herself, but she still deserved exemplary punishment for her disobedience, haughtiness, and stubbornness. She would be corrected further in the future, and the other students warned to show respect for and strict obedience to the school's authorities.

Because of her "abominable and atrocious crime" the inquisitors ordered Mariana's head shaved while she was confined to the stocks. When she was released, they continued, for three days she was to "eat in the refectory at midday, sitting on the floor." For the month that followed, she would be last in all community activities. If she failed to demonstrate her profound obedience and submission, she would be sent to the Casa de las Recogidas.

The inquisitors used this opportunity to change some of the rules. In the future, the students were to wear longer skirts and simpler hairstyles. Disobedient girls would be fed only a small piece of bread daily and would not be given any of the new shoes distributed every month.

Five years later Mariana fled the school to meet up with a man who had asked to marry her, but whose request had been denied. At the time, the school's authorities had argued that he was interested only in the dowry Mariana would receive from the colegio. He was also rejected because as a foreigner with no visible means of support, he could not afford to marry.

Mariana's escape was frustrated when some watchmen encountered her and her intended near the colegio. Although he managed to escape, Mariana was taken back to the school and again locked in the stocks. She was expelled a few days later and returned to doña Francisca Zumarán. She was forbidden to get in touch with her former schoolmates under threat of banishment to the port of Guayaquil.[59]

❧

Illegitimacy was closely linked to the abandonment of children in Lima. Parish registers recorded many children without parents, but qualitative evidence reveals that the absence of parents at the baptismal font did not always mean that children had been abandoned.

Honor, associated with matters of gender, played an important role in child abandonment among the city's white population. Abandoning children born from illicit sexual relationships protected feminine modesty and honor. It also helped resolve any marital problems a man might have should his adultery become public knowledge. Boys and girls of illegitimate birth, whether bastards, spurious, or out of wedlock, enjoyed the privileges of legitimate birth if they were recognized as foundlings. Given the small number of foundlings, this cannot be thought of as a widely used means of upward social mobility.

Many of these abandoned children joined families as servants and were caught up in the hierarchical relationships typical of families at the time. Illegitimacy therefore helped maintain the stratified social system. Child abandonment was one way gender relations were manifested in this society.

The economic problems white women of illegitimate birth had were alleviated in part by institutions like the Colegio de Niñas Expósitas de Santa Cruz de Atocha. These same women experienced many changes in their affective relationships during childhood and later, in lives that were often unstable and troubled. Further investigation of this topic reveals both the events and the social forces that gradually shaped what might be called the psychosocial structure of people living in cities. Without close family ties, they were subject to the vicissitudes of life in colonial society. Any study of the power, authority, and dependency relationships in this setting must take the widespread nature of this phenomenon into account.

Emotional linkages could be and were formed, though, particularly between a wet nurse and the child she was breast-feeding. Although it is impossible to know how frequently this occurred, this relationship was surely a significant event in the lives of abandoned children and probably of many illegitimate children as well. Many women who nursed these children even for short periods refused to return them to the Casa de Huérfanos after weaning them. In contrast to the instability of family life, these bonds gave rise to special relationships that were in many cases characteristic of affective culture in colonial society. These ties must have been an important component in the network of relationships among people and groups living in the city at the time.

By institutionalizing the inherent social problems the existence of children without parents posed, the dominant culture, through bodies like the Colegio de Niñas Expósitas de Santa Cruz de Atocha, was able to continue. Individuals considered potentially disruptive of society at large, and particularly women who, through the accident of birth, were part of the "disorganized" side of social life, were put under the control of city authorities. Physical separation of men and women and asceticism firmly tamed the sexuality and insubordination of white women without families. Extramarital relationships and illegitimacy, in the context of the differing moral codes they gave rise to, led to strict vigilance over the bodies and souls of certain women. Here the dowry system clearly served to control women.

These institutions sought to preserve social hierarchies. This was illustrated by their internal structures and the fate of the people who lived there, subject to their rules. This was certainly the case with the Hospital de los Niños Huérfanos, where gender, social status, and ethnic background were all clearly differentiated.

The creation of the hospital, and the commitments church and civil authorities, as well as laymen and -women, made by establishing it, reveal its meaning in urban colonial society and how other institutions and individuals perceived it. A woman, similar to many others in Lima, donated a piece of land. Luis Pecador, a pious man moved by the physical vulnerability of abandoned children, took the first steps to create the hospital. The royal scribes and those working for the audiencia established a brotherhood responsible for collecting funds to operate it. Those about to die left some of their possessions to the abandoned children of the city. Women, whether white, black, indigenous, free, or slave, breast-fed the children in exchange for a few pesos a month. Parentless children were privileged characters in the city's festivities, and the king himself contributed to their support with his personal wealth. During the seventeenth century, a new parish was founded, named Huérfanos. The presence of abandoned children was a reality for the citizens of Lima, part of the emotional landscape of their everyday lives.

There were institutions and mechanisms whose purpose it was to make clear beyond doubt that illegitimacy was an inferior condition that contaminated the status of the higher group as a whole. Given the high incidence of illegitimacy within this same group, however, its members created ways to protect their status through establishing entities like the Hospital de los Niños Huérfanos and the Colegio de Niñas Expósitas de Santa Cruz de Atocha. The cost of maintaining the social status of whites—strengthening the public authorities' discourse on the control of women's sexuality and increasingly rigid rules governing the behavior of women—was one they were more than willing to pay.

Glossary

Arras Gift a groom gives from his estate to his bride at the time of marriage

Audiencia Supreme colonial tribunal

Beaterio House of the devout, where women who were lay devouts (beatas) lived in community

Casta An individual of mixed blood, usually Spanish and Indian, Spanish and black, or some combination thereof

Cédula Royal decree

Curaca Local chieftain

Encomienda Grant to a Spaniard of the right to collect Indian tribute in exchange for his pledge to protect them and provide Christian instruction

Encomendero Holder of an encomienda

Gentilhombre de cámara Individual of very high social standing who accompanied the king in his private chambers and when he left them

Licenciado Licentiate

Mayorazgo Inalienable entailed estates inherited by the firstborn son

Pardo/a A light-complexioned mulatto/a

Vecino/a A property-owning citizen maintaining permanent residency

Vellón Copper currency circulating in Castile

Zamba A woman of Indian and black descent

Notes

ﬤ

ABBREVIATIONS

AGN Archivo General de la Nación, Perú
ABPL Archivo de la Beneficencia Pública, Lima
AAL Archivo Arzobispal, Lima
BNP Biblioteca Nacional, Perú
C Cuaderno
CC Causas Civiles
f folio
leg. legajo
L Libro
l ley
N Notarios
RA Real Audencia
t Tomo
tít Título

INTRODUCTION

1. See Pablo Macera "Sexo y coloniaje," in *Trabajos de Historia* (Lima: Instituto Nacional de Cultura, 1973), 3:297–312; and Claude Mazet, "Population et société à Lima aux XVI et XVIIe siècles. La Paroisse San Sebastián (1562–1689)," *Cahiers de l'Amérique Latine* 13–14 (1976): 53–100. Also, Luis Martín, *Daughters of the Conquistadores: Women of the Viceroyalty of Peru* (Albuquerque: University of New Mexico Press, 1983).

2. Jean Louis Flandrin, *Orígenes de la familia moderna* (Barcelona: Editorial Crítica, 1979), 231. See also Lawrence Stone, *The Family, Sex, and Marriage in England, 1500–1800* (New York: Harper and Row, 1979); Peter Laslett, *The World We Have Lost: England before the Industrial Age* (New York: Scribners, 1973); and Peter Laslett, ed., *Family and Illicit Love in Earlier Generations* (Cambridge: Cambridge University Press, 1977).

3. Verena Martínez-Alier carefully comments on this problem in light of other studies for the Caribbean region in *Marriage, Class and Colour in Nineteenth-Century Cuba: A Study of Racial Attitudes and Sexual Values in a Slave Society* (Cambridge: Cambridge University Press, 1974).

4. Georges Duby, *El caballero, la mujer y el cura* (Madrid: Taurus, 1987).

5. Stone, *Family, Sex, and Marriage*; Flandrin, *Orígenes*; Duby, *El caballero*; Cissie Fairchilds, "Female Sexual Attitudes and the Rise of Illegitimacy: A Case Study," *Journal of Interdisciplinary History* 8 (spring 1978): 627–67; Edward Shorter, "Illegitimacy, Sexual Revolution and Social Change in Modern Europe," *Journal of Interdisciplinary History* 1 (autumn 1971): 231–72; Louise Tilly, Joan Scott, and Miriam Cohen, "Women's Work and European Fertility Patterns," *Journal of Interdisciplinary History* 6 (winter 1976): 447–76.

6. See Martínez-Alier, especially the analysis and theory in her conclusion, 120–41.

7. Bernard Lavallé, "Divorcio y nulidad de matrimonio en Lima (1650–1700). (La desavenencia conyugal como indicador social)," *Revista Andina* 2 (1986): 427–63; Alberto Flores Galindo and Magdalena Chocano, "Las cargas del sacramento," *Revista Andina* 3 (1984): 403–34.

8. Frederick Bowser, *El esclavo africano en el Perú colonial, 1524–1650* (Mexico City: Siglo Veintiuno, 1977); Christine Hunefeldt, "Los negros de Lima: 1800–1830," *Historica* 3 (1979), 17–51.

9. Marriage has been treated as a social and economic mechanism linking family interests, as an expression of class interests. We know little about aspects linked more to emotions and feelings, that is, to the more intimate and personal dimension of this social fact, so critical to the lives of individuals. We know even less about the world of extramarital relations and illegitimacy, which in colonial Peru was very important.

10. See Asunción Lavrin, ed., *Sexuality and Marriage in Colonial Latin America* (Lincoln: University of Nebraska Press, 1989), which gathers a series of works related to this topic, and Sergio Ortega, ed., *De la santidad a la perversión* (Mexico City: Grijalbo, 1985).

11. See Steve J. Stern, *Peru's Indian Peoples and the Challenge of Spanish Conquest: Huamanga to 1640* (Madison: The University of Wisconsin Press, 1982).

12. Claire Ghilheim, "La devaluación del verbo femenino," in *La inquisición española: Poder político y control social*, ed. Bartolomé Bennassar (Barcelona: Editorial Crítica, 1981), 171–207.

CHAPTER ONE

1. Response given by Beatriz Coya, daughter of Huayna Cápac, when a priest asked her if she wanted to marry Diego Hernández, a Spaniard. Quoted by Inca Garcilaso de la Vega, *Comentarios reales de los Incas* (Lima: Librería Internacional del Perú, 1959). Pte. 2, lib. 6, 610.

2. Statement of encomendero Lucas Martínez Vegazo, who witnessed Atahualpa's capture. Efraín Trelles, *Lucas Martínez Vegazo. Funcionamiento de una encomienda peruana inicial* (Lima: Pontificia Universidad Católica del Perú, 1982), 135.

3. José Antonio Maravall, *Estado moderno y mentalidad social, siglos XV y XVII* (Madrid: Alianza, 1986), 2:27.

4. James Lockhart and Stuart Schwartz, *Early Latin America* (Cambridge: Cambridge University Press, 1983), 7.

5. C. R. Boxer, *Women in Iberian Expansion Overseas, 1415–1815: Some Facts, Fancies, and Personalities* (New York: Oxford University Press, 1975), 52.

6. Lockhart and Schwartz, *Early Latin America*; Martín, *Daughters*; Mariló Vigil, *La vida de las mujeres en los siglos XVI y XVII* (Madrid: Siglo Veintiuno, 1986), 79.

7. Bartolomé Bennassar, *The Spanish Character. Attitudes and Mentalities from the Sixteenth to the Nineteenth Century.* Trans. Benjamin Keen (*L'Homme Espagnol: attitudes and mentalités du XVIe au XIXe siecle*). Librairie Hachette 1975. (Berkeley: University of California Press, 1979), 184.

8. Jeffrey Russel, *Witchcraft in the Middle Ages* (Ithaca: Cornell University Press, 1984), 283.

9. Henry Kramer and James Sprenger's *Malleus Maleficarum* (1484), although not properly the official text, was disseminated and read in the overseas territories. See Pierre Duviols, *Cultura andina y represión. Procesos y visitas de idolatrías y hechicerías. Cajatambo, siglo XVII* (Cuzco: Centro de Estudios Regionales Andinos Bartolomé de las Casas, 1986), lxix.

10. Ricardo Córdoba de la Llave, "Las relaciones extraconyugales en la sociedad castellana bajo medieval," *Anuario de Estudios Medievales* 16 (1986): 571–619.

11. Bennassar, *Spanish Character*, 201.

12. Further proof of flexibility, at least in the civil sphere, was the practice of *barraganía*, which legally and morally legitimized cohabitation between single persons so long as the relationship was based on friendship and fidelity. A contract signed before a public notary laid out the economic responsibilities, the fate of children and inheritances, and certain provisions for the protection of women. The relationship did not imply equality of rights between men and women, however. Women remained under the power of men. In fifteenth-century contracts of this type, men stated that they "had and continued to have the woman," while women affirmed that they were "under his hand and subject to his will and command." Córdoba de la Llave, "Las relaciones," 579.

13. Córdoba de la Llave, "Las relaciones," 611.

14. See chapter five below.

15. It is impossible to ascertain with any degree of accuracy the legitimacy or illegitimacy of the conquistadores. There is interesting information in Lockhart's work on the Spanish men who took part in Atahualpa's capture in Cajamarca. In more than half these cases there is no information about the fathers of the "Men of Cajamarca." It is presumed about a third of the conquistadores knew who their parents were. Only eleven were known to be unmistakably legitimate and four illegitimate. Although both parents are mentioned for the remaining thirty-three, no reference whatsoever is made to their marital status. For seven of those present for Atahualpa's capture, only the father's name is recorded, while in only one case is the mother's name mentioned. Pedro Alconchel, for instance, wrote two wills, but in neither does he reveal his parents' identities. The parents of Juan de Salinas and Miguel Ruiz were known, but it is impossible to determine whether they were legitimate children. James Lockhart, *Los de Cajamarca. Un estudio social y biográfico de los primeros conquistadores del Perú*, 2 vols. (Lima: Milla Batres, 1986).

16. In some regions such as Piura, *capullanas* held significant power. There are more testimonies about the existence of women curacas,

local chieftains. See María Rostworowski, *La mujer en la época pre-hispánica* (Lima: Instituto de Estudios Peruanos, 1986), 7. As Silverblatt mentions, however, we still have to determine the effective power women chiefs wielded in their own ayllus, or extended families, and the way in which they passed their positions on. Irene Silverblatt, *Luna, sol y brujas. Género y clase en los Andes prehispánicos y coloniales* (Cuzco: Centro de Estudios Regionales Andinos Bartolomé de las Casas, 1990), 13–14, 112–14.

17. Gayle Rubin, "The Traffic of Women: Notes on the Political Economy of Sex" in *Toward an Anthropology of Women*, ed. Rayna Reiter (New York and London: Monthly Review Press, 1975), 157–210. See 172–77.

18. Rostworowski, *La mujer*, 8.

19. María Rostworowski, *Doña Francisca Pizarro. Una ilustre mestiza, 1534–1598* (Lima: Instituto de Estudios Peruanos, 1989), 16.

20. The proportionality of men's and women's rights is still unclear. Men and women performed complementary tasks and had mutual obligations to one other. The interaction of male and female efforts was essential for continued social existence. Holding that egalitarian relations derived from their complementary nature is not persuasive, however, as complementarity and hierarchy were not necessarily exclusive. Proof of this can be found in Marisol de la Cadena, "'Las mujeres son más indias': Etnicidad y género en una comunidad del Cusco," *Revista Andina* 1 (1991) 4–35.

21. Felipe Guamán Poma de Ayala, *Nueva corónica y buen gobierno* (Mexico City: Siglo Veintiuno, 1980), 1:192.

22. Contemporary testimonies such as Guamán Poma's underscore this impression. The chronicler's uneasiness about the peasant women's behavior is part of what he perceived as an "upside-down world." The presence of white men, priests, corregidors, and encomenderos had perverted the mating rules of his own and other native people. Indigenous women abused sexually and exploited as workers were giving birth to mestizillos, lowly mestizos, who were jeopardizing the continuity of his race. For him, Indian women were not victims but the willing protagonists in such a situation, for they would lie down with Spaniards or anyone else rather than remain the wives of Indian laborers. Vol I: 189, 192, 199, 205; 2: 462, 468, 474, 476, 489, 495, 500, 501, 511, 523, 526, 534, 538, 542, 544, 555, 566, 575, 668, 824.

23. Colonial authorities did not recognize the right of native women to occupy positions of power and inherit the post of curaca. Spaniards ruled that women could only hold their fathers' curaca positions if there were no male heirs. Women insisted on preserving the matrilineal line to pass on their goods, though, and occasionally chose their sisters and nieces as their heirs. Silverblatt, *Luna, sol y brujas*, 88.

24. Rostworowski, *La mujer*; Silverblatt, *Luna, sol y brujas*, chap. six and eight.

25. Spanish women were present from the very beginning of the conquest of Peru. According to the lists from *Pasajeros de Indias*, there was one woman passenger for every ten men. The high mortality of the Spanish male population lowered the rate to one for every eight men. James Lockhart, *Spanish Peru: 1532–1560, A Colonial Society* (Madison: The University of Wisconsin Press, 1968), 150.

26. José Durand, *La transformación social del conquistador* (Lima: Nuevos Rumbos, 1958), 28.

27. Tzvetan Todorov, *La conquista de América. La cuestión del otro* (Mexico City: Siglo Veintiuno, 1987), 44.

28. Garcilaso de la Vega, *Comentarios*, Pte.2, lib. 8, 814.

29. Maravall, *Estado moderno*, 2:11–17.

30. Bennassar, *Spanish Character*, 215–19.

31. Vigil, *La vida de las mujeres*, 140.

32. Durand, *La transformación*, 50.

33. Durand, *La transformación*, 36.

34. Antonio José Saraiva, *Inquisição e cristãos-novos* (Lisbon: Impresa Universitária, Ed. Estampa, 1985), 132.

35. Silverblatt, *Luna, sol y brujas*, 74.

36. Garcilaso de la Vega, *Comentarios*, Pte. 2, lib. 3, 270.

37. Lockhart, *Los de Cajamarca*, 1:195.

38. Lockhart, *Los de Cajamarca*, 2:50.

39. Raúl Porras Barrenechea, *Pizarro* (Lima: Ediciones Pizarro, 1978), 38.

40. Rostworowski, *Doña Francisca*, 25.

41. Garcilaso de la Vega, *Comentarios*, Pte. 2, lib. 2, 115. John Hemming concurs that Indian women accepted becoming concubines of the conquistadores. John Hemming, *The Conquest of the Incas* (New York: Harcourt Brace Jovanovich, 1970), 180.

42. Quoted by Durand, *La transformación*, 37.

43. Porras, *Pizarro*, 13. He also arranged the marriage of María Alonso, Francisca's mother, to a certain Alonso de Soto.

44. Lockhart, *Los de Cajamarca*, 1:164.

45. Rostworowski, *Doña Francisca*, 18.

46. Lockhart, *Los de Cajamarca*, 1:165.

47. Garcilaso de la Vega, *Comentarios*, lxviii.

48. Hemming, *The Conquest of the Incas*, 181.

49. Hemming, *The Conquest of the Incas*, 181.

50. Lockhart, *Los de Cajamarca*, 1:206.

51. Hemming, *The Conquest of the Incas*, 225.

52. Hemming, *The Conquest of the Incas*, 182–83.

53. During the conquest, relations of Spaniards with native elite women have left the clearest traces. Coyas, ñustas, and pallas are most often mentioned by chroniclers as the conquistadores' concubines. It is therefore risky to speculate about the attitudes of the latter toward these "women of the common" in this specific period. For later decades, especially toward the end of the century, we can refer to Felipe Guamán Poma de Ayala's irreplaceable chronicle to find plentiful information about relations between Spanish men and women of the Andean ayllus, or extended families.

54. Lockhart, *Los de Cajamarca*, 1:64; José Antonio del Busto Duthurburu, "Una huérfana mestiza: La hija de Juan Pizarro," *Revista Histórica* 28 (1965): 103–6.

55. Rostworowski, *Doña Francisca*, 63.

56. Lockhart, *Los de Cajamarca*, 1:148–67.

57. Garcilaso de la Vega, *Comentarios*, lvx.

58. Lockhart, *Los de Cajamarca*, 2:156.

59. Lockhart, *Los de Cajamarca*, 2:48.

60. Lockhart, *Los de Cajamarca*, 2:46.

61. Lockhart, *Los de Cajamarca*, 2:181.

62. Lockhart, *Los de Cajamarca*, 2:224.

63. Hemming, *The Conquest of the Incas*, 180.

64. Lockhart, *Los de Cajamarca*, 1:165.

65. Rostworowski, *Doña Francisca*, 31.

66. Lockhart, *Los de Cajamarca*, 1:191.

67. Lockhart, *Los de Cajamarca*, 1:140.

68. Nancy van Deusen, "Los primeros recogimientos para doncellas mestizas en Lima y Cusco, 1550–1580," *Allpanchis* 1 (1990): 249–91.

69. Hemming, *The Conquest of the Incas*, 353.

70. Lockhart, *Los de Cajamarca*, 2:48.

71. Hemming, *The Conquest of the Incas*, 181.

72. Lockhart, *Los de Cajamarca*, 1:206.

73. Hemming, *The Conquest of the Incas*, 182.

74. Lockhart, *Los de Cajamarca*, 2:50.

75. Lockhart, *Los de Cajamarca*, 2:20–21.

76. Lockhart, *Los de Cajamarca*, 2:43.

77. Lockhart, *Los de Cajamarca*, 2:44.

78. Alonso de Mesa had several other children: Baltazar Hernández de Mesa, a natural child of María Segura; Alonso Hernández de Mesa, born to Luisa de Balboa; Bernardo de Mesa; and Alonso de Mesa, the latter mestizo. Lockhart, *Los de Cajamarca*, 2:26–28.

79. It is sometimes difficult to trace descent and determine if illegitimate mestizo children were the offspring of one or several mothers. Martín de Florencia, an artisan present in Cajamarca, is a case in point. In his will he recognized three mestizo children, Luis, Pedro, and Isabelica, born from his two Indian women, Isabel and Tocto. This occurred in many other documented cases. Locating these three experiences properly in time is also hard. Miguel de Cornejo, for instance, married in Peru and eventually fathered numerous progeny, including four legitimate children. He also fathered three natural children, though it is unknown whether children were born before or during his marriage. Presumably, the natural and legitimized children were born before legal marriage, as the children's bastard condition would otherwise have hampered their recognition and standing in the family. This information is taken from Lockhart, *Los de Cajamarca*. Martin de Florencia, vol: II, 178, Miguel de Cornejo, vol: II, 116.

80. This suggests a link between Mesa's preference for Indian women and the philanthropic actions toward Indians in his will. Lockhart, *Los de Cajamarca*, 2:28.

81. Daisy Rípodas Ardanaz, *El matrimonio en Indias. Realidad social y regulación jurídica* (Buenos Aires: Conicet, 1977), 10.

82. *Recopilación de leyes de los reynos de las Indias*, 4 vols. (1681; reprint, Madrid: Ediciones Cultura Hispánica, 1973), Lib. 6, tít. 9, ley 36.

83. Garcilaso de la Vega, *Comentarios*, Pte. 2, lib. 3, 122.

84. Lockhart, *Spanish Peru*, 154.

85. Garcilaso de la Vega, *Comentarios*, Pte. 2, lib. 2, 115.

86. Durand, *La transformación*, 38.

87. Lockhart, *Los de Cajamarca*, 1:170.

88. Lockhart, *Los de Cajamarca*, 217.

89. Garcilaso de la Vega, *Comentarios*, Pte. 2, lib. 2, 115.

90. Ella Dumbar, "El testamento inédito de doña Beatriz Clara Coya de Loyola, hija del Inca Sayri Túpac," *Fénix* (Revista de la Biblioteca Nacional, Lima) 7 (1950): 111–22.

91. Dumbar, "El testamento inédito," 111–22.

92. Héctor López Martínez, *Rebeliones de mestizos y otros temas quinientistas* (Lima: P. L. Villanueva, 1972), 26.

93. Hemming, *The Conquest of the Incas*, 281.

94. Hemming, *The Conquest of the Incas*, 134.

95. Trelles, *Lucas Martínez Vegazo*, 37.

96. Trelles, *Lucas Martínez Vegazo*, 122.

97. Trelles, *Lucas Martínez Vegazo*, 135.

98. Lockhart, *Los de Cajamarca*, 2:158.

99. Lockhart, *Los de Cajamarca*, 2:58.

100. Lockhart, *Los de Cajamarca*, 2:60.

Chapter Two

1. Bowser, *El esclavo*, 409.

2. Bowser, *El esclavo*, 410.

3. Miguel Jaramillo, "Formación de un mercado laboral urbano e indígena en Lima de comienzos del siglo XVII" (tesis de bachiller, Pontificia Universidad Católica del Perú, 1986), 11.
*The baptismal records from these parishes provided the quantitative

data used throughout this work to investigate illegitimacy among city residents.

4. Fray Antonio de Calancha, *Crónica moralizadora del orden de San Agustín en el Perú*, 6 vols. (1638; reprint, Lima: Universidad Nacional Mayor de San Marcos, 1975), 2:557.

5. Fray Diego de Córdova y Salinas, *Crónica franciscana*, 1651, in *Los cronistas de convento*, a compilation by Pedro Benvenutto Murrieta and Guillermo Lohmann Villena, edited by José de la Riva-Agüero, Biblioteca de Cultura Peruana, Primera Serie No. 4 (Paris, Desclée, de Brouwer, 1938), 260.

6. [Pedro de León Portocarrero], *Descripción del Virreinato del Perú*, ed. Boleslao Lewin (Rosario: Universidad Nacional del Litoral, 1958), 42.

7. The percentage of Spanish women who migrated to the Indies changed over time. Initially, compared to men, few women came. When the colonial regime was well established, cities became increasingly safe and comfortable for Spanish women. Over time, travel by single men to the New World was increasingly limited. It should also be noted that women coming from Spain preferred to go to Lima, as opposed to other colonial destinations. See Peter Boyd-Bowman, "Patterns of Spanish Emigration to the Indies until 1600," *Hispanic American Historical Review* 56 (1976): 599.

8. *Numeración general de todas las personas de ambos sexos, edades y calidades que se ha hecho en esta ciudad de Lima, año de 1700* (Lima: COFIDE, 1985).

9. *Numeración general.*

10. Enrique Torres Saldamando, *Libro primero de cabildos de Lima*, 3 vols. (Paris: Paul Dupont, 1900), 1:203.

11. The town had its own priest, hospital, and a school for the Indian caciques. Already in the seventeenth century, the Cercado was on its way to becoming a parish of the city and had a population that had been strongly influenced by Spanish culture. Torres Saldamando, *Libro primero*, 1:203.

12. *Numeración general.*

13. *Numeración general.*

14. Alvaro Barnechea, "Marginación, informalización y cambio cultural en la ciudad de Lima en el siglo XVII" (memoria de bachiller, Pontificia Universidad Católica del Perú, 1988), 95–96.

15. Louis Mumford, *La ciudad en la historia* (Buenos Aires: Infinito, 1966), 2:461.

16. [León Portocarrero], *Descripción*, 33.

17. Calancha, *Crónica moralizadora*, 2:556; fray Juan Meléndez, *Tesoros verdaderos de las Indias* (*1681–82*) in *Los cronistas de convento*, ed. José de la Riva-Agüero, comp. Pedro Benvenutto Murrieta and Guillermo Lohmann Villena (Paris: Desclée, de Brouwer, 1938), 226–27.

18. In what follows, references to the physical layout of the city are taken from Juan Bromley, "La ciudad de Lima en el año 1630," *Revista Histórica* 24 (1959): 268–317, and from [León Portocarrero], *Descripción del Virreinato del Perú*, dating to the beginning of the seventeenth century. Other sources are indicated in the corresponding references.

19. [León Portocarrero], *Descripción*, 34.

20. "Court life reached true magnificence and splendor under the administration of the second Marqués de Cañete, don García. He arrived in 1589 with his wife, doña Teresa de Castro y de la Cueva, surrounded by an entourage of two hundred. All this display was presided over by the vicereine's senior chambermaid, doña Ana de Zúñiga, a noble widow from Guadalajara. Under the vicereine's patronage, court functions became more frequent and solemn." Riva-Agüero y Osma; José de la Riva-Agüero, Estudios de Historia Peruana. *La Conquista y el Virreinato*. Prólogo de Guillermo Lohmann Villena. Recopilación y notas de César Pacheco Vélez. Lima: PUCP, 1968, 475p. (Obras completas, VI, Publicaciones del Instituto Riva-Agüero, #4).

21. *Recopilación*, Lib. 2, tít. 16, ley 82; Lib. 3, tít. 3, ley 32; Lib. 5, tít. 2, ley 7; Lib. 8, tít. 2, ley 7.

22. [León Portocarrero], *Descripción*, 59.

23. [León Portocarrero], *Descripción*, 59.

24. [León Portocarrero], *Descripción*, 58.

25. Riva-Agüero, "Lima española," 390.

26. Boyd-Bowman, "Patterns," 596.

27. Boyd-Bowman, "Patterns," 583; *Recopilación*, Lib. 9, tít. 26, ley 29.

28. Riva-Agüero, "Lima española," 381.

29. Riva-Agüero, "Lima española," 381.

30. The only women's monastery that was not part of this group in the eastern quarter was La Encarnación, located to the southwest, almost on the border with the farming belt around the city.

31. Riva-Agüero, "Lima española," 387.

32. *Numeración general.*

33. *Numeración general.*

34. All the women here wore the habits of Nuestra Señora del Carmen and Santa Teresa de Jesus. Some, probably the younger ones, were taken to Catalina María by their own parents. Others were poor orphans. They lived in seclusion, and communicated only with their parents in the outside world. They received a conventional contemporary education consisting of some Latin, reading and writing, prayers, and music. In 1627 the school was officially authorized to operate. Bernabé Cobo, S. J., *Obras*, ed. Francisco Mateos, S. J., 2 vols. (Madrid: Atlas 1964), 2:435–36.

35. This figure includes homes of ten or more people that were nucleated around five or more Spanish, indigenous, or adult mulatta women and also lodged a small number, generally two or three, of young children, slaves, and/or servants. *Numeración general.* My thanks to Luz Peralta for the information on this subject. We have worked together on the quantitative information from this source, which appears throughout this document.

36. Luz Peralta, "El Hospital de la Caridad de Lima. Siglos XVI–XIX," Tesis de maestría, Pontificia Universidad Católica del Perú, in preparation.

37. Peralta, "El Hospital."

38. Martín, *Daughters*, 201–79.

39. Amedeé Frézier, in *El Perú visto por viajeros*, comp. Estuardo Núñez (Lima: PEISA, 1973), 15.

40. Francisco de Echave y Assú, *La estrella de Lima convertida en sol sobre sus tres coronas* (Antwerp: Juan Baptista Verdiussen, 1688). I am grateful to Carlos Villanueva for this information.

41. Meléndez, *Tesoros*, 229.

42. The sense of stage and representation of public life in preindustrial societies has been proposed by Richard Sennet, *O declínio do homem público. As tiranias de intimidade*, (São Paulo: Companhia das Letras, 1988).

43. Religious holidays included those the Councils of Lima established in the sixteenth century, organized for indigenous people and Spaniards, either separately or together. The "table" feasts were attended by the viceroy and other high authorities. The secular holidays with no fixed date included royal feasts such as the king's birthday and wedding anniversary. Also in this group were local holidays such as carnivals and the arrival of the viceroy and other civil authorities. Other secular holidays without definite dates included royal inaugurations and the viceroy's excursion to Amancaes on 24 June. Rosa María Acosta, "Una aproximación al estudio de la fiesta colonial en el Perú (Fiestas oficiales urbanas)" (tesis de bachiller, Pontificia Universidad Católica del Perú, 1979), 31–35.

44. Acosta, "Una aproximación," 30–32.

45. Acosta, "Una aproximación," 30–32.

46. Acosta, "Una aproximación," 71.

47. Acosta, "Una aproximación," 30–32.

48. Bartolomé Arzáns de Orsúa y Vela, *Historia de la Villa Imperial de Potosí*, ed. Lewis Hanke and Gunnar Mendoza (Providence, RI: Brown University Press, 1965), quoted by Acosta, "Una aproximación."

49. Calancha, *Crónica moralizadora*, 556.

50. *Libros del Cabildo de Lima*, vol. 2, 27 November 1600 (Biblioteca Nacional, Lima).

51. Torres Saldamando, *Libro primero*, 2:237, quoting Cobo in "La Fundación de Lima."

52. Frézier, in Núñez, *El Perú visto*, 16.

53. Fray Gaspar de Villarroel y Ordóñez, *Gobierno eclesiástico pacífico y unión de los dos cuchillos Pontificio y Regio*, in *Los cronistas*, 336.

54. The scaffold, for example, was initially placed in the Plaza Mayor, as shown by the illustration in Guamán Poma de Ayala's *Nueva corónica*, 3:950. During the viceregal administration of the first Marqués de Cañete, (1555–59) it was placed behind the viceregal palace, next to the hermitage of the Virgen de los Desamparados. Still, it remained in full view of the city's residents. Riva-Agüero, "Lima española," 380.

55. Torres Saldamando, *Libro primero*, ordenanza 21, 3:54.

56. Bowser, *El esclavo*, 210.

57. Fernando de Trazegnies, *Ciriaco de Urtecho. Litigante por amor* (Lima: Pontificia Universidad Católica del Perú, 1981), 94.

58. Trazegnies, *Ciriaco de Urtecho*, 95.

59. Bowser, *El esclavo*, 208.

60. *Recopilación*, Lib. 7, tít. 5, ley 28.

61. Juan Antonio Suardo, *Diario de Lima, 1629–1634*, 2 vols. (Lima: Imprenta Vázquez, 1935), 1:155.

62. These categories are taken from the work by Norbert Elias, *El proceso de la civilización. Investigaciones sociogenéticas y psicogenéticas* (Mexico City: Fondo de Cultura Económica, 1987).

63. Bowser, *El esclavo*, 143–44.

64. We assume the proportion of slave population in households headed by men was even higher. The figures come from the *Numeración general*.

65. Bowser, *El esclavo*, 143.

66. Bowser, *El esclavo*, 147.

67. Bowser, *El esclavo*, 149–50.

68. *Numeración general*, 357–58.

69. These figures were prepared based on the *Numeración general*.

70. *Numeración general*.

71. Frézier, in Núñez, *El Perú visto*, 20.

72. Mumford has noted the distribution of a house's internal space and its relation to sexual habits in *La ciudad*, 254.

73. Héctor Velarde, "Apreciaciones generales sobre la Casa de Pilatos," *Revista Peruana de Cultura* 1 (1963): 11–17.

74. Frézier, in Núñez, *El Perú visto*, 20.

75. "What we call a platform is, like in Spain, a six- to seven-inch-high dais generally found to one side of the reception hall; men, though, sit on armchairs and only when they are very close to the family will they be allowed to sit on the platform. Otherwise, women have as much freedom in their house as they do in France. They receive their visits with much pleasure and like to entertain, playing the harp or guitar, and singing. If asked to dance, they will do so with much pleasure and grace." Frézier, in Núñez, *El Perú visto*, 20–21.

76. Mumford, *La ciudad*, 523.

77. Frézier, in Núñez, *El Perú visto*, 16.

78. Frézier's comments, however, are tempered by Riva-Agüero's remarks about the quality of nobility based on the types of objects usually bequeathed in the wills of city aristocrats: tableware in precious metals engraved with coats of arms, candelabra and large candlesticks, nets, damask draperies, tapestries and cupboards, figurines, paintings, and dressing tables with carved columns. Riva-Agüero, "Lima española," 372.

79. Frézier, in Núñez, *El Perú visto*, 20.

80. Mary Douglas, *Pureza y peligro. Un análisis de los conceptos de contaminación y tabú* (Madrid: Siglo Veintiuno, 1973), 17.

Chapter Three

1. AAL, Amancebados, leg. 3, 1618–37, trial of Juan Sánchez and María Criolla, 1625.

2. Juan Machado de Chávez noted that when a man deflowered a woman, he was legally obligated to marry her. If he did not, he was then living in mortal sin. Antonio Machado de Chávez y Mendoza, *El perfeto confessor i cura de almas*, 2 vols. (Madrid: La viuda de Francisco Martínez, 1646–47), 1:428.

3. "Un místico del siglo XVII. Autobiografía del venerable Padre Francisco del Castillo de la Compañía de Jesús" (Lima: Rubén Vargas Ugarte, S. J., 1960), 34.

4. Castillo, "Un místico," 35.

5. José Toribio Medina, *Historia del Tribunal del Santo Oficio de Lima 1569–1820*, 2 vols. (Santiago: Nascimento, 1956), 1:306.

6. The Council of Trent stated that "marital status cannot be placed above celibacy. On the contrary, it is better and more virtuous to remain a virgin or single." Laura Mello e Souza, *O diabo e a terra de Santa Cruz. Feitiçaria e religiosidade popular no Brasil Colonial* (São Paulo: Companhia das Letras, 1986), 105.

7. Medina, *Historia del Tribunal*, 1:177.

8. Medina, *Historia del Tribunal*, 1:307.

9. Medina, *Historia del Tribunal*, 1:178.

10. Undoubtedly, the urban colonial society of the seventeenth century used different time notions. Few people knew with certainty, for example, how old they were. Days were organized in accord with liturgical activities. Longer periods also referred to the religious calendar, "after Lent," "during Easter," and these expressions were commonly used to refer to time elapsed. These references come from fifty-eight files in the archiepiscopal archives of Lima that correspond to the seventeenth century and concern individuals who were engaged in concubinage.

11. Witnesses and those who made accusations could and surely did generally exaggerate the length of extramarital relationships to make the crime more serious. It must be kept in mind, however, that those making false statements incurred sanctions. People who testified must have given some thought to this.

12. Jorge René González, "Clérigos solicitantes, perversos de la confesión," in *De la santidad a la perversión*, ed. Sergio Ortega. (Mexico City: Grijalbo, 1985), 139.

13. Medina, *Historia del Tribunal del Santo Oficio de la Inquisición de Lima (1569–1820)*, prológo de Marcel Bataillon (Santiago de Chile: Nascimento, 1956, 2 T).

14. Medina, *Historia del Tribunal*, 1:299.

15. Medina, *Historia del Tribunal*, 1:298.

16. Medina, *Historia del Tribunal*, 1:288.

17. This case is discussed at length in Medina, *Historia del Tribunal*, 1:243–67.

18. Medina, *Historia del Tribunal*, 1:243–67.

19. Frézier, in Núñez, *El Perú visto*, 15.

20. All the seventeenth-century files on concubinage were reviewed, a total of fifty-eight. All referred to people living in Lima, but it was impossible to determine precisely what barrio or parish they came from. These trials apparently originated in the periodic inspections archiepiscopal authorities made in accord with ordinances issued by the Council of Trent. The number of cases is small, however, and it is almost certain they were only a fraction of the trials carried out during that period. There is no way to know what the total number was.

21. AAL, Amancebados, leg. 1, 1589–1611, trial of Catalina González and Melchor de Cintar, Portuguese, 1606.

22. AAL, Amandebados, unnumbered leg., trial of Juan de Castro and María de Ayllón, free black, 1632.

23. Elias, *El proceso*, 203.

24. AAL, Amancebados, leg. 4, 1640–58, trial of Francisco Escudero, 1645.

25. AAL, Amancebados, leg. 3, 1618–37, trial of don Miguel Dávila and doña Antonia de Escobar, 1634.

26. It is interesting to note that when female witnesses appeared, the quality of information was different. They tended to give more details about everyday life than did men.

27. AAL, Amancebados, leg. 1, 1589–1611, trial of Melchora de los Reyes and Juan Romero, 1610.

28. AAL, Amancebados, unnumbered leg., trial of Francisco de Espinosa, Spaniard, and Isabel Escalante, 1635.

29. AAL, Amancebados, unnumbered leg., trial of Antonio Pérez, cleric of minor orders, and Margarita Gutiérrez, 1627.

30. AAL, Amancebados, leg. 1, 1589–1611, trial of Pedro de Godoy, 1610.

31. Machado de Chávez, *El perfeto*, 1:409.

32. AAL, Amancebados, leg. 2, 1612–18, trial of Diego Loarte and Gerónima de Loyola, 1615.

33. AAL, Amancebados, leg. 1, 1589–1611, trial of Ramón González and Marina García, 1610.

34. AAL, Amancebados, leg. 4, 1640–58, trial of Francisco de Saldaña and doña María de los Reyes, 1645.

35. AAL, Amancebados, leg. 1, 1589–1611, trial of Isabel, Indian, and Sebastián Moreno, 1606.

36. AAL, Amancebados, leg. 1, 1589–1611, trial of Mariana de Bicuña and Juan Susarte, 1611.

37. AAL, Amancebados, unnumbered leg., trial of Juan Gómez, married, and Juana Ramírez, 1627.

38. AAL, Amancebados, leg. 5, 1658–1808, trial of Francisco de Saldías and Nicolaza, zamba, 1668.

39. Duby, *El caballero*, 97.

CHAPTER FOUR

1. Machado de Chávez, *El perfeto*, 2:429.

2. Machado de Chávez, *El perfeto*, 2:429.

3. Córdoba de la Llave, "Las relaciones," 592.

4. Machado de Chávez, *El perfeto*, 2:429.

5. Machado de Chávez, *El perfeto*, 1:413.

6. Machado de Chávez, *El perfeto*, 1:413.

7. Machado de Chávez, *El perfeto*, 2:454.

8. Suardo, *Diario de Lima*, 1:189.

9. Suardo, *Diario de Lima*, 1:197.

10. Suardo, *Diario de Lima*, 1:259.

11. Suardo, *Diario de Lima*, 1:154.

12. Suardo, *Diario de Lima*, 1:104.

13. AAL, Amancebados, leg. 1, 1589–1611, trial of Diego Gil, 1609. Files are sometimes incomplete. Many contain only the complaint. Others have only the sentence, while failing to state the reasons. In some instances, witnesses' testimonies, as well as administrative and economic subjects, are presented. When files are complete, they usually follow a fixed form: complaint, defense, proof from witnesses, the woman's situation and her goods during the trial, sentence, and finally, though not always, secondary trials related to dowry, properties, and goods in general. Each bundle of documents has a different number of cases, eleven in some, more than twenty in others. The theme of adultery sometimes only appeared between the lines. This happened, though infrequently, with occasional fragmented and incomplete files. Files for the 1620s and 1680s were missing, and they would be needed to determine frequency. The problem of establishing series and frequencies based on this type of documentation is that documents may have been mishandled or lost over time, making it impossible to know whether the frequency found in them was the true one.

14. AAL, Amancebados, leg. 1, 1589–1611, trial of Juana, Indian, and Diego de Castro, 1611.

15. AAL, Amancebados, leg. 3, 1618–37, trial of Sebastián Gómez and Florentina Catalán, 1624.

16. AAL, Divorcios, leg. 31, 1655, suit of doña Juana de Pedraza against Damián de Montesinos, 1665.

17. Bennassar, *Spanish Character*; Flandrin, *Orígenes*.

18. AAL, Divorcios, leg. 30, suit of Francisca de Salcedo against Francisco Corbeto, 1653.

19. AAL, Divorcios, leg. 20, suit of doña Maior de Espino against Francisco Guisado, 1634.

20. AAL, Divorcios, leg. 15, suit of doña Francisca de la Mota against Pablo Domínguez, 1640.

21. AAL, Divorcios, leg. 30, suit of doña María Magdalena de Rojas y Sandoval against Juan Bautista de Porras, 1653.

22. AAL, Divorcios, leg. 45, suit of Josefa Bernarda, Indian, against José Arias, 1672.

23. AAL, Divorcios, leg. 45, suit of María Inés against Juan Agustín, 1672.

24. AAL, Divorcios, leg. 49, suit of Clemente de Torres against doña Angela de Gutiérrez, 1678.

25. AAL, Divorcios, leg. 45, suit of don Juan Bravo de Laguna against Juana de Franco, 1671.

26. AAL, Divorcios, leg. 33, suit of María de Aspitia against Francisco Portierra, 1659.

27. AAL, Divorcios, leg. 31, suit of doña Francisca de Campos against Juan Salvador, 1655.

28. AAL, Divorcios, leg. 45, suit of doña Sebastiana de Tello against José de Paredes, 1671.

29. AAL, Divorcios, leg. 1, suit of doña María de Marmolejo against Capt. Rafael Escoto, 1600.

30. AAL, Divorcios, leg. 29, suit of Leonor Pascuala against Alonso Esteban, 1651.

31. AAL, Divorcios, leg. 20, suit of doña Blasa de Guzmán against Francisco de la Mota, 1640.

32. AAL, Divorcios, leg. 31, suit of María de las Nieves against Hernando de Cuevas, 1656.

33. AAL, Divorcios, leg. 20, suit of doña María Rodríguez Giraldo against Pedro Gerónimo de Mello, 1640.

34. AAL, Divorcios, leg. 60, suit of doña Ana Sabala against José Lozano, 1700.

35. AAL, Divorcios, leg. 20, suit of Francisca de Ampuero against Ambrosio de Torres, 1640.

36. AAL, Divorcios, leg. 31, suit of doña Ursula de Avilés against Manuel de Rivero, 1656.

37. AAL, Divorcios, leg. 15, suit of doña Luisa de los Ríos against Pedro de Bohórquez, 1633.

38. AAL, Divorcios, leg. 20, suit of doña Catalina de Uceda against Martín Francisco Alemán, 1639.

39. AAL, Divorcios, leg. 30, suit of María Gertrudis against Jusepe de los Ríos, 1653.

40. AAL, Divorcios, leg. 15, suit of María de Andrada, Indian, against Francisco de Ortega, 1633.

41. AAL, Divorcios, leg. 29, suit of doña María Cuyniva, Indian, against Pedro de Angulo, 1650.

42. AAL, Divorcios, leg. 15, suit of Lorenza Criolla against Antonio Bermúdez, 1634.

43. AAL, Divorcios, leg. 20, suit of Ana Delgado against Francisco Rodríguez, 1639.

44. AAL, Divorcios, leg. 30, suit of Ana María de la Zerba against Martín de Espinosa, 1654. Italics are the author's.

45. AAL, Divorcios, leg. 32, suit of doña Josefa de Monterrey against Juan Rivadeneyra, 1658. Italics are the author's.

46. AAL, Divorcios, leg. 31, suit of María de Tineo against Roque de Dueñas, 1655. Italics are the author's.

47. AAL, Divorcios, leg. 1, suit of Ana Ruiz against Marcos Fernández, 1601. Italics are the author's.

CHAPTER FIVE

1. Macera, "Sexo y coloniaje"; Martín, *Daughters*, chap. 4, n33.

2. Bowser, *El esclavo*, 230.

3. Edith Clarke, *My Mother Who Fathered Me* (London: 1957), quoted by Martínez-Alier, *Marriage, Class and Colour*, 125.

4. Laslett, *World We Have Lost*, 52.

5. John J. Tepaske and Herbert S. Klein, "The Seventeenth-Century Crisis in New Spain: Myth or Reality?" *Past & Present* 90 (Feb. 1981): 116–35. See also Luis Miguel Glave, *Trajinantes. Caminos indígenas en la sociedad colonial siglos XVI/XVII* (Lima: Instituto de Apoyo Agrario, 1989).

6. This can be attributed in part to the Inquisition's persecution of New Christians. Many were merchants and confiscation of their goods seriously hampered their economic power. See Alfonso Quiroz, "La expropiación inquisitorial de cristianos nuevos portugueses en Los Reyes, Cartagena y México," *Histórica* 2 (1986): 237–303; Alberto Flores Galindo, *Aristocracia y plebe. Lima, 1760–1830* (Lima: Mosca Azul, 1984).

7. William Goode, *La familia* (Mexico City: UTHEA, 1966), 52.

8. Law 11 of the Laws of Toro, quoted by José Ots Capdequí, *Manual de Historia del Derecho español en las Indias y el Derecho propiamente indiano*, 2 vols. (Buenos Aires: Facultad de Derecho y Ciencias Sociales, 1943), 1:117.

9. Ots Capdequí, *Manual*, 1:117.

10. Juan de Solórzano y Pereyra, *Política indiana*, 2 vols. (Madrid: Compañía Iberoamericana de Publicaciones, 1972), 2:214–15.

11. Solórzano y Pereyra, *Política indiana*, 2:214.

12. Solórzano y Pereyra, *Política indiana*, 2:215.

13. Solórzano y Pereyra, *Política indiana*, 2:214.

14. Ots Capdequí, *Manual*, 1:107.

15. Richard Konetzke, *Colección de documentos para la historia de la formación social de Hispanoamérica, 1493–1810*. 3 vols. in 5. (Madrid: Consejo Superior de Investigaciones Científicas, 1950), 2:14.

16. Solórzano y Pereyra, *Política indiana*, 1:357.

17. Solórzano y Pereyra, *Política indiana*, 2:58.

18. Laws 6 and 28 from the Laws of Toro and Lib. 10, tít. 20, leyes 1, 8, from the *Novísima Recopilación*, quoted by Ots Capdequí in *Manual*, 1:149.

19. Lib. 15, tít. 9, part. 6 from the *Novísima Recopilación*, quoted by Ots Capdequí in *Manual*, 1:151.

20. Law 12 from the Laws of Toro and Lib. 10, tít. 7, from the *Novísima Recopilación*, quoted by Ots Capdequí in *Manual*, 1:166. As for the father's goods, when there were no legitimate or legitimized children, natural children inherited two of the twelve parts into which the estate was divided. Spurious children could not inherit from their fathers. Adulterine children or the sacrilegious offspring of a priest or nun were barred from inheriting from their fathers and mothers. Ots Capdequí in *Manual*, 166.

21. The figures for illegitimacy come from the baptismal certificates of the El Sagrario and San Marcelo Parishes. The figures for the seventeenth century are in five-year cycles. In 1593, the cathedral parish had gathered 8,770 people, some 3,980 blacks and mulattoes and 4,790 whites. Around 1600, the city's population was 14, 262. El Sagrario thus had 61.49 percent of Lima's total population at the beginning of the century. Around 1619, the four parishes in Lima, El Sagrario, Santa Ana, San Sebastián, and San Marcelo, counted 24,275 people. El Sagrario had 15,012 people or 61.84 percent, a percentage similar to the one previously mentioned. San Marcelo had 1,874, or 7.1 percent of the city's population. Bowser, *El esclavo*, 410.

22. Ann Twinam, "Honor, Sexuality, and Illegitimacy in Colonial Spanish America," in *Sexuality and Marriage in Colonial Latin America*, ed. Asunción Lavrin (Lincoln: University of Nebraska Press, 1989), 118–55.

23. Natural children were born of single parents who, despite no impediment, chose not to marry.

24. AGN, RA, CC, leg. 239, C. 898, proceedings of doña Francisca de Sosa against don Pedro Luque, her father's executor, so she may be recognized as her father's natural daughter, 1682.

25. AGN, N. 605, Antonio Marcelo Figueroa, Antonio Pérez de Losada, Will, 1680. These statements also lead to a different matter: the tendency for illegitimate births to be underrecorded. It is highly probable that a number of legitimate children were actually offspring of extramarital relationships. The inverse figure—that legitimate children who did not appear as such—is virtually impossible to establish, especially if we consider that legitimacy in part defined status in all different social

sectors. For the underrecording of illegitimacy, see Stone, *Family, Sex, and Marriage*, 380.

26. Goode, *La familia*, 50. Louis Dumont's book, *Homo hierarquicus. Ensayo sobre el sistema de castas en la India* (Madrid: Aguilar, 1973) has been very influential in my understanding of how illegitimacy affected social hierarchies in Lima.

27. AGN, N. 809, Pablo González Romo, José de Quesada, Will, 1682.

28. Incest was another structural form of illegitimacy though I have been unable to find statements alluding to it. It is equally difficult to trace illegitimacy resulting from relations between women and priests. We know that celibacy for priests was established by the Western Church around the eleventh century, but the church was not always able to control the sexual habits of its ecclesiastical hierarchy. It is likely that many of the children unrecognized by their fathers were priests' children, but it is impossible to determine the precise number. As was seen in chapter three, the concubinage trials in the archive of the archiepiscopal court provide evidence that priests were involved in illicit sexual relationships.

29. AGN, RA, CC, leg. 3, C. 28, proceedings of the defender of minors for don Domingo Hernández's natural daughters against Lic. Don Bartolomé de Brey, executor and guardian of Hernández's goods, over the execution of his will, 1643.

30. AGN, N. 163, Cristóbal Rodríguez de Linpias, Juan Mendoza, Will, 1612.

31. It is nevertheless difficult to accurately establish the single status of fathers of illegitimate children. In the baptismal books of both parishes, the category "single parents" seldom occurs: 14 (0.6 percent) in San Marcelo and 95 (1 percent) in El Sagrario. This indicates that this category is unreliable. Paternity patterns among the illegitimate population in both parishes are a better indication.

32. AGN, N. 303, Juan Casas y Morales, Antonio de Lorsa, Will, 1668.

33. AGN, N. 68, Cristóbal Aguilar Mendieta, Diego Morales Gallinato, Will, 1641.

34. AGN, N. 50, Cristóbal Aguilar Mendieta, Juan Martín Guillermo, Will, 1607.

35. AGN, N. 613, Antonio Marcelo Figueroa, Juan Otasso de Normat, Will, 1652.

36. Otasso was definitely a generous man. He made several donations to women and had a benevolent attitude toward his slaves, particularly María Angola, who had served him for more than twenty-four years. Otasso said that María Angola should remain with Micaela, his daughter, "so that she will not be left unaided and there will be someone to take care of her and sustain her." He even considered the fact that María might not want to live with Micaela, but do something else with her life. The final decision would remain with the owner, who should act in good will, "considering that María had been her wet nurse." AGN, N. 613, Antonio Marcelo Figueroa. Juan Otasso de Normat, Will, 1652.

37. AGN, N. 809, Pablo González Romo, María de Salamanca, Will, 1682.

38. AGN, RA, CC, leg. 165, C. 617, proceedings of doña Jordana de Orihuela, natural daughter of don Rodrigo Paz de Orihuela, against his executor and heirs over the execution of the legacy arranged by her father's will, 1659.

39. AGN, RA, CC, leg. 239, C. 898, proceedings of doña María Francisca de Cosar Bueno against Capt. Luque Cosar over being declared his natural daughter and her right to support to purchase food, 1682.

40. AGN, RA, CC, leg. 211, C. 799, proceedings of don Francisco and Antonio del Cerro, don Lorenzo de Cerro's natural sons, against doña Francisca de Acevedo, his widow, executrix and guardian of his goods, over their descent from don Lorenzo and their right to their inheritance from him, 1673.

41. The meaning of arguments like this is analyzed in chapter six.

42. AGN, RA, CC, leg. 267, C. 1006-A, proceedings of doña Baltasara de Villegas against Juan de Villegas's heirs over her descent from Juan de Villegas and that she should be declared his natural daughter and given support, 1690.

43. AGN, Cabildo, CC, leg. 14, C. 155, proceedings of doña Francisca de la Vega Laso, doña María Narváez's natural daughter, against Capt. don Manuel Vélez de Guevara, her mother's executor, over the executor's account and the surrender of her maternal legitim, 1695.

44. AGN, N. 1494, Pedro Pérez Landero, Gerónimo de Oliva, Will, 1690.

45. AGN, N. 604, Antonio Marcelo de Figueroa, Gerónimo de Montenegro, Will, 1650.

46. AGN, Cabildo, CC, leg. 8, C. 96, proceedings of don Pedro Fernández de Moreda, Pedro Fernández de Moreda's natural son, against Alonso Jiménez Vela de Lara, his father's executor, over the executor's account, 1687.

47. AGN, N. 1494, Pedro Pérez Landero, Alonso de Gameroz, Will, 1690.

48. AGN, N. 281, Juan Casas y Morales, José Carrillo de Albornoz, Will, 1681.

49. AGN, RA, CC, leg. 188, C. 712, proceedings of Pedro de Mendoza, natural son of don Juan de Monte, against his father's estate over his right to the sixth part of his father's goods, 1666.

50. Goode, *La familia*, 50.

51. Goode, *La familia*, 51.

52. AGN, RA, CC, leg. 165, C. 618, proceedings of Fernando Cuadrado, tutor and guardian of minor José de Ribera, don Juan de Ribera's son, against the alferez, Fernando de Arco, tutor and guardian of Juan de Ribera's legitimate children, over the guardianship account, 1659.

53. AGN, RA, CC, leg. 140, C. 517, proceedings of don Roque Lorenzo García de Bobadilla against don Lorenzo de Arnedo, his father's executor, over his descent from his father and his right to his father's estate, 1619.

54. Elias, *El Proceso*, 223.

55. Elias, *El Proceso*, 223.

Chapter Six

1. AAL, Apelaciones, Cuzco, doña Juana de los Remedios, nun from the convent of Nuestra Señora de los Remedios in the city of Cuzco, against doña Mencía de San Bernardo, nun in the same convent, who sought the annulment of the former's election as prioress there, 1644.

2. Flores Galindo, *Aristocracia*, 26.

3. Iberian law was less discriminatory than Anglo-Saxon legislation, where women's access to the distribution of family goods was particularly restricted. Boxer, *Women in Iberian Expansion*, 52.

4. Ots Capdequí, *Manual*, 114.

5. Lavallé, "Divorcio," 438.

6. Machado de Chávez, *El perfeto*, 2:447.

7. Machado de Chávez, *El perfeto*, 2:448.

8. This precept is virtually universal, although different transgressions may present themselves according to particular social conditions. In stratified societies, this norm inspired many legal formulae and their subsequent reformulation. In Lima's colonial society, it served as a significant indicator of gender identity. Social stratification became more complex and further redefined when the ethnic component was added.

9. Vigil, *La vida de las mujeres*, 88.

10. Martínez-Alier, *Marriage, Class, and Colour*, 124.

11. Vigil, *La vida de las mujeres*, 125.

12. Quoted by Goode, *La familia*, 46.

13. [León Portocarrero], *Descripción*, 39.

14. [León Portocarrero], *Descripción*, 71.

15. Frézier, in Núñez, *El Perú visto*, 25.

16. See also Raquel Chang-Rodríguez, *Cancionero peruano del siglo XVII* (Lima: Pontificia Universidad Católica del Perú, 1983), 31–32.

17. "Memoria de Juan de Mendoza," in *Memorias de los virreyes que han gobernado el Perú durante el tiempo del coloniaje español*, ed. Manuel Atanasio Fuentes, 6 vols. (Lima: Librería Central de Felipe Bailly, 1859), 1:35.

18. "Memoria de Virrey Luis de Velasco de 1604," in *Colección de memorias o relaciones que escribieron los virreyes del Perú*, ed. Ricardo Beltrán y Róspide (Madrid: Imprenta de Asilo de Huérfanos, 1921), 2 vols., 2:133.

19. "Memoria," 2:133.

20. Carta de Francisco de Saldaña, Lima, 20 May 1634, Emilio Lisson, *La iglesia de España en el Perú*, 4 vols. (Seville: Escelicer, 1944), 4:7, 556.

21. Nancy van Deusen, *Dentro del cerco de los muros* (Lima: Cuadernos de Trabajo, CENDOC Mujer, 1987), 22.

22. "Memoria del Virrey Melchor de Liñan," in *Memorias de los virreyes*, ed. Fuentes, 1:286.

23. "Memoria del Virrey Melchor de Liñan," in *Memorias de los virreyes*, ed. Fuentes, 1:286.

24. "Memoria del Virrey Melchor de Liñan," in *Memorias de los virreyes,* ed. Fuentes, 1:294–95.

25. AGN, Colección Santa María, no folios, 1684.

26. In 1548, in a royal cédula issued in Valladolid, the king commented that he knew many mestizas committed adultery while married to Spaniards. The problem was that these women were not prosecuted under any canon, as there was no specific body of laws for adulterous mestizas. In this case, the monarch determined mestizas should be governed by the same laws applying to Spanish women. *Disposiciones complementarias a las leyes de Indias* (Madrid: Ministerio de Trabajo, 1930), 1:237.

27. Several authors have analyzed the colonial dowry system. John Kicza's "The Great Families of Mexico: Elite Maintenance and Business Practices in Late Colonial Mexico City," *Hispanic American Historical Review* 62 (1982): 429–57, and Doris Ladd's *The Mexican Nobility at Independence, 1780–1826* (Austin: University of Texas Press, 1976), for Mexico reveal the importance of this mechanism for elite configuration and social-group alliances. The same can be said of Susan Socolow's *The Merchants of Buenos Aires, 1778–1810: Family and Commerce* (Cambridge: Cambridge University Press, 1978), for the Buenos Aires commercial elite of the eighteenth century. Asunción Lavrin and Edith Couturier, "Dowries and Wills: A View of Women's Socioeconomic Role in Colonial Guadalajara and Puebla, 1640–1790," *Hispanic American Historical Review* 59 (1979): 280–304, have analyzed aspects of dowry as related to feminine identity, its matrimonial function, and the role of women in the Mexican economy. In Peru, colonial dowries have not been much studied. Paul Rizo-Patrón has dealt with the topic in connection with Lima's elites of the eighteenth century in "Familia, matrimonio y dote en la nobleza de Lima: Los de la Puente, 1700–1850" (tesis de bachiller, Pontificia Universidad Católica del Perú, 1989).

28. The *Siete Partidas* specified several forms of dowry. "Advertencia" was the kind made up with goods that did not come from the father and that reverted to the woman and her heirs. "Profeticia" was the sort coming from the father, and if the daughter died with no children, it returned to him. If a divorce occurred and the dowry had been given back to the father, once he died, the daughter was completely entitled to it. "Voluntaria" was a dowry provided by

the woman herself or someone not obliged to. A dowry that was "necesaria" was given by those obliged by law to grant it: fathers (to legitimate and minor daughters), a paternal grandfather, a mother who professed different religion than that of her Catholic daughter, a curator in charge of a minor, or anyone obliged to do so by contract or a last will. If a dowry was "estimada," its goods had been valued; if "inestimada," they had not.

The husband was the owner of the dowry from the wedding day forward. He had some accountability, but was entitled to transfer it, unless it was "inestimada." Any profits the dowry produced increased the marriage goods. A dowry was returned if the husband's bad behavior jeopardized those goods, but not because of some misfortune he suffered. It was also given back when matrimonial bond was broken.

The Laws of Toro made a distinction between donations—even *propter nuptias*, those made to children—from dowries granted to daughters and introduced some innovations in dowry regulation. Dowries could not exceed the legitim. The goods making up the dowry had to come from matrimonial earnings if given by both parents. If the father alone granted the dowry to a common daughter, it also came from the earnings or if there were none, from the father's and not the mother's goods. María Isabel López Díaz, "Arras y dote en España. Resumen histórico," in *Nuevas perspectivas sobre la mujer. Actas de las primeras jornadas de investigación interdiciplinaria.* (Madrid: Seminario de Estudios de la Mujer, Universidad Autónoma de Madrid, 1982), 1:96–97.

29. López Díaz, "Arras y dote," 97.

30. ABPL, Libro de la Congregación de Nuestra Señora de la O, fol. 1.

31. ABPL, Libro de la Congregación de Nuestra Señora de la O, fol. 1.

32. Archivo Histórico Nacional de Madrid, Consejo de la Inquisición, Lima, fol. 392.

33. Martínez-Alier, *Marriage, Class, and Colour*, 120. See also J. G. Peristiany's classic studies on the subject, *Ensayos de antropología del honor. El concepto de honra en la sociedad mediterránea* (Barcelona: Nueva Colección Labor, 1968), and Julian Pitt-Rivers, *Antropología del honor o política de los sexos. Ensayos de antropología en la sociedad mediterránea* (Barcelona: Grijalbo, 1979).

34. On the contrary, although perhaps not formally acknowledged, men's worth has also rested on the conquest of women. Virility,

somehow a component of honor, had to do with the seduction of women. It is worth noting, however, that at no time during research for this work did sufficient evidence appear to affirm that men boasted about having successfully seduced women. It is likely that at this time in colonial history, public and feminine opinion of a sort had developed sufficiently to inhibit this kind of masculine attitude. See Elias, *El proceso*, 221–23.

35. AGN, N. 809, Pablo González Romo, doña María Gabriela Espinosa, Will, 1671.

36. AGN, RA, CC, leg. 285, C. 1082, proceedings of Juan Jacinto Gelder against Julián Avila, doña Francisca de Morales's executor, over being acknowledged as her natural son with a right to his maternal legitim, 1696.

37. AGN, RA, CC, leg. 10, C. 124, proceedings of don Diego Damián de León against don Diego León y Andrade's goods and heirs, over his acknowledgment as his natural son with a right to his paternal legitim, 1690.

38. AGN, RA, CC, leg. 270, C. 1021, proceedings of doña Jacoba de Córdova, Andrés de Parra's natural mother, over his declared natural son of the deceased and with an acknowledged right to his paternal legitim, 1691.

39. AGN, RA, CC, leg. 5, C. 57, attested copy of the proceedings of Esteban, Manuela, and Leonor Jiménez, doña Juana de Lorca's natural children, against doña Agustina de Lorca Sarmiento for some pesos, 1667.

40. AGN, RA, CC, leg. 241, C. 903, proceedings of doña Teodora Gómez Barahona, don Juan Gómez Barahona's natural daughter, against her deceased father's estate, over her right to her paternal legitim, 1682.

41. AGN, RA, CC, leg. 211, C. 799, proceedings of don Francisco and Antonio del Cerro, don Lorenzo del Cerro's natural sons, against doña Francisca de Acevedo, his widow, executrix and guardian of his goods, over their descent from don Lorenzo and their right to their inheritance, 1673.

42. AGN, RA, CC, leg. 227, C. 857, proceedings of Josefa de Herrera, don Sebastián de Herrera's natural daughter, against her father's estate over her right to her paternal legitim, 1679.

43. Doña Josefa de Herrera's trial was incomplete, since the sentence of the royal audiencia was provisional. Although it is unknown whether this case was reopened later, it clearly shows the difficulties a daughter born out of wedlock could encounter when seeking to be formally acknowledged.

44. This case, which occurred in Cuzco, could have happened in Lima, too. Since it took place in a religious institution, the same criteria would have been invoked in any convent of the Viceroyalty of Peru. The nuns' behavior and the authorities' opinion were general enough to have been shared with the population in Lima. See note 1 in this chapter for the citation for this material. I thank Kathryn Burns for informing me of this file.

45. AGN, RA, CC, leg. 185, C. 694, proceedings of María Magdalena de San Juan y Santa Lucía, Capt. don Juan de Urrutia's natural daughter, against his estate over the surrender of bequests arranged by her father, 1665.

46. AGN, N. 809, Pablo González Romo, María de Salamanca, Will, 1682.

47. AGN, N. 809, Pablo González Romo, Catalina Gil de Pastrana, Will, 1689.

48. AGN, N. 609, Marcelo Antonio Figueroa, Francisca de Campoverde, Will, 1651.

49. AGN, N. 615, Marcelo Antonio Figueroa, Pascuala de Sarmiento, Will, 1653.

50. Donald Ramos commented on this topic in "Marriage and Family in Colonial Vila Rica," *Hispanic American Historical Review* 55 (1975): 200–225.

51. For a synthesis of this debate, see Eugene D. Genovese, *In Red and Black: Marxian Explorations in Southern and Afro-American History* (Knoxville: University of Tennessee Press, 1984).

52. In his *Descriptión*, León Portocarrero was struck by white men's affection for black women. "Since they are their wet nurses, white men are fonder of them than of Spanish women," 39.

53. Part. 4, tít. 5, ley 1, cited by Trazegnies, *Ciriaco de Urtecho*, 112.

54. Part. 4, tít. 5, ley 1, cited by Trazegnies, *Ciriaco de Urtecho*, 112.

55. Part. 4, tít. 5, ley 1, cited by Trazegnies, *Ciriaco de Urtecho*, 110.

56. It is important to clarify that these observations refer to formal marriage, since the possible forms of conjugal life among the slave population in Lima are unknown. Unfortunately, there are no studies similar to those carried out in other slave societies where alternative kinds of family life and conjugal links have been found among the slave population. See Herbert Gutman, *The Black Family in Slavery and Freedom, 1750–1925* (New York: Random House, 1977).

57. Bowser, *El esclavo*, 314–17.

58. There is no research on how this came about in cities, but it was certainly true of slaves working in the haciendas belonging to religious orders. In his study of Jesuit haciendas north of Lima in the colonial period, Nicholas Cushner noted that priests had policies concerning their slaves' conjugal lives that favored marriage among them. *Lords of the Land: Sugar, Wine, and Jesuit Estates of Colonial Peru, 1600–1767* (Albany: State University of New York Press, 1980). See also Bowser, *El esclavo*, 298.

59. At the beginning of the seventeenth century, the Spanish crown received a number of reports stating that most of the black population, which in Lima alone numbered twenty thousand, were unassimilated insofar as religion was concerned. These statements were rebutted some years later when the judges of Lima's audiencia argued that according to the 1600 census, there were only sixty-six hundred blacks and parochial institutions and the church in general were able to take care of their spiritual needs. Bowser, *El esclavo*, 298.

60. These figures are similar to those of other studies on this topic for urban centers in colonial Latin America. See, for example, Elizabeth A. Kuznesof, "Sexual Politics, Race and Bastard Rearing in Nineteenth-Century Brazil: A Question of Culture or Power?" *Journal of Marriage and Family History*, 16 (1991): 241–60.

61. The predominance of extramarital relationships among the African population and their offspring makes it difficult to determine whether or to what extent African conjugal and family patterns survived in the colonial setting.

62. *Disposiciones*, 1:244.

63. AAL, Amancebados, unnumbered leg., trial of Juan Gómez and Juana Ramírez, 1627.

64. AGN, RA, CC, leg. 87, C. 323, proceedings of doña María Arias against don Salvador Arias, her natural father, over support, 1632.

CHAPTER SEVEN

1. John Boswell, *The Kindness of Strangers: The Abandonment of Children in Western Europe from Late Antiquity to the Renaissance* (New York: Pantheon Books, 1988).

2. Birth control was not unknown. Coitus interruptus was practiced, though not widely. Faced with unwanted pregnancies, women could resort to abortifacients, but those were seldom effective. Vigil, *La vida de las mujeres*, 121.

3. Boswell, *The Kindness*.

4. León Carlos Alvarez Santalo, *Marginación social y mentalidad en Andalucía Occidental: Expósitos en Sevilla (1613–1910)* (Seville: Consejería de Cultura de la Junta de Andalucía, 1980), 34.

5. Aries.

6. At this time, the only census with information on the population of children, the *Numeración general de Lima*, has been studied. It contains interesting but to date unexplored, data on the city's children.

7. This distinction is similar to what Philippe Ariès finds in his study on childhood in Ancient Regime France. See P. Ariès, *Centuries of Childhood*.

8. The quantitative and demographic information here comes from the baptismal records of the same parishes mentioned in earlier chapters, San Marcelo and El Sagrario, during the seventeenth century.

9. AAL, Bautizos, San Marcelo, Lib. 5B, fol. 46r, 1635.

10. Machado de Chávez, *El perfeto*, 1:190–91.

11. [León Portocarrero], *Descripción*, 63.

12. See original.

13. AAL, Bautizos, San Marcelo, Españoles, Lib. 4, fol. 23, 1675.

14. AAL, Bautizos, El Sagrario, Españoles y Mestizos, Lib. 8, fol. 48, 1685.

15. AAL, Bautizos, El Sagrario, Españoles y Mestizos, Lib. 6, fol. 56, 1665.

16. In almost all cases the newborns were abandoned at family homes. No cases of children left at convents or churches have been found. This does not seem to have been a common practice among city inhabitants. Children might be left at the Hospital de los Niños Huérfanos, an institution created to shelter them, but this only occurred once in San Marcelo in 1620, when a girl was abandoned there.

17. Alvarez Santalo, *Marginación social*, 139.

18. AGN, RA, CC, leg. 140, C. 517, proceedings of don Roque Lorenzo García de Bobadilla, don Andrés García Bobadilla's natural son, against don Lorenzo de Arnedo, his father's executor, over his descent from don Andrés and his right to his inheritance from his father, 1649.

19. Cobo, *Obras*, 2:453.

20. AGN, Inquisición, Fundaciones, leg. 2, 1746–87, file of Bonifacia del Espíritu Santo, 1748.

21. Rubén Vargas Ugarte, S. J., *Historia general del Perú*, 6 vols. (Lima: Milla Batres, 1966), 2:31.

22. Hesperiophylo [pseud.], "Noticia histórica del hospital de los Niños Huérfanos," *Mercurio Peruano* (1791: facsimile ed., Lima: Biblioteca Nacional de Perú, 1964), 2:298.

23. ABPL, Huérfanos, Antecedentes, 1.

24. Vargas Ugarte, *Historia general*, 2:31.

25. Vargas Ugarte, *Historia general*, 2:300.

26. Cobo, *Obras*, 2:453.

27. Hesperiophylo, "Noticia histórica," 2:303.

28. Cobo, *Obras*, 2:453.

29. If carried out, these measures probably enhanced wet nurses' standing and prestige, since many women who performed this labor were from the margins of society. There is no evidence, however, that these changes occurred.

30. At the end of the eighteenth century, wet nurses took care of children in their own homes until they reached the age of twelve months, but this period could be extended. Within the hospital itself, twenty nursemaids provided domestic service. ABPL, Huérfanos, Antecedentes I.

31. Ilder Mendieta Ocampo, *Los hospitales de Lima colonial. Siglos xvii–xix*, (Lima: Seminario de Historia Rural, Universidad Nacional Mayor de San Marcos, 1990).

32. Cobo, *Obras*, 2:308.

33. Cobo, *Obras*, 2:301.

34. Mendieta, *Los hospitales*, 110.

35. Cobo, *Obras*, 2:310.

36. In other societies, the widespread availability of wet nurses brought with it a high infant mortality rate and differing fertility patterns for women from different social classes. At the end of the eighteenth century in Rouen, France, 90 percent of abandoned children fed by wet nurses died before the age of one. Of those nursed by their mothers, 18.7 percent died. Flandrin, *Orígenes*, 258. In Spain, infant mortality in the sixteenth century was rather high. See Vigil, *La vida*, 137.

37. In spite of moralists' advice, women in Spain, at least those who had the means, continued to hire wet nurses to breast-feed their children until the mid-nineteenth century. Vigil, *La vida de las mujeres*, 127. In Peru, advertisements for wet nurses appeared in the newspapers almost until the end of the century. There has not, however, been any research on this and what it might mean.

38. Nothing is known about the infant mortality rates of abandoned children who could not be assured sufficient breast-feeding to survive, but they were probably high.

39. AGN, Inquisición, Fundaciones, leg. 1, file of Paula de Atocha, 1783. For our purposes, using the applications of foundling women for places in the Colegio de la Santa Cruz de Atocha that correspond to the eighteenth century does not adversely affect their relevance to the period under study. In terms of the information they contain, the early eighteenth-century applications, for example, from 1703, are virtually identical to those from the end of the century.

40. AGN, Inquisición, Fundaciones, leg. 1, file of Paula de Atocha, 1783.

41. AGN, Inquisición, Fundaciones, leg. 2, file of María Pasquala de Atocha, 1758.

42. AGN, Inquisición, Fundaciones, leg. 2, file of María Pasquala de Atocha, 1758.

43. AGN, Inquisición, Fundaciones, leg. 1, file of María Antonia de Atocha, 1772.

44. AGN, Inquisición, Fundaciones, leg. 2, file of María Josefa Florentina de Atocha, 1745.

45. AGN, Inquisición, Fundaciones, leg. 2, file of Vicenta de las Mercedes de Atocha, 1750.

46. AGN, Inquisición, Fundaciones, leg. 2, file of María Juliana de Atocha, 1705.

47. AGN, Inquisición, Fundaciones, leg. 1, file of Alfonsa de Atocha, 1711.

48. AGN, Inquisición, Fundaciones, leg. 2, file of María Liberata de Atocha, 1753.

49. AGN, Inquisición, Fundaciones, leg. 2, file of María Ascensión de Atocha, 1786.

50. Vigil, *La vida de las mujeres*, 130–31.

51. AGN, RA, CC, leg. 178, C 667, proceedings of don Diego de Villagómez against Josefa de Toro's estate over his descent from his mother his right to a share of his deceased mother's goods, 1663.

52. AGN, Inquisición, Fundaciones, leg. 4, 1602–61, don Mateo Pastor, Will, 1653–55.

53. AGN, Inquisición, Fundaciones, leg. 1, file of María de los Santos, 1674.

54. AGN, Inquisición, Fundaciones, leg. 1, file of María del Carmen de Atocha, 1770.

55. AGN, Inquisición, Fundaciones, leg. 1, file of María Dolores de Atocha, 1772.

56. BNL, Sala de Investigaciones, B237, Constituciones del Colegio de Niñas Expósitas de Santa Cruz de Atocha, 1659. The references to the school administration that follow are from this source, unless otherwise indicated.

57. "La educación en al Virreynato del Perú. El Colegio de Santa Cruz para niñas expósitas," *Revista del Archivo Nacional del Perú* 24 (1960): 34.

58. BNL, Sala de Investigaciones, B514, Colegio de Niñas de Santa Cruz de Atocha, 1708. This is a list of thirty-six women, twenty-three of whom decided on marriage. Seven chose convent life.

59. AGN, Inquisición, Fundaciones, leg. 2, file of Mariana de Atocha, 1771.

Bibliography

Acosta, Rosa María. "Una aproximación al estudio de la fiesta colonial en el Perú (Fiestas oficiales urbanas)." Tesis de bachiller, Pontificia Universidad Católica del Perú, 1979.

Alvarez Santalo, León Carlos. *Marginación social y mentalidad en Andalucía Occidental: Expósitos en Sevilla (1613–1910)*. Seville: Consejería de Cultura de la Junta de Andalucía, 1980.

Aries, Phillipe. *Centuries of Childhood*. New York: Penguin Books, 1976.

———, y Georges Duby. *Historia de la vida privada. La alta edad media. T. 2. Poder privado y poder público en la Europa feudal*. T. III. Madrid: Taurus, 1987.

Ballesteros, Tomás de. *Tomo primero de las ordenanzas del Perú*. Lima: Imprenta de Francisco Sobrino, 1572.

Barnechea, Alvaro. "Marginación, informalización y cambio cultural en la ciudad de Lima en el siglo XVII." Memoria de bachiller, Pontificia Universidad Católica del Perú, 1988.

Beltrán y Róspide, Ricardo. *Colección de memorias o relaciones que escribieron los virreyes del Perú*. 2 vols. Madrid: Imprenta del Asilo de Huérfanos, 1921.

Bennassar, Bartolomé. *The Spanish Character. Attitudes and Mentalities from the Sixteenth to the Nineteenth Century*. Trans. Benjamin Keen (*L'Homme Espagnol: attitudes and mentalités du XVIe au XIXe siecle*). Librairie Hachette 1975. (Berkeley: University of California Press, 1979), 184.

Boswell, John. *The Kindness of Strangers: The Abandonment of Children in Western Europe from Late Antiquity to the Renaissance*. New York: Pantheon Books, 1988.

Bowser, Frederick. *El esclavo africano en el Perú colonial, 1524–1650*. Mexico City: Siglo Veintiuno, 1977.

Boxer, C. R. *Women in Iberian Expansion Overseas, 1415–1815: Some Facts, Fancies, and Personalities*. New York: Oxford University Press, 1975.

Boyd-Bowman, Peter. "Patterns of Spanish Emigration to the Indies until 1600." *Hispanic American Historical Review* 56 (1976): 588–604.

Bromley, Juan. "La ciudad de Lima en el año 1630." *Revista Histórica* 24 (1959): 268–317.

Busto Duthurburu, José Antonio del. "Una huérfana mestiza: La hija de Juan Pizarro." *Revista Histórica* 28 (1965): 103–6.

Cadena, Marisol de la. "'Las mujeres son más indias': Etnicidad y género en una comunidad del Cusco." *Revista Andina* 1 (1991): 4–35.

Calancha, fray Antonio de. *Crónica moralizadora del orden de San Agustín en el Perú*. 6 vols. 1638. Reprint. Lima: Universidad Nacional Mayor de San Marcos, 1975.

Castillo, Francisco del. "Un místico del siglo XVII. Autobiografía del venerable Padre Francisco del Castillo de la Compañía de Jesús." Lima: Rubén Vargas Ugarte, S. J., 1960.

Chang-Rodriguez, Raquel. *Cancionero peruano del siglo XVII*. Lima: Pontificia Universidad Católica del Perú, 1983.

Cobo, Bernabé, S. J. *Obras*. Edited by Francisco Mateos, S. J. 2 vols. Madrid: Atlas, 1964.

Córdoba de la Llave, Ricardo. "Las relaciones extraconyugales en la sociedad castellana bajo medieval." *Anuario de Estudios Medievales* 16 (1986): 571–619.

Córdova y Salinas, fray Diego de. *Crónica franciscana*, 1651, in *Los cronistas del convento*, edited by José de la Riva-Agüero, compiled Pedro Benvenutto Murrieta and Guillermo Lohmann Villena. Biblioteca de Cultura Peruana, Primera Serie No. 4. Paris, Desclée, de Brouwer, 1938.

Cushner, Nicholas. *Lords of the Land: Sugar, Wine, and Jesuit Estates of Colonial Peru, 1600–1767*. Albany: State University of New York Press, 1980.

Disposiciones complementarias a las leyes de Indias. Vol. 1. Madrid: Ministerio de Trabajo, 1930.

Douglas, Mary. *Pureza y peligro. Un análisis de los conceptos de contaminación y tabú.* Madrid: Siglo Veintiuno, 1973.

Duby, Georges. *El caballero, la mujer y el cura.* Madrid: Taurus, 1987.

Dumbar Temple, Ella. "El testamento inédito de doña Beatriz Clara Coya de Loyola, hija del Inca Sayri Túpac." *Fénix* (Revista de la Biblioteca Nacional, Lima) 7 (1950): 111–22.

Dumont, Louis. *Homo hierarquicus. Ensayo sobre el sistema de castas en la India.* Madrid: Aguilar, 1973.

Durand, José. *La transformación social del conquistador.* Lima: Nuevos Rumbos, 1958.

Duviols, Pierre. *Cultura andina y represión. Procesos y visitas de idolatrías y hechicerías. Cajatambo, siglo XVII.* Cuzco: Centro de Estudios Regionales Andinos Bartolomé de las Casas, 1986.

"La educación en el Virreynato del Peru. El Colegio de Santa Cruz para niñas expósitas." *Revista del Archivo Nacional del Perú* 24 (1960): 72–98.

Echave y Assú, Francisco de. *La estrella de Lima convertida en sol sobre sus tres coronas.* Antwerp: Juan Baptista Verdiussen, 1688.

Elias, Norbert. *El proceso de la civilización. Investigaciones sociogenéticas y psicogenéticas.* Mexico City: Fondo de Cultura Económica, 1987.

Fairchilds, Cissie. "Female Sexual Attitudes and the Rise of Illegitimacy: A Case Study." *Journal of Interdisciplinary History* 8 (spring 1978): 627–67.

Flandrin, Jean Louis. *Orígenes de la familia moderna.* Barcelona: Editorial Crítica, 1979.

Flores Galindo, Alberto. *Aristocracia y plebe. Lima, 1760–1830.* Lima: Mosca Azul, 1984.

Flores Galindo, Alberto, and Magdalena Chocano. "Las cargas del sacramento." *Revista Andina* 3 (1984): 403–34.

Fuentes, Manuel Atanasio. *Memorias de los virreyes que han gobernado el Perú durante el tiempo del coloniaje español.* 6 vols. Lima: Librería Central de Felipe Bailly, 1859.

Garcilaso de la Vega, Inca. *Comentarios reales de los Incas.* 3 vols. Lima: Librería Internacional del Perú, 1959.

Genovese, Eugene D. *In Red and Black: Marxian Explorations in Southern and Afro-American History.* Knoxville: University of Tennessee Press, 1984.

Ghilheim, Claire. "La devaluación del verbo femenino." In *La inquisición española: Poder político y control social*, edited by Bartolomé Bennassar. Barcelona: Editorial Crítica, 1981.

Glave, Luis Miguel. *Trajinantes. Caminos indígenas en la sociedad colonial siglo XVI/XVII*. Lima: Instituto de Apoyo Agrario, 1989.

González, Jorge René. "Clérigos solicitantes, perversos de la confesión." In *De la santidad a la perversión*, edited by Sergio Ortega. Mexico City: Grijalbo, 1985.

Goode, William. *La familia*. Mexico City: UTEHA, 1966.

Guamán, Poma de Ayala, Felipe. *Nueva corónica y buen gobierno*. 3 vols. Mexico City: Siglo Veintiuno, 1980.

Gutman, Herbert. *The Black Family in Slavery and Freedom, 1750–1925*. New York: Random House, 1977.

Hemming, John. *The Conquest of the Incas*. New York: Harcourt Brace Jovanovich, 1970.

Henry, Louis. *Manual de demografía histórica*. Barcelona: Grijalbo, 1983.

Hesperiophylo [pseud.]. "Noticia histórica del hospital de los Niños Huérfanos." *Mercurio Peruano*. Facsim. Ed., Lima: Biblioteca Nacional del Perú, 1964.

Hollingsworth, T. H. "Mortality in British Peerage Families Since 1600," *Population Studies*, (special number) 32 (1964): 323–54.

Hunefeldt, Christine. "Los negros de Lima: 1800–1830." *Histórica* 3 (1979): 17–51.

———. *Mujeres: esclavitud, emociones y libertad*, 427–63. (Documento de trabajo). Lima: Instituto de Estudios Peruanos, 1988.

Jaramillo, Miguel. "Formación de un mercado laboral urbano e indígena en Lima de comienzos del siglo XVII." Tesis de bachiller, Pontificia Universidad Católica del Perú, 1986.

Johansson, S. Ryan. "Centuries of Childhood/Centuries of Parenting: Phillipe Aries and the Modernization of Privileged Infancy." *Journal of Family History*, 12 (1987): 343–65.

Kicza, John E. "The Great Families of Mexico: Elite Maintenance and Business Practices in Late Colonial Mexico City." *Hispanic American Historical Review*, 62 (1982): 429–57.

Konetzke, Richard. *Colección de documentos para la historia de la formación social de Hispanoamérica, 1493–1810*. 3 vols. in 5. Madrid: Consejo Superior de Investigaciones Científicas, 1950.

Kuznesof, Elizabeth A. "Sexual Politics, Race and Bastard Rearing in Nineteenth-Century Brazil: A Question of Culture or Power?" *Journal of Marriage and Family History* 16 (1991): 241–60.

"La educación en al Virreynato del Perú. El Colegio de Santa Cruz para niñas expósitas," *Revista del Archivo Nacional del Perú* 24 (1960): 72–98.

Ladd, Doris. *The Mexican Nobility at Independence, 1780–1826.* Austin: University of Texas Press, 1976.

Laslett, Peter. *The World We Have Lost: England before the Industrial Age.* New York: Scribners, 1973.

———, ed. *Family and Illicit Love in Earlier Generations.* Cambridge: Cambridge University Press, 1977.

Lavallé, Bernard. "Divorcio y nulidad de matrimonio en Lima (1650–1700). (La desavenencia conyugal como indicador social)." *Revista Andina* 2 (1986): 427–63.

Lavrin, Asunción, ed. *Sexuality and Marriage in Colonial Latin America.* Lincoln: University of Nebraska Press, 1989.

Lavrin, Asunción, and Edith Couturier. "Dowries and Wills: A View of Women's Socioeconomic Role in Colonial Guadalajara and Puebla, 1640–1790." *Hispanic American Historical Review*, 59 (1979): 280–304.

León Portocarrero, Pedro de. *Descripción del Virreinato del Perú.* Edited by Boleslao Lewin. Rosario: Universidad Nacional del Litoral, 1958.

Lisson, Emilio. *La iglesia de España en el Perú.* 4 vols. Seville: *Libros del Cabildo de Lima*, vol. 2, 27 November 1600 (Biblioteca Nacional, Lima).

Lockhart, James. *Spanish Perú, 1532–1560: A Colonial Society.* Madison: The University of Wisconsin Press, 1968.

———. *Los de Cajamarca. Un estudio social y biográfico de los primeros conquistadores del Perú.* 2 vols. Lima: Milla Batres, 1986.

Lockhart, James, and Stuart Schwartz. *Early Latin America.* Cambridge: Cambridge University Press, 1983.

López Díaz, María Isabel. "Arras y dote en España. Resumen histórico." In *Nuevas perspectivas sobre la mujer. Actas de las primeras jornadas de investigación interdisciplinaria.* Vol. 1. Madrid: Seminario de Estudios de la Mujer, Universidad Autónoma de Madrid, 1982.

López Martínez, Héctor. *Rebeliones de mestizos y otros temas quinientistas.* Lima: P. L. Villanueva, 1972.

Macera, Pablo. "Sexo y coloniaje." In *Trabajos de Historia*. Vol. 3. Lima: Instituto Nacional de Cultura, 1973.

Machado de Chávez y Mendoza, Juan. *El perfeto confessor i cura de almas.* 2 vols. Madrid: La viuda de Francisco Martínez, 1646–47.

Maravall, José Antonio. *Estado moderno y mentalidad social, siglos* XV y XVII. 2 vols. Madrid: Alianza, 1986.

Martín, Luis. *Daughters of the Conquistadores: Women of the Viceroyalty of Peru.* Albuquerque: University of New Mexico Press, 1983.

Martínez-Alier, Verena. *Marriage, Class and Colour in Nineteenth-Century Cuba: A Study of Racial Attitudes and Sexual Values in a Slave Society.* Cambridge: Cambridge University Press, 1974.

Mazet, Claude. "Population et société à Lima aux XVIE et XVIIE siècles. La Paroisse San Sebastian (1562–1689)." *Cahiers de Amérique Latine* 13–14 (1976): 53–100.

Medina, José Toribio. *Historia del Tribunal del Santo Oficio de Lima (1569–1820).* 2 vols. Santiago: Nascimento, 1956.

Meléndez, fray Juan. *Tesoros verdaderos de las Indias (1681–82).* In *Los cronistas de convento*, edited by José de la Riva-Agüero, compiled by Pedro Benvenutto Murrieta and Guillermo Lohmann Villena. Paris: Desclée, de Brouwer, 1938.

Mello e Souza, Laura. *O diabo e a terra de Santa Cruz. Feitiçaria e religiosidade popular no Brasil Colonial.* São Paulo: Companhia das Letras, 1986.

Mendieta, Ilder. *Los hospitales de Lima colonial. Siglos XVII–XIX.* Lima: Seminario de Historia Rural, Universidad de San Marcos, 1990.

Mumford, Lewis. *La ciudad en la historia.* Buenos Aires: Infinito, 1966.

Numeración general de todas las personas de ambos sexos, edades y calidades que se ha hecho en esta ciudad de Lima, año de 1700. Lima: COFIDE, 1985.

Núñez, Estuardo, comp. *El Perú visto por viajeros.* Lima: PEISA, 1973.

Ortega, Sergio, ed. *De la santidad a la perversión.* Mexico City: Grijalbo, 1985.

Ots, Capdequí, José María. *El Derecho de Familia y el Derecho de Sucesión en nuestra legislación de Indias.* Madrid: Imprenta Helénica, 1921.

———. *Manual de historia del Derecho español en las Indias y el Derecho propiamente indiano.* 2 vols. Buenos Aires: Facultad de Derecho y Ciencias Sociales, 1943.

Peralta, Luz. "El Hospital de la Caridad de Lima. Siglos XVI–XIX." Tesis de Maestría en Historia. Pontificia Universidad Católica del Perú, in preparation.

Peristiany, J. G. *Ensayos de antropología del honor. El concepto de honra en la sociedad mediterranea.* Barcelona: Nueva Colección Labor, 1968.

Pitt-Rivers, Julian. *Antropología del honor o política de los sexos. Ensayos de antropología en la sociedad mediterránea.* Barcelona: Grijalbo, 1979.

Porras Barrenechea, Raúl. *Pizarro.* Lima: Ediciones Pizarro, 1978.

Quiroz, Alfonso. "La expropiación inquisitorial de cristianos nuevos portugueses en Los Reyes, Cartagena y México." *Histórica* 2 (1986): 237–303.

Ramos, Donald. "Marriage and Family in Colonial Vila Rica." *Hispanic American Historical Review* 55 (1975): 200–225.

Recopilación de leyes de los reynos de las Indias. 4 vols. 1681. Reprint. Foreword by Ramón Menéndez y Pidal, and a preliminary study by Juan Manzano Manzano. Madrid: Ediciones Cultura Hispánica, 1973.

Rípodas Ardanaz, Daisy. *El matrimonio en Indias. Realidad social y regulación jurídica.* Buenes Aires: Conicet, 1977.

Riva-Agüero, José de la, *Estudios de Historia Peruana. La Conquista y el Virreinato.* Prólogo de Guillermo Lohmann Villena. Recopilación y notas de César Pacheco Vélez. Obras completas, VI, Publicaciones del Instituto Riva-Agüero, #4. (Lima: PUCP, 1968).

Riva-Agüero, José de la. "Lima española." In *La conquista y el Virreinato.* Vol. 4 of *Obras completas.* Lima: Pontificia Universidad Católica del Perú, 1968.

Riva-Agüero, José de la. ed., and Pedro Benvenutto Murrieta and Guillermo Lohmann Villena, comps. *Los cronistas de convento.* París: Desclée, de Brouwer, 1938.

Rizo-Patrón, Paul. "Familia, matrimonio y dote en la nobleza de Lima: Los De la Puente, 1700–1850." Tesis de bachiller, Pontificia Univerdidad Católica del Perú, 1989.

Rostworowski de Diez Canseco, María. *La mujer en la época pre-hispánica.* Lima: Instituto de Estudios Peruanos, 1986.

———. *Doña Francisca Pizarro. Una ilustre mestiza, 1534–1598.* Lima: Instituto de Estudios Peruanos, 1989.

Rubin, Gayle. "The Traffic of Women: Notes on the Political Economy of Sex." In *Toward an Anthropology of Women*, edited by Rayna Reiter. New York and London: Monthly Review Press, 1975.

Russel, Jeffrey. *Witchcraft in the Middle Ages*. Ithaca: Cornell University Press, 1984.

Saraiva, Antonio José. *Inquisição e cristãos-novos*. Lisbon: Impresa Universitária, Ed. Estampa, 1985.

Sennet, Richard. *O declínio de homem público. As tiranias de intimidade*. São Paulo: Companhia das Letras, 1988.

Shorter, Edward. "Illegitimacy, Sexual Revolution and Social Change in Modern Europe." *Journal of Interdisciplinary History* 1 (autumn 1971): 231–72.

Silverblatt, Irene. *Luna, sol y brujas. Género y clase en los Andes prehispánicos y coloniales*. Cuzco: Centro de Estudios Regionales Andinos Bartolomé de las Casas, 1990.

Socolow, Susan. *The Merchants of Buenos Aires, 1778–1810: Family and Commerce*. Cambridge: Cambridge University Press, 1978.

Solóranzo y Pereyra, Juan de. *Política indiana*. 2 vols. Madrid: Compañía Iberoamericana de Publicaciones, 1972.

Stern, Steve J. *Peru's Indian Peoples and the Challenge of Spanish Conquest: Huamanga to 1640*. Madison: The University of Wisconsin Press, 1982.

Stone, Lawrence. *The Family, Sex, and Marriage in England, 1500–1800*. New York: Harper and Row, 1979.

Suardo, Juan Antonio. *Diario de Lima, 1629–1634*. 2 vols. Introduction and notes by Rubén Vargas Ugarte, S. J. Lima: Imprenta Vásquez, 1935.

Tepaske, John J., and Herbert S. Klein. "The Seventeenth-Century Crisis in New Spain: Myth or Reality?" *Past & Present* 90 (Feb. 1981): 116–35.

Tilly, Louise, Joan Scott, and Miriam Cohen. "Women's Work and European Fertility Patterns." *Journal of Interdisciplinary History* 6 (winter 1976): 447–76.

Todorov, Tzvetan. *La conquista de América. La cuestión del otro*. Mexico City: Siglo Veintiuno, 1987.

Torres Saldamando, Enrique. *Libro primero de cabildos de Lima*. 3 vols. Paris: Paul Dupont, 1900.

Trazegnies, Fernando de. *Ciriaco de Urtecho. Litigante por amor*. Lima: Pontificia Universidad Católica del Perú, 1981.

Trelles, Efraín. *Lucas Martínez Vegazo. Funcionamiento de una encomienda peruana inicial.* Lima: Pontificia Universidad Católica del Perú, 1982.

Twinam, Ann. "Honor, Sexuality, and Illegitimacy in Colonial Spanish America." In *Sexuality and Marriage in Colonial Latin America,* edited by Asunción Lavrin. Lincoln: University of Nebraska Press, 1989.

van Deusen, Nancy. "Los primeros recogimientos para doncellas mestizas en Lima y Cusco, 1550–1580." *Allpanchis* 1 (1990): 249–91.

———. *Dentro del cerco de los muros.* Lima: Cuadernos de Trabajo, CENDOC Mujer, 1987.

Vargas Ugarte, Rubén, S. J. *Historia general del Perú.* 6 vols. Lima: Milla Batres, 1966.

Velarde, Héctor. "Apreciaciones generales sobre la Casa de Pilatos." *Revista Peruana de Cultura* 1 (1963): 11–17.

Vigil, Mariló. *La vida de las mujeres en los siglos* XVI y XVII. Madrid: Siglo Veintiuno, 1986.

Villarroel y Ordóñez, fray Gaspar de. *Gobierno eclesiástico pacífico y unión de los dos cuchillos Pontificio y Regio.* In *Los cronistas de convento,* edited by José de la Riva-Agüero, compiled by Pedro Benvenutto Murrieta and Guillermo Lohmann Villena. Paris: Desclée, de Brouwer, 1938.

Index

The letters *t* or *n* following a page number refer to a table or note on that page. The number following the *n* is the note number.

adultery: divorce and, 59, 67–68, 70; double standard and, 58–60, 70; female, 64–65; geographic mobility and, 63, 70; male, 58; marriage and, 62–63; premarital sex and, 62–63; public domain and, 59–60; violence and, 66

Aguila, Gabriela del, 86–87

Alconchel, Pedro de, 13

archiepiscopal court, 24, 57, 170n13; concubinage and, 41–42, 49, 52

Archivo Arzobispal, xv

Archivo General de la Nación, xv

Arias, María, 121–22

Atahualpa, 8

Azarpay, 8

Barahona, Teodora Gómez, 112

barragania, 156n12

Benalcázar, Sebastián, 10

Bernarda, Josefa, 63–64

Bowser, Frederick, x

Calancha, Antonio, 20

capullanas, 156–57n16

Caraccioli, Viceroy, 135

Casa de Divorciadas, 26

Casa del Divorcio, 48, 62

Casa de Niños Expósitos, 133

Casa de Recogidas, 102

Casas, Bartolomé de las, 7

castas, 19; illegitimacy and, 35, 81, 95

Castelar, Conde de, 39

Castillo, Francisco del, 39

Castro, Alfonso de, 59

Castro, Américo, 5–6

Catalán, Florentina, 60–62

Cerro, Lorenzo del, 87–88, 113

Chávez y Mendoza, Juan Machado de, 58–59, 99, 130–31

child abandonment, 127–33; affection and, 128; charitable contributions and, 132–33; children's rights and, 131–32; Colegio de Niñas Expósitas de Santa Cruz de Atoche and, 149; convent residents and, 137–38; free children, population of, 128–29; illegitimacy and, 128–29, 130–31, 148–49; mothers and, 139–40; private homes and, 132, 184n12; registry and, 129; wet nurses and, 135–39, 149, 185n25–26, 185n32, 186n33

Chinchón, Conde de, 20

Chocano, Magdalena, x

clergy, behavior of, 43–44

Cobo, Bernabé, 135; *Historia de la fundación de Lima*, 31

Colegio de Niñas Expósitas de Santa Cruz de Atoche, 141–48, 150; admission to, 142–43; boys and, 143; Cristóbal de Castilla y Zamora and, 143–44; daily life in, 145; dowries and, 146–47; education and, 144; "enclosure and confinement" and, 145–46; financial administration of, 144; Inquisition and, 143–44; punishment in, 147–48; residents of, 142–43; slaves and, 146

colonialism, social hierarchies and, 18

Columbus, Christopher, 5

concubinage: archiepiscopal court and, 41–42, 49, 52; auto de fé of 1600 and, 42; the church and, 39; clergy and, 42–44; control of, 53; conversation concerning, 39–40; ecclesiastical authorities and, 45–46; false accusations of, 46–47; guilt feelings and, 39, 53; Inquisition and, 41, 42; marital status and, 50–51; privacy and, 44–45; prosecution for, 48–49, 54; punishments for, 53; recidivism and, 51; social strata and, 47–48, 54; sources, 168n20; visitas and, 44; women and, 54

conquistadores: legitimacy and, 156n15; marriage and, 12–13; native women and, 5, 7–12, 159n53

Corbeto, Francisco, 62

Córdova, Jocoba de, 110–11

Córdova y Salinas, Diego de, 20

Council of Trent, xiii, 54; ecclesiastical inspections and, xiii, 44, 50, 60; illegitimacy and, 75, 115; marriage and, 62, 167n6

curaca, native women and, 158n23

data sources, xiii–xiv, xv

Descripción del Virreinato del Perú (León Portocarrero), 20, 101, 131

Diario de Lima (Suardo), 59

divorce, 62, 65–66; adultery and, 67–68; material support and, 67; respect and, 69–70; social strata and, 65–66, 68–69, 71

Dongo, Bartolomé, 88–89

double standard: adultery and, 58–60, 70; barragania and, 156n12; illegitimacy and, 114–16; morality and, 122; property transfers and, 98; religious orders and, 122

dowry system, xv, 28, 123–24, 179n27;
arranged marriages and, 70;
Colegio de Niñas Expósitas de
Santa Cruz de Atoche and, 146–
47; control of women and, 150;
definition of women and, 103–5;
divorce and, 98; female orphans
and, 104–5; Laws of Toro and,
179–80n28; *Siete Partidas* and,
179–80n28
Duby, Georges, x

Elías, Norbert, 93
El Sagrario parish, xii, 129;
acknowledgment and, 109–10;
female population, 19, 20t; free
children population, 129–30;
illegitimacy, 79–80, 85–86, 120,
129; illegitimacy in, 76t; Indian
population, 130; paternity
patterns, 78t; slaves in, 119–20,
129–30
encomienda system, gender relations
and, 15–16
endogamy, 99, 178n8
Escalante, Isabel, 48
Espinosa, Francisco, 48
Espinosa, María Gabriela de, 106
Esquilache, Príncipe de, 134
Esquivel, Doña de Esquivel, 134

Flandrin, Jean Louis, x
Frézier, Amedeé, 28, 34–35, 101,
167n78

Galindo, Alberto Flores, x
García, Marina, 50–51

Garcilaso de la Vega, 5–6, 7, 14
Gasca, Pedro de la, 10–11
Godoy, Pedro, 49
Gómez, Sebastián, 60–62
González, Ramón, 50–51
Gregory XVI, 130
Gutiérrez, Margarita, 49

Hemming, John, 9
Hernández, Domingo, 83
Herrera, Josefa de, 113–14
Historia de la fundación de Lima
(Cobo), 31
Hospital de la Caridad, 61
Hospital de los Niños Huérfanos,
130–31, 133, 140–41; 1687
earthquake and, 134; casta
children and, 135
Huérfanos parish, 150
Hunefeldt, Christine, x

illegitimacy: acknowledgment
and, 80, 84, 90–92;
child abandonment and,
128–29; double standard
and, 114–16; economic
stability and, 74; ethnic
groups and, 76t, 77t;
hierarchical system of,
93; honor and shame and,
81; incest and, 175n28;
inheritance and, 84–85, 86,
94; legitimizations and, 78–
80; meaning of, 77–78, 81, 94;
mestizo children and, 160n79;
paternity patterns and, 78t,
79t; religious orders and,
114–16; slaves and, 118–20;

social conditions and, ix; social disorganization and, 74; social standing and, 83, 89–90, 93, 116–17, 125; sources, 174n21; stigma of, 91–92; women's roles and, 92–93

illegitimate children, 17–18, 127; care of, 9–11; categories of, 74; gender of, 85–86; inheritance and, 10–11, 75–76; legitimization of, 10–11; male attitudes and, 11–12; religious orders and, 75; Santa Clara retreat for girls and, 10; slaves and, 12; Spanish crown and, 10–11, 18. *See also* child abandonment

Indian society, men-women relationships in, xiv, 3–4, 157n20; adultery and illegitimacy, 157n22

La Caridad, 28, 70

Lavallé, Bernard, x, 99

Laws of Toro, 2, 76, 104, 115; dowry system and, 179–80n28

Lemos, Conde de, 102, 134

León Pinelo, Antonio de, 75

León Portocarrero, Pedro de, 100–101, 130–31; *Descripción del Virreinato del Perú*, 20, 101

Lima, x–xi, 160n79; archiepiscopal court, 24; architectural symmetry of, 22; autos de fé, 30; beaterios, 27; civic and religious core of, 23; commerce and, 24, 35; convents, monasteries, and schools, 26, 27; courtly life, 23, 163n20; diversity, ethnic and social, 19–22, 35; ecclesiastical spaces, 28; enclosure and separation of the sexes, 27–28, 36–37; female population, 20–22; gender relations and, 36; hospitals, 26; households, internal order of, 33–34, 164n35, 166n75; indigenous people in, 22; monastic life in, 28; parishes, 29; plazas, 22–25; population, 19; privacy in, 37; public functions, 29–30, 36–37, 165n43; regulation of life, 31–32; religious houses for men, 27; royal audiencia, 23; sexes, separation of, 35; shopping areas, 24–25; slaves in, 22, 32–33, 36; Spanish population, 20–21, 162n7; women, segregation of, 30–31

Macera, Pablo, x

Maldonaldo, Diego, 11, 14–15

Malleus Maleficarum, 2–3

marriage, 12, 154n9; conquistadores and, 12–13; consolidation of power and, 14–15; dowry system and, 70; encomiendas and, 13; government officials and, 23–24; slaves and, 118–19, 183n56, 183n58, 183n61; social processes and, x. *See also* dowry system

Martinez-Alier, Verena, 100

matrifocal families, x

Mazet, Claude, x

Mendoza, Juan de, 84

Mesa, Alonso de, 12

methodology, xii–xiv

Miranda, Diego Frías de, 41

Monclova, Conde de la, 20

Montañés, 42–43

Morales, Francisca de, 106–9

Mota, Francisca de la, 63

Mugaburu, Josephe de, 29

native women: conquistadores and, 5, 7–12, 159n53; curaca and, 158n23

natural children, inheritance and, 87–88, 91, 95, 174n20

New Laws, 13

Nicolasa, María, 52

Novísima Recopilación, 76

Numeración general, 21, 27

Ochoa, Antonio de, 113

Olivitos y Esquivel, Angela de, 105

Orihuela, Rodrigo Paz de, 86–87

overview, xiv–xvi

Parra, Diego de, 110–11

Parra, Francisco Arce de la, 81–82

Pastor, Mateo, 141–42

Paul V, 134

Pecador, Luis, 133, 150

Pérez, Antonio, 49

Peruvian society: Bourbon rule and, xi–xii; Spanish women and, 158n25

Pizarro, Francisco, 7–8

Pizarro, Gonzalo, 6–8, 10–11

Pizarro, Pedro, 8

Pizarro family, 9

Poma de Ayala, Felipe Guamán, 3–4

Porras, Juan Bautista de, 63

property transfers, double standard and, 98

Recopilación, illegitimacy and, 115

religious orders, 43–44; double standard and, 22; illegitimacy and, 114–16

Reyes, Maria de los, 51

Rojas y Sandoval, María Magdalena de, 63

royal audiencia, xii–xiii

Salcedo, Francisca de, 62

Saldaña, Francisco de, 51, 102

Saldías, Francisco de, 52

San Bernardo, Mencía Pérez Martel de, 114

San Juan de la Penitencia, 10

San Marcelo parish, xii; acknowledgment in, 78–79, 85–86, 109–10; female population, 20, 21t; free children population, 129–30; illegitimacy, 77t, 129; paternity patterns, 79t; slaves in, 109–10, 119–20, 129–30

Santiago del Cercado, 22, 162n11, 164n34

seventeenth century, xi

sexual culture, x

sexuality, the church and, xii–xiii

Siete Partidas, 2, 5, 57, 74, 76, 115; dowry system and, 179–80n28; slaves and, 118

Sisa, Quispe, 7–8

slaves: baptismal records of, 129–30; family units and, 126; marriage and, 118–19, 125, 183n56, 183n58, 183n61; *Siete Partidas* and, 118; virginity and, 120

Solórzano y Pereyra, Juan de, 75

Soto, Hernando de, 8, 11

Spain: extramarital relations, 3; family structures in, 2; illegitimacy, 3; matrimony, 2–3; Muslim legacy and, 2; women's status and, 2–3, 6, 16; xenophobia, 6

Spaniards, code of honor and, 5–6, 16–17

Spanish empire, colonization and, xi

Stone, Lawrence, x

Suardo, Juan Antonio: *Diario de Lima*, 59

time notions, 41, 168n10

Toledo, Francisco de, 14

Toro, Alonso de, 15–16

Torres, Sebastián de, 11–12

Tribunal of the Inquisition, 26, 41; New Christians and, 173n6

Twelfth Council of Toledo, 58

Ulloa, Gutiérrez de, 42–43

Universidad de San Marcos, 26

Vargas, Francisco de, 11

Vega, Garcilaso de la, 9

Vegazo, Lucas Martínez, 15

Velarde, Héctor, 34

Velasco, Luis de, 101, 134

Verdugo, Melchor, 7

Vigil, Mariló, 100

women, 2–3; appropriate behavior of, 122; conquistadores and, xiv, 5; definition of, 103–5; exchange of, in Andean societies, 3–4, 17; extramarital relations and, 106–9; family control over, 109–10; family units and, 126; "feminine state" and, 99; honor and, 123, 125–26; illegitimacy and, 123; perceptions of, 99, 100–101; property transfers and, 98; religious orders and, 114–16; segregation of, 101–2; sexuality, honor and, 100; social hierarchies and, 102–3; Spaniards in Peru, 158n25; Spanish code of honor and, 5–6, 16–17; status of, in Andean societies, 3–4, 17; status of, in Spain, 2–3, 6, 16. *See also* double standard; dowry system; native women